DWARF CAMPANULAS

Dwarf Campanulas

AND ASSOCIATED GENERA

Graham Nicholls

Timber Press

To Rick Lupp, a valued and generous friend, who like me has a passionate love of campanulas, and to the memory of H. Clifford Crook, who spent more than 30 years of his life in the study of this genus.

Published in 2006 by
Timber Press, Inc.
The Haseltine Building
133 S.W. Second Avenue, Suite 450
Portland, Oregon 97204-3527, U.S.A.

www.timberpress.com

For contact information regarding editorial, marketing, sales,
and distribution in the United Kingdom, see www.timberpress.co.uk.

Designed by Dick Malt.
Printed in China.

Library of Congress Cataloguing-in-Publication Data
Nicholls, Graham, 1935-
   Dwarf campanulas and associated genera / Graham Nicholls.
      p. cm.
   Includes bibliographical references and index.
   ISBN-13: 978-0-88192-810-5
   ISBN-10: 0-88192-810-0
   1. Campanula. 2. Campanulaceae. I. Title.
   SB413.C2N53 2006
   635.9'3398--dc22
                        2006013495

A catalogue record for this book is also available from the British Library.

Contents

Acknowledgments

I never cease to be amazed by the assistance freely given from both friends and total strangers when I ask them to loan me slides, write or check text, or simply supply information regarding the plants I am researching. As with my previous book, *Alpine Plants of North America*, this book could not have been written without that help.

Many choice campanulas from the Caucasus would have been omitted but for the assistance of Vojtěch Holubec and Tatyana Shulkina, both of whom supplied information. Robert Rolfe gave up much of his valuable time to write the foreword and check sections of the draft text. Brian Burrow also spent a lot of time checking draft text, for which I am extremely grateful. My thanks to Jane Leeds, who enthusiastically threw herself into the section on *Codonopsis*, without which this book would have been short-changed. Rick Lupp provided a description of the habitat in North America, as did Panayoti Kelaidis of the habitat in Greece. Julie Ritchie of Hoo House Nursery in the United Kingdom, who holds the National Collection of *Platycodon*, checked the *Platycodon* text for me.

Many photographers throughout the world generously loaned me their slides for possible inclusion in this book. Whether I approached them as a personal friend or as a stranger on Alpine-L, that splendid electronic rock garden on the Internet, all responded without hesitation, even knowing the slides would be away for a long time during the production process. I would like to offer my heartfelt thanks to all for their assistance, including Winnie Bevington, Cliff Booker, Ann Borrill, Trevor Cole, Lesley Cox, John Crellin, Jean Elliott, Jon Evans, Phyllis Gustafson, Franz Hadacek, Vojtěch Holubec, Ellen Hornig, Mike Ireland, Panayoti Kelaidis, Jane Leeds, Rod Leeds, Harold McBride, David McDonald, Dave Mountfort, Aalt Musch, Carolyn Parker, John Purcell, Paul Ranson, Robert Rolfe, Tatyana Shulkina, Bob Wallis, Penny Watt, Richard Wilford, and Zdeněk Zvolánek. Thanks, too, to the North American Rock Garden Society (NARGS) for use of Dick Redfield's photo of *Campanula piperi*.

My thanks also go to all those campanula growers at Alpine Garden Society (AGS) shows who were patient under my close questioning, and to all those friends and strangers who replied positively to my e-mails about campanula cultivation.

Additional thanks go to all the research facilities I used, including the comprehensive AGS library at Pershore, dozens of Web sites maintained by nurseries, botanical gardens, private sites, and databases and research sites, which helped me no end. How easy it is nowadays to sit in a chair, type in the plant you want, and click a mouse. Plant research has a lot to thank the Internet for.

I sincerely hope I have left no one out. If so, I apologise.

Finally, I am indebted to Clifford Crook for writing such a fine monograph in the first place. His *Campanulas* (1951) set the standard and is a hard act to follow.

Foreword

ROBERT ROLFE

As I write this in midwinter, most campanulas are soundly asleep, building up reserves for their early to high summer extravaganzas. But in the alpine house, some of the most precocious have already developed bright green fledgling rosettes, sheltered underneath tuffets of dead foliage, while outdoors, in the paving around the house, that most rampant of colonisers, *Campanula poscharskyana*, boasts spasmodic trusses of bloom, long past its main flowering period. The latter, a wolf that was inadvertently purchased under the guise of one of its meeker, sheepish relatives almost 40 years ago, is far from alone when it comes to misidentification and muddle. A further awkwardness relating to this indispensable but sometimes inscrutable genus is that while there are indeed many species, there are many, many more names, whose synonyms and sometimes spurious affinities can be very tricky to disinter, whether you are a taxonomist, a "specialist," a nurseryman, or simply a gardener keen to know (as precisely as possible) what is what.

It is now more than 50 years since Clifford Crook's landmark work *Campanulas* was published. You might imagine that the very extensive fieldwork and the innumerable plant introductions made in the interim would have dispersed the mists through which that mordant monographer was obliged to chart his course—well, yes, and then again, no. Names continue to spill forth in quantity—the most recent supplements of *Index Kewensis* churn out further additions to the corpus—but such is our unfamiliarity with some of the plants latterly introduced that they either arrive under an unlikely-to-be-decoded collector's number, or else are assigned to a complex or group (those from northeastern Turkey and the Caucasus in particular) from whose all-embracing, overlapping descriptions they cannot at present be satisfactorily disentangled.

Of course, such difficulties do not bedevil the genus across the board; in Europe, and in North America for that matter (two strongholds of the genus), things are pretty much clear-cut, even if horticulturists muddy the waters by making indiscriminate hybrids and launching them under labels such as *Campanula pseudoraineri*. Anyone who has seen the Californian *C. shetleri* threading through the granite crevices above Castle Lake, *C. cenisia* exuberant in the lake-fringing moraines at Mattmark (Switzerland), or *C. barbata* more abundant still in the alpine meadows overlooking the Lac de Mont Cenis on the French-Italian border, will have a very clear idea of these species delimitations, and perhaps a sense of incomprehension when it comes to the confusions rife elsewhere: in mitigation, it should be said that matters are by no means always so easily settled.

Indeed, the boundaries that distinguish *Campanula* from some of its closer allies have also been called into question, though at present it is usual to maintain the distinctions that exist between *Adenophora, Asyneuma, Symphyandra, Trachelium*, and others. A study of *Campanula* relatives can take you almost around the globe, with surprising excursions, such as the semi-woody *Lightfootia* (South Africa) and that mid-Atlantic outcast, *Azorina vidalii*: no continent is exempt from their presence. From Alaska to New Zealand, and from Japan across China to central and western Asia, Europe, and the Rockies, almost the only place where you will search more or less fruitlessly is South America, where genera hitherto aligned (*Hypsela* and *Lysipomia* chief among them) are presently allied with the Lobeliaceae in most modern accounts.

Some areas have been effectively out of bounds to plant hunters until recently, and the early introductions had long since slipped from the collections of the few people that grew them the first time round. A few of these reintroductions have been revelations to a new generation of gardeners. Picking at random, the Caucasian *Campanula autraniana* has proved more diverse and more enticing than previous reports suggested, while from Iran there have been several reintroductions of *C. humillima*, which, as illustrations in at least one book on the Iranian flora shows, can be a delight, with bicoloured flowers patterned in the manner of California's fivespot (*Nemophila maculata*)—check earlier accounts and you will find it dismissed as "small" and "insignificant." On a broader level, displays at garden centres and even local greengrocers of mass-produced lines such as *Platycodon grandiflorus* in its several dwarf cultivar groups (variously available in white, pink, blue, and even double morphs) attest to the broad-based appeal of the family.

Aside from the generally robust pantheon of campanulas and close relatives that perform exuberantly in herbaceous borders during high summer, there is a very considerable coterie of much dwarfer, more concise plants, generally rewardingly floriferous, and typically inhabiting the mountainous parts of the world, largely saxatile, intermittently moraine-dwelling, chasmophytic, and scree-segregated or more generally alpine-associated throughout their range. Some frustrate the efforts of all but the most skilled growers; rather more respond magnificently if their none-too-demanding needs are met. It is mostly a matter of understanding their diverse natures—some are soundly perennial, others monocarpic, a few are biennial—and catering for their various needs (clearly defined in this long-awaited book, written by someone who has had a sustained interest in Campanulaceae for almost as long as he has been a gardener). Determined wanderers in the main, relatively few will repeat-perform without your further intervention, but suitably provided for, they will provide exuberant performances rivalling those of almost anything else in the gardening year.

Preface

I have been growing members of the Campanulaceae family since 1959, and I love them. Not just the tall border herbaceous perennials like *Adenophora* or *Platycodon* but also the small, compact genera that are suitable for rock gardens, troughs, and pots, like *Cyananthus* or *Edraianthus*. The genus *Campanula*, however, contains some of the very best of the standard rock garden plants, and there can be few gardens in the world that are without at least one campanula in their collection. They are a mainstay for the summer perennial border and sunny rock garden, and the majority are easy to grow, increasing in size every year or even becoming a nuisance by seeding around. They are showy and bloom for a long period, some into late autumn. They are versatile, some making mounds while others flow down over rock formations, and the flowers are endearing, from the blowsy large saucers of *Campanula carpatica* to the delicate and unusual flowers of *C. zoysii* and *C. excisa*. They can be grown in pots, troughs, or raised beds, as well as in the rock garden, enabling the grower to see the plants at close quarters. And enthusiasts can exhibit campanulas to a high standard at shows, bringing to the attention of the general public many of the plants that aren't commonly seen. For example, when *C. zoysii* 'Lismore Ice', the rare white form of the species, or a large pot of the delicate *C. jaubertiana* or *C. hercegovina* 'Nana', or maybe a 36 CM pot overflowing with *C. thessala*, appears on the show bench, everyone, from the general public to the experienced gardener, becomes hungry for more knowledge and wants to grow it. Although some campanulas are evergreen, the majority die back to underground rhizomes or a taproot over winter. In an alpine house or cold frame, however, many of these will keep some green leaves.

In spite of *Campanula* being such a large genus, in the wild the 300 or so species are found only in the northern hemisphere, with a large proportion inhabiting the Mediterranean region and eastward into Turkey, the Caucasus, Iran, Tajikistan, and Japan. Europe has its fair share of campanulas, and these are considered by many to rank among the finest, although that is debatable. The United States can lay claim to nine species. The flowers come in a range of colours, from deep purple to blue, violet, lavender, and pink paling to white. These flowers can be stellate to campanulate, tubular, or almost circular. Leaves also vary from small or large, oval, and toothed, to lanceolate and linear, and can be bright green and smooth to grey and densely hairy.

Campanulas vary in height from a few centimetres to well over a metre, but the plants discussed in this book are those that I consider to be dwarf forms of the genus—in effect, the species, cultivars, and hybrids that are suitable for growing in a rock garden or alpine house and grow no taller than 50 CM. This arbitrary height was determined by myself as the most appropriate for this book, border campanulas having been discussed in other publications. Many of the plants discussed here are easily grown, while others are more challenging. Although quite happy outside during summertime, the more demanding plants require protection against winter damp and humidity to prevent rotting off during winter and are therefore best cultivated in an alpine house or cold frame. Species like the North American *Campanula piperi* and *C. shetleri* are examples of this.

The Early Years

Thinking back over all those years, like many others before me I must have bought my first plant at a plant sale or local nursery, because garden centres were few and far between at that time. Without doubt it was *Campanula portenschlagiana*, one of the most floriferous and easily grown plants of the genus, and the most popular for nursery or plant sales. *Campanula carpatica* and *C. cochleariifolia* were soon to follow, keeping *C. portenschlagiana* company in the rock garden. (Some 45 years and three gardens later, I still have all three, although not the original plants.) Those remained my sole species until I joined the Alpine Garden Society (AGS) in the early 1970s and began reading the quarterly bulletins. Although the photographs were in black and white, and line drawings were used far more than they are now, there were descriptions of campanulas at the shows and of those that had received plant awards from the Royal Horticultural Society (RHS) Joint Rock Garden Plant Committee. For example, in 1976 Brian Mathew wrote that "mention must be made of the recently described (1970) *Campanula shetleri*, which, though not in flower, was a fine healthy plant with the appearance of a very reduced *C. piperi*." Nowadays *C. shetleri* is fairly common at summer shows thanks to the many seed and plant lists that make it available, and yet at that time the species was just a curiosity. Reading the description certainly didn't excite me.

Two years later Eric Hilton wrote in the AGS bulletin, "I had for instance a thriving plant of *Campanula zoysii* in the wall and when I returned (from holiday) expecting it to be dead I found that it was flowering splendidly." He went on to say, "In the autumn it became the target for attacks by woodlice and in spite of nightly inspections and every effort at protection the plant eventually succumbed." A black-and-white photo of *C. morettiana* appeared in the same bulletin, but how can you appreciate the beauty of this species without seeing it in colour? Not having seen *C. zoysii* or *C. morettiana* in real life at that time, I was not enthused by a black-and-white photo and the knowledge that woodlice are lethal. Also in 1978, the plant award report included a description of "a very promising new hybrid of *C. morettiana* × *C. raineri* discovered as a seedling in a pot of *C. morettiana*." This was *C.* 'Joe Elliott', and it received an RHS Award of Merit. Since then it has featured in many a nursery catalogue and graces the show bench every year. In 1978, though, no coloured photo was available, and where could I have obtained the plant anyway?

I had started to exhibit some of my plants at the West of England show in Bristol by then and in 1980 became the secretary of that show. Although this was an early spring show, it encouraged me to travel to other shows, including the summer shows at Woking, where I saw such rarities as *Campanula cenisia*, *C. hawkinsiana*, and a lovely pan of *C. petrophila*, which took a Farrer Medal there. By the mid-1980s I was growing some of the more choice campanulas, including *C. bornmuelleri* raised from seed collected in Turkey under the collection number McP. & W. 5813, and *C. alpina* raised from seed collected in Romania. In 1987 I received an award for the *C. alpina*.

With the advent of colour photos in AGS bulletins in 1985, plants could now be seen and enjoyed to the full. March 1991 finally saw the AGS bulletin published in full colour, including front and rear covers, and as a result many more campanulas appeared in colour. *Campanula topaliana* and *C. rupestris*, for example, were shown side by side so that we could see the difference between them. By this time I was becoming interested in more of the dwarf Campanulaceae and began growing several other genera in the family. *Adenophora nikoensis*, a couple of *Edraianthus* species, and *Physoplexis comosa* made their appearance in my alpine house to go alongside the increasing number of campanulas. I planted many dwarf campanulas in my rock gardens. Easy and accommodating species like *C. carpatica* and *C. garganica* made fairly large clumps, while smaller plants like *C. cochlearifolia* or *C.* 'Haylodgensis' were grown in troughs.

Recent Years

I started my nursery in 1990 and as a result my collection of *Campanula* species and hybrids increased in number. Not only that, but I was showing more. Soon, in addition to the common species, rarities like *C. zoysii*, both blue and white forms, *C. petrophila*, *C. jaubertiana*, *C. lasiocarpa*, *C. piperi*, *C. shetleri*, and in 1994 the new introduction *C. choruhensis*, featured in my catalogue. Hand in hand with the techniques of growing these species to exhibition quality came propagation knowledge in producing plants for the nursery. Although there is great demand for the rare species, I still propagate the more common campanulas, but nowadays there are so many easy-to-grow cultivars and hybrids in the trade that they can be purchased anywhere. Garden centres, nurseries, or sales tables at AGS shows or local meetings make getting a nice collection together straightforward, but I would advise anyone new to campanulas to gain experience with these easy forms before moving on to the more difficult species. There are others that are quite rare, only appearing at AGS shows and hanging on by their fingertips in cultivation. I continually urge growers to propagate these: we have to keep these rare plants in cultivation, as so many have been lost in the past. These rarities are available from one or two specialist nurseries or have to be grown from seed available from commercial seed lists. In recent years Czech seed collectors like Vojtěch Holubec, Josef Jurášek, Josef Halda, and Vladislav Piatek have added to our knowledge of campanulas by listing many of the rare species from Turkey or the Caucasus.

Some readers may wonder why I mention AGS shows so much. I love shows and have exhibited for many years, but the main thing is that shows are where you can see all those rare and beautiful campanulas and their relatives—not just the odd one or two, but dozens of different species, hybrids, and cultivars. Exhibitors cultivate them to a high standard, and seeing them growing well in cultivation is the next best thing to seeing them in the wild. I recommend that every campanula enthusiast visit at least one AGS summer show in their lifetime. You will be amazed.

This Book

At the commencement of this project it was felt that a book containing not just campanulas but also other members of the Campanulaceae would be of more interest to readers. However, a decision had to be made regarding the height of the species to be included, as the intention was not to include all Campanulaceae but only those suitable for the small rock garden and trough or pot culture. As mentioned previously, I had decided that a maximum height of 50 CM was suitable for the campanulas to be included. This rule came unstuck, however, when it came to the allied genera, as I realised that some species had a range of 40–60 CM in height. I finally decided that as long as the minimum height for these species was below 50 CM, I could include them.

As with *Alpine Plants of North America*, I have tried to make this book reader-friendly, and although I use botanical terms in the descriptions, I feel this in no way detracts from the book's usefulness for beginners, gardeners, and enthusiasts wishing to increase their knowledge of the Campanulaceae. Although I grow a great many campanulas, I am in no way an expert, just a passionate grower. In fact I do not think there can be any "expert" of this complicated genus. On the one hand there are wide differences within *Campanula*; on the other hand, while most species are quite easy to recognise, there are many so similar to one another that even Clifford Crook, who spent 30 years or more of his life travelling and writing his famous monograph *Campanulas* (1951), couldn't tell the difference. In this book I have as far as possible used the specific names that are in current use and listed any synonyms. I have written a general propagation and cultivation section, but where I felt that more specialist information was needed within a plant description, I have included it.

Crook's *Campanulas* and Lewis and Lynch's *Campanulas* (1998) are both excellent publications. However, in Crook's book the photos are in black and white, and only limited cultivation information is given; and while it is the standard, it is also more than 50 years old. The Lewis and Lynch publication contains many border campanulas but only a few of the more specialised species. In *Dwarf Campanulas*, by comparison, I have included colour photos, species and new hybrids not previously described, and more extensive propagation and cultivation information, and am confident that the resulting book will be suitable for everyone interested in campanulas.

The Main Campanula-Growing Areas of the World

Campanulas grow naturally in many regions of the world, in mountains, sub-alpine pastures, and at the roadside, mainly in the northern hemisphere. Many of these regions are home to only one or two species, which may be endemic (restricted to that particular locality) or which may grow in other areas as well. Other regions have a wealth of campanulas and are recognised as the best places to visit if you wish to see campanulas growing in the wild. During my research I became more and more aware of these campanula-rich regions and decided to include brief descriptions of those that I consider to be the best, in the hope that this information may aid campanula hunters. I accept that some well-travelled readers may disagree with my selection and so must emphasise that the areas described here were chosen based purely on my own experience and research. In addition to the regions in this chapter, campanulas can be found growing in Algeria, the Balkans, the Carpathians, the Himalaya, Iran, Iraq, Japan, Morocco, Norway, Portugal, Siberia, Spain, Syria, and the United Kingdom.

CAUCASUS

Someone once said to me that the Caucasus is the *Campanula* epicentre of the world, and when looking at my collection of campanulas, how can I argue? About 50% of my collection has its roots in the Caucasus, having either been grown by me from seed collected there or by someone else who had passed a plant on to me. Nowhere else in the world can you find such a tremendous richness of bell-flowers. *Flora of the Caucasus* by A. A. Grossheim (1939–1967) contains about 5000 species of plants, including about 1000 endemics, the Campanulaceae being widely represented by seven genera, of which *Campanula* comprises 88 species.

Nearly two-thirds are endemic to the territory of Caucasus, where most of the large-flowered *Campanula* species have made their homes. Some occur over a vast area stretching the entire length, or at least most of the ridge. Others are restricted to just one region or occasionally are more localised still and found only on a single mountain or in just one valley. They can be found in many habitats: woods, meadows, among rocks (frequently in the alpine and subalpine zones), and occasionally in steppe and semi-desert. Those with rather large areas of distribution have made life very difficult for taxonomists, since they differ slightly from area to area in many or most of their characteristics, and moreover, they hybridise and produce unusual offspring. Such diversity makes them difficult to determine. Nevertheless, their beauty is extraordinary, and rock gardeners and plant lovers know it, many struggling and occasionally succeeding in growing them to a high standard. Beautiful species such as *C. anomala*, which grows in limestone crevices in the northern Caucasus, *C. autraniana*, which grows in grassland on Mt. Fisht in the western Caucasus, the lovely but testing *C. hypopolia*, which colonises rock fissures throughout the Greater Caucasus, and *C. dzaaku*, which is endemic to the western end of the Russian Caucasus, are all much sought after. Many Caucasian campanulas are of great horticultural value, and the very large flowers for which some species are noted make them highly desired alpines for rock gardeners. Without doubt this is the most campanula-rich region in the world.

The Caucasian Mountains lie between the Black Sea and the Caspian Sea to the north of Turkey and Iran. There are two main ranges, the Greater Caucasus and the Lesser Caucasus, which run parallel from the northwest to the southeast for about 1500 KM. It is generally recognised that these are divided into two parts, the northern Caucasus and the Transcaucasus. The former consists of the northern slopes and ranges of the Greater Caucasus and includes a number of members of the Russian Federation (former autonomous republics and regions of the former Soviet Union). The Transcaucasus comprises the southern ranges of the Greater Caucasus and all of the Lesser Caucasus, and includes Georgia, Azerbaijan, and Armenia. The Greater Caucasus is traditionally divided into western, central, and eastern regions. The borders of these regions go along meridians that cross Mt. Elbrus (the highest mountain in Europe, at 5642 M) in the west and Mt. Kazbek (5033 M) in the eastern part of the central Caucasus. It is between these peaks that the majority of the most beautiful mountains lie. The Baksan River flows along the central valley, with many smaller side valleys branching out and

Mt. Kazbek, Caucasus.

Photo by Vojtěch Holubec

Mt. Oschten, Caucasus.

Photo by Vojtěch Holubec

leading up to the most dramatic peaks of the Caucasus, including Mt. Donguz-Orun (4468 M) and the magnificent ridges of Mt. Shkhelda (4300 M).

The western Caucasus covers a large part of the extreme western end of the Caucasus chain and is located 50 KM northeast of the Black Sea. This is one of the few large mountain areas of Europe that has not experienced significant human contact and has a great diversity of ecosystems, with many endemic flora and fauna. The central Caucasus contains the highest mountains in the Caucasus system. Vast glacier basins are a feature of the area, with huge peaks towering above. Large expanses of snow and ice are present year-round in the upper alpine zone, with high meadows and pine-forested valleys further down. In the eastern Caucasus, the weather is drier than in the western and central ranges, and the mountains form isolated massifs rather than glaciated chains. At the far eastern end, humidity decreases dramatically. There is a rain shadow behind the main ridge on the northern slopes on the Russian side. Dagestan in the east is the driest region of the Caucasus, and here semi-desert conditions prevail as the range approaches the Caspian Sea. It has a relatively poor flora, but a lot of species are very restricted endemics such as *Edraianthus owerinianus*.

The Caucasus has a very diverse climate thanks to its geographic position and length. The prevailing winds from the west (namely from the Black Sea) bring moisture to the southwestern slopes, and the vegetation of the Caucasus here is very luxuriant and rich. While a large proportion of the mountains are covered by forests, once you are near the alpine level at around 2100–2700 M, you can find some wonderful alpine plants thriving in this harsh world. Overall these alpine conditions give a range of different microclimates from west to east. Above 3600 M, snow and ice are present year-round, making for wonderful and spectacular scenery. Photographers intending to concentrate solely on the plants need only look up at the surrounding snow-capped peaks and they will be seduced into capturing the breathtaking vistas.

This region has yet to be fully botanised—who can say how many more species will be discovered? Luckily for us, intrepid Czech seed collectors such as Vojtěch Holubec are willing to botanise the area. Without the efforts of such people, particularly in the last decade, many of these Caucasian campanulas would not be in cultivation.

Turkey

Turkey has a unique position in the world, sitting astride the point where southeastern Europe and southwestern Asia meet (although that portion of Turkey west of the Bosporus is geographically part of Europe). It is bordered by the Black Sea, the Aegean Sea, and the Mediterranean, and by Armenia, Azerbaijan, Bulgaria, Georgia, Greece, Iran, Iraq, and Syria. It is divided into seven regions: the Black Sea region, the Marmara region, the Aegean, the Mediterranean, central Anatolia, eastern Anatolia, and southeastern Anatolia.

In spite of Turkey being situated in a geographical location where climatic conditions are quite temperate, the varying topography, and especially the existence of mountains that run parallel to the coasts, results in significant differences in climatic conditions from one region to another. While the coastal areas enjoy a climate of hot, dry summers and mild, wet winters, inland the Anatolian plateau experiences harsh extremes of hot summers and cold winters with limited rainfall. Turkey also suffers very severe earthquakes, especially in the north.

In the Mediterranean region located in the south of Turkey, the western and central Taurus Mountains (commonly known as the Rockies of Turkey) suddenly rise up behind the coastline, and the Nur Mountains lie at the southeastern extreme of this area. When seen from the sea, the range presents a formidable crest line of steep rocky peaks, dozens of them over 3000 M. The range is snow-covered in winter, and patches of snow remain permanently on the higher slopes. In spring the rivers swell from the snowmelt and run swiftly to the Mediterranean. In the Aegean region the mountains in general rise perpendicularly from the coastline, and the plains run from east to west. In the northwest the Marmara region covers the area encircling the Sea of Marmara, including the entire European part of Turkey and the northwestern Anatolian plain. However, while this is the smallest of the regions of Turkey (after southeastern Anatolia), it has the highest population density. Central Anatolia is exactly in the middle of Turkey and, with a high plateau that has an average height of 915 M, appears to be less mountainous compared with the other regions. The main peaks here are Karadağ, Karacadağ, Hasandağ, and especially Erciyes, which reaches 3917 M. Eastern Anatolia is Turkey's largest and highest region. About three-quarters of it is at an altitude of 1500–2000 M, composed of isolated mountains and whole mountain ranges, such as the eastern Taurus Mountains, with vast plateaus and plains. There are numerous inactive volcanoes in the region, including Turkey's highest peak, Mt. Ağri (also known as Mt. Ararat), which is 5165 M high and capped year-round with snow and ice. This is where, it is said, Noah's Ark came to rest. Southeastern Anatolia is notable for the uniformity of its landscape, although the eastern part of the region is comparatively more uneven than its western areas.

Turkey is home to an astonishingly rich and varied flora: while there are about 12,000 different species in Europe and Turkey, about 10,000 of them occur in Turkey, and of these, about 3500 are endemic. The unusual diversity of Turkey's flora is due to both climatic and topographical characteristics. A wide range of rare and beautiful bulbous plants grow in Turkey, from genera such as *Crocus*, *Fritillaria*, *Galanthus*, *Iris*, *Lilium*, and *Tulipa*, making this a photographer's paradise. Turkey has traditionally been (and remains) a major supplier of flowering bulbs in international markets.

The alpine flora ranges from the steppes to alpine levels only free from snow for four months of the year. Among this wonderful flora grow campanulas, rivalling those from Greece and the Caucasus in their rarity and beauty. *Campanula betulifolia* and *C. bornmuelleri* can be found growing in cracks and crevices of limestone and granite, and one of the best introductions of recent years, *C. choruhensis*, inhabits crevices in volcanic rock. All three of these beautiful species are very rewarding if grown under cold glass. Two others species, both compact and choice, are *C. hakkiarica*, from southeastern Turkey (where it grows on limestone cliffs), and *C. coriacea*, which is endemic to a small area of eastern Turkey. Numerous other species have been described, a number within the last few years.

GREECE

If the Caucasus is the campanula epicentre of the world, then Greece must come a close second, not just for campanulas but also for many of the allied genera in the family, such as *Asyneuma*, *Edraianthus*, *Michauxia*, and *Phyteuma*. Two distinctive genera, *Petromarula* and *Trachelium*, are practically restricted to Greece, and almost every ancient site in Greece harbours its own endemic race or species of *Campanula*, which is commonly sprayed by herbicide or scraped off by conscientious caretakers, often to the horror of visiting botanists.

Greece occupies 131,900 square KM—almost precisely the same area as England. But nearly 5000 species of vascular plants are native to Greece, while perhaps

only 1500 species occurred in England in preagricultural times. The extraordinary biodiversity of Greece is the result of many factors. Glaciation during the last ice age in Greece was minimal, with small glaciers occurring only on its highest peaks, whereas England was completely covered with continental glaciation. Few countries are as mountainous and fragmented as Greece, which comprises 1400 islands (169 of which are inhabited) and many thousands of mountain peaks that are effectively sky islands. Just as Darwin's finches have speciated dramatically in the Galápagos, the fantastic reticulation of the Greek landscape has led to isolation and accelerated speciation in many plant groups, especially Campanulaceae. The very ruggedness of the Greek landscape is a boon to *Campanula*: a large proportion of the campanulas of Greece are chasmophytes, plants that have evolved to grow in the tiny crevices of sheer rock faces. Most of the cliffs and rock faces in Greece are limestone, derived from the marine deposits of the Mesozoic sea of Tethys, the Dinosaur-age antecedent of the Mediterranean Sea. But there are extensive granitic, volcanic, and serpentine outcrops throughout Greece, many of which have their own special campanulas. *Campanula hawkinsiana*, for instance, is a notable serpentine endemic of northern Greece, while *C. oreadum* is restricted to the limestones of Thessaly (primarily Mt. Olympus), and *C. rupicola*

Rock-face habitat of *Campanula rupestris* in Delphi, Greece.

Photo by Panayoti Kelaidis

is the noted specialty of Mt. Parnassus above Delphi. The Greek islands have their own endemic species. *Campanula carpatha*, for example, is restricted to Karpathos, while *C. hierapetrae* is endemic to Crete. Many of the species are monocarpic or biennial, such as *C. formanekiana* and *C. incurva*, both of which are like smaller versions of *C. medium*, Canterbury bells. With such a range and diversity of species, it is no wonder that so many campanula lovers continually return to Greece.

EUROPEAN ALPS

The Alps is the collective name given to one of the great mountain range systems of Europe, which stretches from France in the west, through Germany, Liechtenstein, Switzerland, Italy, Slovenia, and Austria in the east. The highest peaks are on the eastern edge, forming a natural barrier with Italy. Mont Blanc in the French Alps is the highest mountain in western Europe at 4807 M. Included within this vast area are smaller ranges, such as the Maritime Alps (extending in an arc along the French-Italian border for around 190 KM) and the Ligurian Alps (following on into the northern and central Apennines of Italy). In Switzerland the mountains are dominated by the spectacular granite formation known as the Matterhorn, at a height of 4478 M; further east, the Dolomites are a large limestone range allocated in equal parts to the provinces of South Tyrol, Trentino, and Belluno, all in northern Italy. Other ranges include the Julian Alps (Slovenia) and the Velebit Mountains (Croatia).

The climate in the Alps is controlled by the effects of the mountain chains on the prevailing winds, with the warm air rising, expanding, and eventually cooling so that precipitation falls in the form of snow or rain. The accumulation of vast masses of snow has gradually been converted into permanent glaciers, but there are also running streams, fed by snow and melting ice. The many different climates and microclimates between the foot of the mountains and the upper levels are reflected in the diversity of the flora, amounting to thousands of alpine and subalpine plants. Some plants are restricted to the high screes where snowmelt percolates, some inhabit rock crevices on sheer limestone cliffs, and others revel in meadows or even light woodland conditions.

Some species of *Campanula*, such as *C. rotundifolia* or *C. persicifolia*, are widespread throughout the Alps; others, such as *C. excisa* (from a very restricted

Campanula thyrsoides
on Furka Pass,
Switzerland.

Photo by Ann Borrill

area in the southwestern and south-central Alps) and *C. morettiana* (endemic to the Dolomites), are comparative rarities. Tall species, like the yellow-flowered *C. thyrsoides*, contrast with compact, ground-hugging (and difficult to cultivate) species, such as *C. cenisia* from the western Alps and *C. raineri* and *C. zoysii* from the southeastern Alps. *Campanula alpestris* from the southwestern Alps is a dwarf, suckering species with beautiful large flowers, and *C. pulla* from the northeastern Alps has flowers that are probably the deepest blue of the genus. All these and more are very photogenic and richly reward photographers who search for them in their high homelands.

Pyrenees

When great mountain regions of western Europe are discussed, the Pyrenees rank second only to the Alps, although they are of similar age, being formed 50–100 million years ago during the Tertiary period. Although the Pyrenees were glaciated in the distant past, they have just one alpine glacier now, the Ossoue Glacier. The lower slopes are made up of folded limestone, but at higher elevation exposed crystalline rock can be found.

Campanula speciosa in the Valle de Pineta, Pyrenees.

Photo by Harold Bevington

The Pyrenees mountain chain runs in an almost straight line between France and Spain, from the Bay of Biscay on the west to the Mediterranean Sea on the east, a total of 435 KM in length, with a maximum width around 130 KM. It covers an area of about 55,374 square KM, with about two-thirds of its area in Spain and the rest in France, although the principality of Andorra is located among the peaks. The Pyrenees are a climatic divide between France and Spain. The French slopes are much steeper than the Spanish side, with waterfalls and cascades fed by the large rainfall they receive, while the Spanish slopes are much drier and have a steppe-like climate.

There are three main ranges, of which the central section is the highest. The Pico de Aneto is the highest peak, at 3404 M, and is located in Spain, as is Monte Perdido (3355 M). Two other peaks, the Pic de Vignemale and the Pic du Midi d'Ossau, are in France. *Campanula jaubertiana* and *C. cochlearifolia* can be found growing alongside one another in the central Pyrenees. The Cantabrian Mountains are a western extension of the range.

North America

Given the huge area encompassed by North America, it is rather surprising that there is such a paucity of *Campanula* species that are of interest to growers of alpine plants. Those species are mostly found in just a few scattered areas over a wide range of habitats and, with a couple of exceptions, are not especially common plants where they do exist. The needs of the plants in cultivation are much influenced by their natural habitat, and this should be kept in mind when growing them.

Alaska is home to several species of interest, including *Campanula lasiocarpa*, *C. chamissonis*, and the very widely distributed *C. rotundifolia*, which is found in many widely separated areas of North America and around the northern hemisphere. *Campanula lasiocarpa* is very widespread throughout the mountains of Alaska, while *C. rotundifolia* is found in the southern coastal areas and a few locales in central Alaska. Very good dwarf forms of *C. rotundifolia* are also found in Canada, especially on the east coast. In North America, *Campanula chamissonis* is only found in the far western reaches of the Aleutian Islands.

Alaska has cold winters, with lows to about −34°c in the area of Anchorage on the south coast, and even colder winters in the interior, with lows below −45°c in Fairbanks. Snow cover is generally dependable and protects the plants from the extreme cold. Rainfall is modest in all but southeastern Alaska, with Anchorage receiving about 41 cm of precipitation a year, and even less falls in the interior. Afternoon thunderstorms are common in the mountains of interior Alaska in summer. The Aleutian Islands have a much more moderate climate due to the influence of the Pacific Ocean, but they do receive much more rainfall than the south coast and interior of Alaska.

Campanula piperi is one of North America's finest campanulas and is an endemic of Washington State's Olympic Mountains. The west side of the mountain range receives in excess of 635 cm of precipitation a year, but the eastern Olympics, where *C. piperi* makes its home, is in a rain shadow and receives only about 38 cm of annual precipitation. The plant is found at elevations of about 1690–2000 m, mostly on western exposures with good airflow and reliable winter snow cover. This combination of habitat and climate with the typical low humidity in the area makes this a difficult plant to grow in the open garden, where it falls prey to fungal blights. Winter temperatures are moderate, with lows to about −18°c and summer highs to about 27°c in the plant's range.

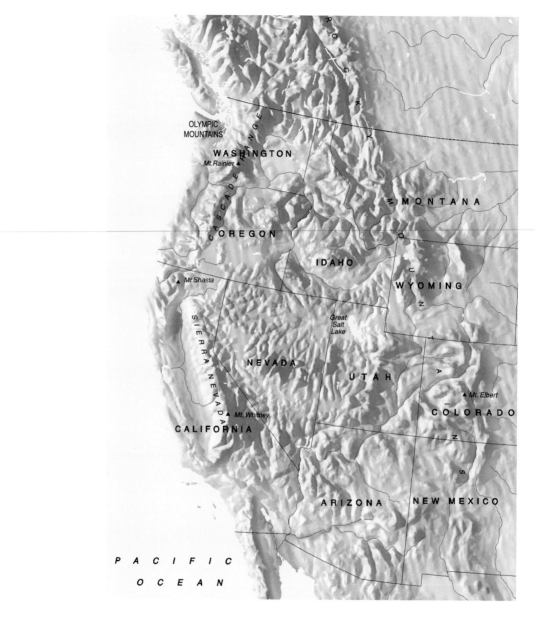

Another outstanding species that likes it dry is *Campanula scabrella*, which is found growing in the rain shadow on the east side of the Cascade Range, extending from central Washington to northern California. It prefers a habitat consisting of sandy, rocky soil or volcanic scoria. The precipitation in the range of

C. *scabrella* averages about 25–38 CM annually, with reliable snow cover in winter. The summers are rather hot, with temperatures to 32°C or more, and with winter lows to about −26°C.

Campanula shetleri is native to northern California and is found at elevations of about 1540–2155 M, growing mainly on granite. It prefers cooler situations such as northern or eastern exposures on cliffs and among rocks. The summer high temperatures here usually range from the mid 20s to low 30s, with winter lows of about −12°C. Precipitation averages about 102 CM annually, with good winter snow cover.

The Rocky Mountains are home to two good species of alpine *Campanula*. *Campanula parryi* is found in alpine meadows from northern Arizona to Montana. *Campanula uniflora* is found in alpine tundra areas from Alaska through the mountains of western Canada and down through the Rocky Mountains to Colorado. These areas are subject to extreme temperatures in both winter and summer, with lows to −29°C or more on occasion, although the plants are generally protected in winter by snow cover. The central and southern Rocky Mountains get a fair amount of precipitation in both summer and winter, as a rule, while the northern Rockies are drier. The high-alpine tundra areas stay quite cool year-round, while the alpine meadows where *C. parryi* grows can reach 27°C or more in summer.

Mt. Shasta, California

Growing Campanulaceae

Like many other enthusiastic beginners to gardening, when I bought my first plants I positioned them as I thought fit and where I could see and enjoy them, with no thought of the plants' needs. Sometimes it was a success and the plants thrived, but other times they slowly died. There was, of course, greater frustration when the plant was an irreplaceable gift. In this chapter I give advice on propagation and cultivation, mainly of campanulas (although there is some discussion of other members of the Campanulaceae), in the hope that readers will have greater successes and fewer disappointments than they may have had in the past.

PROPAGATION

Why bother with propagation, you may ask, when it is so easy to buy a replacement plant? After all, you only have to pay another visit to the nursery and put your hand in your pocket. Well, not quite. Propagation of your plants is essential for a number of reasons, and anyway, most of us cannot afford to let them die and then buy another.

As you become more skilled and experienced in growing Campanulaceae, you will find that you want to try some of the more difficult species. This in itself is a problem, as the more difficult it is to grow the plant, the more chance you have of killing it. Thus insurance comes into the equation: propagate your plant in case you end up killing it. What if you were given a never-to-be-replaced rarity? You wouldn't want that to die and not have a replacement, would you? Furthermore, some species are monocarpic, biennial, or just intrinsically short-lived and need raising from seed almost annually. Usually these set an abundance of seed, so normally there is no problem.

This need to reproduce goes for all plants, of course, and when I give talks I always implore the audience to *propagate, propagate,* and *propagate,* even if it is only to produce a couple of plants for the group sales table. Propagation of all genera in Campanulaceae is reasonably easy from seed, cuttings, or division, and for myself as a nurseryman, it is a necessity.

PROPAGATION BY SEED

I always encourage growers of campanulas to collect their own seed. From experience I know that good cultivars can arise this way, although I have found that seed from most of the species I grow produces plants that are true to type. One emphatic exception to this rule is *Campanula rotundifolia*, which will produce a vast number of variants.

Most of the hybrid seedlings grown from your garden-collected seed will be inferior to their parents (the flowers too small, perhaps, or of poor colour, or sparsely produced): consign these to the compost heap, retaining only the most promising. From these select for vigour, a neat habit, overall balance, and flower quality, and discard the remainder. When you grow on seedlings it can be difficult to throw so many away, as they almost become your babies, but throw them away you must.

"But where is the seed?" I am quite often asked. The main reason for this question is that unlike many plants, members of the Campanulaceae develop seed-pods or capsules below the base of the petals. This is to say that the ovary is inferior, and the seed capsule and calyx are united. With most campanulas and adenophoras, as the capsule ages and gradually turns brown, small pores can be seen near to the stem at the base of the capsule. These are covered with a thin membrane, which disintegrates once the capsule and seed are ripe, opening the pores. This in turn allows the seed to fall out, and in a wind it can be carried quite a way. In species such as *Campanula cashmeriana* and *C. rotundifolia* the seed is almost dust-like, while in *C. collina*, for example, it is bigger, and individual seeds can easily be seen. You have to keep a close watch, though, because some species can catch you unawares. When the flowers are pendant, as in *C. sarmatica*, the resultant seed capsule is also pendant, and the open pores are at the top of the capsule, making it easy to collect seed before it has dispersed in the wind. However, when the flowers are upward-facing, the seed capsules are upright, as in *C. scabrella*, and the open pores are at the bottom of the capsule. This makes it much more difficult to catch the seed, and in these cases it is recommended that the capsules are removed using scissors before they turn completely brown and the pores open.

Ripe seed capsule of
Campanula scabrella

Ripe seed capsule of
Campanula sarmatica

I always try to catch the capsules before the pores open, when they are brown and not quite ripe, but always when they are dry, which is essential. I sever them from the stem and put them in a seed envelope. Even if I do this too late, when the pores have already opened, it is still possible to collect seed if there hasn't been a strong wind. In some cases the capsules will have been completely skeletonised and yet there will still be seed there. In these cases, tapping the capsule over the open envelope will cause the seed to fall out. Sometimes if there are a lot of capsules, to save time and space I hold the capsule over an envelope and, using scissors, cut across it just above where the stems join. Ripe seed will then drop into the envelope, and the capsule can be discarded.

Codonopsis and *Platycodon* differ from *Campanula* in that the pores open at the top of a fairly large capsule in front of the sepals. This makes it easier to collect seed, as it is less likely to fall out or blow away. *Edraianthus* is similar but not so obvious, and the whole capsule has to be removed from the plant and be pinched and shaken to release any seed present. With *Physoplexis* and some species of *Campanula*, the capsule gradually reduces in size as it ages, until it is very small. This makes it difficult to know whether seed has been set. If this is the case, remove the crisp, brittle capsule and remnants of the corolla, crunch them gently between thumb and forefinger, and check with a magnifying glass to see if the seed has developed. If still in doubt, sow all the remnants of the capsule and corolla. This also applies for the species that set seed late.

Sometimes you will be disappointed when trying to collect campanula seed. What may seem like fat seed capsules when the plants are flowering will gradually get smaller as the flower dies, eventually almost disappearing and containing no seed. I have known this to happen with species that have set seed in the past quite happily year after year. You just have to accept that for a season you will not have any seed.

It is perhaps appropriate at this point to discuss the ways in which campanulas are pollinated. The anthers normally ripen within the flower while it is still at the bud stage; even then, pollen is shed onto the hairs that cover the style. But it is only when the flower opens that the stigma becomes ripe and receptive. Typically, cross-pollination takes place, whereby an insect gathers pollen from the anthers of one flower and transfers it onto the style of (usually) another plant of (usually) the same species. A second method, representing something of an insurance policy, is known as *selfing* and refers to the transfer of pollen from one flower to another on the same plant. Additionally, if you keep an eye on a selected stigma, you will notice that with age it will split distally into three, the tripartite lobes curling over and downward to receive pollen, so effecting a secondary fertilisation should the above mechanism not come into play.

This brings me to an interesting exercise in cross-pollination that you might like to try. Hybridising two species generally produces seedlings intermediate between the two parents, especially with regard to habit and flower colour. However, crossing an albino plant with a typically blue-flowered one will almost invariably produce uniformly blue-flowered offspring, as will crossing two blue-flowered species. If two albino plants are crossed, the result is usually the same. Nonetheless, a small percentage of the seedlings in the second generation of a white × white cross will likely be white, and if you have the time, experimenting with this is well worth pursuing. In some cases genetic mutation will produce a white-flowered plant from seed collected from a blue-flowered one. I had an example of this when raising plants of *Campanula morettiana* from seed. Having sown seed from three of my own blue-flowered plants, which in turn I had raised from seed given to me, ten plants were produced. Of these second-generation seedlings, three turned out to be white-flowered. Unfortunately, I had previously given away two of them, something I only discovered when told by the customer, who was somewhat delighted. White-flowered plants are most sought after, since most campanulas are blue. Just look at *C. raineri* var. *alba*, *C. carpatha* var. *alba*, *C. zoysii* 'Lismore Ice', *C. morettiana* var. *alba*, and so on. I cannot propagate enough of them.

This rough-and-ready guide can be amplified by referring to specialist accounts of the processes and outcomes involved; further reading of such literature is recommended, since other variations (in the shape and size of the flowers, particularly) can be expected.

Apart from collecting your own seed, you can obtain it from commercial seed lists or society seed exchanges. Commercial vendors have a reputation to maintain, and therefore such seed is almost guaranteed to be true to name. Be wary of seed obtained through exchanges, however, as it is only as true as the accuracy of the donor's plant. This isn't to say that all seed from exchanges is wrongly named; on the contrary, most will be correct. But even so, be wary. I have had a number of disappointments in the past with seed obtained from such sources, and even with seed from botanic gardens. Also remember that wild-collected seed is more likely to come true than seed collected in the garden, where hybridity may result from the comparatively large number of campanulas grown in close proximity.

A great many campanulas from the Caucasus are new in cultivation, with still many more to be discovered. Seed of these choice species is very difficult to obtain, with just a few Czech collectors listing them. Maybe future expeditions to the Caucasus will enable more of these gems to be brought into cultivation.

I always sow seed in a soil-based compost rather than in one with peat as its main constituent. Although germination is probably about the same in either medium, the peat-based compost encourages too great a fibrous root system. And once the seedlings are big enough to be planted in the rock garden or potted up, not only will their roots be tangled, but the root systems will also have a very difficult time adapting to normal soil, and quite often will fail. Anyone who has bought a plant from a nursery that has been grown in a peat-based compost will know what I mean. When I purchase plants grown in this manner, I remove as much of the compost as possible (the technique comes close to the process commonly referred to as bare rooting) before replanting in a soil-based medium.

When sowing fine seed, I fill a plastic pot that is 7 cm square almost to the top with compost, barely cover this with grit, and place the seed on top. If the seed is very fine, I mix a small amount with fine, dry, silver sand and sow the complete mixture. Next I set the pot in a dish of water and leave it to soak for approximately one hour. This draws the seed down slightly into the grit so that it is protected but still able to receive the light needed to germinate. (This is better than sowing fine seed on top of the compost and then covering it with a layer of grit, in which case the light will be removed altogether.) It is all too easy to sow fine seed and think that you are only sowing a small amount; the resulting mass germination will show you that you have sown too thickly and face the problem of disentangling the root systems when it comes to pricking out the seedlings. In such cases, choose the earliest opportunity to do so, or the seedlings could damp off because they are so crowded. When dealing with larger seeds, I sow them individually, or thinly (scattered from the tips of my thumb and forefinger) on top of the compost, covering them with a layer of grit. The grit I use for either kind of seed is approximately 2–4 mm in diameter. Most grits can be used, from normal horticultural grit to Cornish grit, chicken grit, or plain granite grit. Wash it thoroughly prior to use in order to prevent clogging.

Once I have sown the seed, I label the pots with the name of the plant, the origin of the seed, and the date of sowing, and then place them outside. Most of my seed is sown during autumn and will germinate the following spring. In recent years I have had seed germinate in autumn, within six weeks of sowing; this causes slight problems in keeping the seedlings over winter. Seed sown in early spring will usually germinate the same year, although some seed will wait another year before germination takes place. *Campanula morettiana* is one example of this.

Propagation by Vegetative Means

Vegetative propagation is carried out for a number of reasons. You may require plants that will be identical to the mother plant, or you may require mature plants of the same clone more quickly than can be obtained by growing from seed. Vegetative propagation is also useful if no seed was set that season by a plant you wish to reproduce.

Cuttings. This is the most common form of vegetative propagation used, and more plants can be reproduced quickly using it than with any other method. Cuttings of fresh shoots are taken in spring when new growth is under way. The bottom leaves are removed and the shoots are inserted into the cutting medium, which in turn is placed in a closed cutting frame or box. The medium I use is nothing more than moist, fine Cornish grit or silver sand. Others use a mix of peat, vermiculite, or pumice and sand. No cutting mix is indispensable, so if you are successful at present with your own mix, stay with it. Rooting time depends upon the weather, but on average a cutting should root in about four to six weeks, sometimes sooner. Just give the cuttings a gentle tug now and again: resistance usually means rooting has taken place. Once they have rooted, remove them and pot them on into a 7 cm pot, or a pot of a similar size, using a balanced compost such as the John Innes compost number 1 (for a recipe, see "Cultivation" later in the chapter). If you miss the spring cuttings, do not worry: spent flower stems that still retain foliage can also be used as cuttings later in the season as long as they are removed as near to the base of the stem as possible.

Division. Traditionally division is carried out as the plants come into growth in very late winter or early spring, but I find that division can be carried out over a long period from late winter until well into late autumn, as long as good growing conditions exist. In the United Kingdom, with our increasingly mild autumns and winters, I have divided campanulas as late as early December (though this late stage carries more risk, particularly if a cold spell follows).

Campanula root systems vary from a taproot, as in *C. betulifolia*, to a mass of matted rhizomes, as in *C. lasiocarpa*. Most campanulas with taproots have to be propagated by cuttings or seed, but occasionally they will throw out stems that have rooted below ground level, as with *C. portenschlagiana* or *C. cespitosa*, and these can be detached and potted up. In my experience with propagating campanulas, most species without taproots have been easy to divide. I have simply dug them up or emptied them from their pots, pulled them apart, and replanted. *Campanula arvatica* and *C. carpatica* are good examples of species that are easy to grow and propagate by division. *Campanula jaubertiana*, *C. piperi*, and *C. zoysii* need more careful treatment but nonetheless divide easily. These species are always in demand, and I have to grow as many plants as possible from the divisions. In these cases I remove most of the soil and then bare root the plants by washing off as much remaining soil as possible. Using scissors I snip off any stem that has a piece of root attached, pot these pieces up, and keep them in a cold frame until they are growing away. These are like rooted cuttings. Not all pieces will survive, but the survival rate is pretty high. Then there are those species with dense mats of rhizomes, such as *C. lasiocarpa* and *C. petrophila*. These *must* be bare rooted. Even when you hold the soil-free mass of rhizomes in your hand, it can still be a puzzle. Patience is important here: by gently teasing and pulling apart the crowns, you will eventually have pieces that can be potted up to form new plants.

Cultivation

Most campanulas bloom in the summer and require a sunny spot, resenting too much shade or excessive winter wet (a deep topdressing of grit and covering in winter help to counteract such conditions). In the rock garden, try planting the smaller species in a rock crevice. A crevice will allow the plant to get its roots way down, so that it can access moisture in a hot summer, but will provide quick drainage over winter. The taller species can be planted in the open rock garden or border if given a gritty soil and sunny aspect. The smaller species can also be planted in troughs or grown as pot plants in the alpine house. This will enable you to keep a wary eye out for pests yet still grow the plants as in nature, especially if you make up the trough or pot as a crevice garden. Campanulas that resent winter wet and subsequently rot off during that period must have some form of cover from the wet or be grown in the alpine house.

Contrary to some opinions, campanulas are greedy plants and if grown in pots need repotting every year. A liquid feed can also be applied during the growing season. It is quite a good idea when repotting a plant grown for exhibition to take any pieces popping up at the side of the pot (and not used for propagation) and reposition them into the main central mass of growth to make the appearance more uniform. A word of warning here if you grow campanulas in pots in the alpine house: Those that make a mass of roots or spread by shoots running under the surface (for example, *Campanula zoysii* and *C. morettiana*) tend to become dry in winter and this can occur without you realising it. Although these plants do not require as much moisture in winter as they do during the growing season, they still need some water to survive. Gently watering around the edge of the pot just will not do. The tangled mass of roots and underground shoots cannot take up moisture from the edge of the pot, and therefore they must be watered in the middle or from below. When I first grew *C. zoysii*, I wondered why I lost it over successive winters. Once I realised that the compost was dry on each occasion, the penny dropped, and I now ensure that all campanulas with this root system are kept watered in the middle. Taprooted species are not as sensitive, with water permeating to the centre of the pot. However, do not try to hurry the plants into growth once winter appears to be over, as too much water too early can lead to dieback or "sulking."

If growing in pots, I always use a loam-based compost, and here in the United Kingdom I am able to obtain the John Innes composts. These are numbered 1, 2, or 3, depending on the amount of base fertiliser in the mix; the higher the number, the more base fertiliser is used. I use John Innes compost number 1 for most plants, but campanulas cry out for numbers 2 or 3. If you have access to the ingredients and can steam sterilise the soil, you can always make your own using the following recipes. All ingredients are for 0.76 cubic M (1 cubic yard) of soil mix.

John Innes seed mix	*John Innes potting compost number 1*
2 parts sterilised soil	7 parts sterilised soil
1 part moss peat	3 parts moss peat
1 part lime-free coarse grit	2 parts lime-free coarse grit
1 KG (2 LB) superphosphate	2.2 KG (5 LB) complete base fertiliser
500 G (1 LB) chalk	500 G (1 LB) chalk

If you want to make up the equivalent of John Innes compost numbers 2 and 3, note that number 2 has twice the amount of base fertiliser as number 1, or 4.5 KG (10 LB), and number 3 has three times the amount, or 6.8 KG (15 LB).

Pests and Diseases

I think we can all agree that slugs and snails are by far the worst enemies of campanulas. Even in the alpine house I have to use slug bait to prevent the plants from being eaten by these creatures. (Be careful in the wintertime—the bait soon acts as a focus for botrytis.)

Powdery mildew will affect any plant that has dense foliage and becomes wet in the centre, unless there is a good flow of air around the plant. This is more prevalent in the alpine house, where airflow can be limited. It also bedevils older, more congested plants. Remove all dead foliage as soon as it is noticed to help keep mildew at bay.

Red spider mite will badly affect plants grown under glass unless the problem is treated immediately, and aphids can infest both new and, where mild winter conditions are the norm, overwintering growth. My advice is to use a systemic insecticide that can be applied as a drench, watering into the compost as early as possible at the start of the growing season. Some systemic insecticides give protection for several months when used as a drench, so will be best if applied well before the problem arises.

A–Z of Dwarf Campanulas

Campanula (commonly known as the bellflowers, bluebells, or harebells) is the largest genus in the Campanulaceae, but it is impossible to give an exact number of species. Many campanulas are so similar to one another, differing only in small botanical variations, that the total is continually being revised. For example, in 1830 Alphonse de Candolle described 137 distinct species, with many having a subspecies or variety. In 1907 this total was increased to 206 species and a list was published in the RHS *Journal,* while a few years later Reginald Farrer in his book *The English Rock Garden* (1918) partially described some 220 species. More species and varieties have been discovered since then, while botanists have either split or lumped others already described. The total has increased to at least 300, and no doubt that total will continue to rise over time, especially as more of the Caucasian and Turkish species are discovered. This total consists of perennials and annuals from the northern temperate zone, with just a few on tropical mountains, and ranges from the tightest compact forms to the tall plants we gardeners love to grow in the perennial border. The many attractive hybrids and cultivars send the total even higher.

As explained elsewhere, I have described only the campanulas with a maximum height of approximately 50 CM. Many are well known and common in cultivation, while many others will be new to most readers.

SPECIES

Campanula acutiloba comes from Turkey, Iran, and Iraq, where it grows in vertical crevices and rock fissures in limestone cliffs. It is a tufted plant growing from rhizomes, with hanging, curving stems 10–15 CM long spreading out from the rocks. The hairy leaves are to 1.3 CM long, reniform to ovate-cordate, with the hairs lying almost flat along the leaves, and the margins are lobed. The lower leaves are on long petioles. The light mauve to lilac to pinkish flowers are to 8 MM long, narrowly infundibular, have spreading lobes, and are in stalked racemes of one to three, growing from the leaf axils and blooming in late summer. Propagate by seed sown in autumn or spring, or by division of the rhizomes in spring. If grown in the rock garden or trough, this plant will need a warm crevice.

Campanula aghrica comes from Turkey, where it grows in limestone rock crevices at 1400–1700 M. It makes tufts of grey, hirsute basal leaves 8–13 MM long that are spatulate or narrowly obovate, irregularly dentate, and on petioles. The ascending stems, 10–15 CM tall, have lanceolate stem leaves and carry one to six solitary, bright lilac flowers to 8 MM wide on 4–6 MM pedicels. Propagate by seed sown in winter or by division in early spring and autumn. In the rock garden this plant needs well-drained soil and a sunny spot with protection from winter wet. It also makes a good alpine house plant.

Campanula albanica (synonym *C. hellenica*) grows in stony and rocky areas in the Balkan Peninsula. A spreading species, it grows from slender rhizomes that eventually form colonies. The basal leaves are cordate, dentate, and wither at flowering time. The erect to ascending stems are 8–15 CM long and have linear-ovoid leaves. The blue to blue-purple flowers are to 1.8 CM long and usually solitary though occasionally in pairs or threes, blooming in summer. Propagate by seed or by division of the rhizomes in spring. This species grows best in the rock garden, but be aware of its spreading capabilities.

Campanula albertii comes from Uzbekistan, where it grows among subalpine rocks. It is a tufted species with many erect, thin stems 20–30 CM tall. Stems leaves are few, almost grass-like, and denticulate. The dark violet flowers are solitary, occasionally two or three, and campanulate, with deeply cut lobes. Propagate by seed, if available, sown in spring or autumn. I do not think this species is in cultivation, but if it is it would make an attractive plant for the alpine house.

Campanula albovii comes from the western Caucasus, where it grows in sub-alpine meadows, spreading by its creeping underground rootstock. Slender, branched stems grow 50–70 CM tall, with lanceolate, crenate leaves on petioles 15–20 CM long. The dark blue or violet, infundibular flowers are in groups of two to nine in lax racemes 2 CM long, blooming midspring to early summer. Propagate by seed sown in autumn or spring, or by division in spring. This species grows well in a semi-shaded site in a large rock garden or border.

Campanula alliariifolia (synonyms *C. lamiifolia*, *C. microphylla*) comes from the Caucasus and the Turkish mountains, where it grows among rocks in conifer forests, in open scrub, occasionally on cliffs, and quite often on steep banks. It is a taprooted species and makes tufts of hairy, slightly serrate, ovate-cordate basal leaves to 10 CM long and 6 CM wide, with petioles 15–20 CM long. Erect, thick, hairy, leafy stems 50–70 CM tall have leaves to 7 CM long and to 3 CM wide, with shorter petioles, upper leaves sessile and much reduced. The light violet or white, campanulate flowers are to 5 CM long and 3.8 CM wide, have widely flared lobes, and are in one-sided racemes. They bloom for a long time, from early summer to late autumn.

Campanula alliariifolia var. *minor* is a form collected in the central Caucasus (Russia) at 1500 M, where it grows in screes. There is doubt, however, as to whether this is a valid name. It is similar to the more common form of the species but is only 10–20 CM tall, with large, pale yellow flowers. This is a nice form for the small rock garden, as it keeps its size in cultivation. *Campanula alliariifolia* 'Ivory Bells' is creamy white and is the usual form seen for sale. *Campanula alliariifolia* 'Flore Plena' is an infrequently seen double; however, those that have seen it tell me that it is not very attractive.

This species sets plenty of seed, and sowing in autumn or spring is the easiest way to propagate it. Some say it becomes a menace, seeding itself all over the place, but I have not found this happening in my garden. It prefers a sunny place and is not worried about the type of soil. It is hardy, long-lasting, and good for group planting. In fact group planting is preferable, as this plant is not very elegant on its own, the stems tending to fall flat on the ground. I debated whether to include this species, as one reference told me that it can grow up to 122 CM.

However, since I grow it in my own garden, where it only reaches 55 CM, and since I bought the plant from a respectable alpine nurseryman, I decided to include it.

Campanula alpestris (synonym *C. allionii*) comes from the southwestern European Alps, where it grows in rock crevices and screes at around 1400–2800 M, spreading by slender rhizomes. It has linear to lanceolate, entire leaves that form mats or clumps. Stems 5–10 CM high have solitary, cylindrical and campanulate, blue to deep violet-purple, horizontal flowers 3–4.5 CM long in late May onward that look like small Canterbury bells. It is a beautiful, striking species and is considered by some to be not easy in cultivation. It usually produces plenty of seed and can be kept going by sowing the seed or by careful division of the rhizomes in early spring. In the rock garden it likes a cool or east-facing position and soil that isn't too rich. If grown in an alpine house, some shade during summer is needed. A white form, *C. alpestris* var. *alba*, has been recorded.

Campanula alpestris,
French Alps.

Photo by Harold Bevington

Campanula alpigena comes from Turkey (Asia Minor), particularly the Pontic Mountains, where it grows on rocky slopes in the alpine zone. From a much-branched root system it makes rosettes of spatulate-lanceolate, serrate leaves, to 30 MM long and 5–7 MM wide, on short petioles and appressed-hairy on both surfaces. Ascending to erect stems 7–15 CM tall are covered with short pubescence and have blunt, spatulate-lanceolate leaves. The solitary, violet-blue, campanulate flowers are 2.5–3 CM long, with a hairy exterior and a tomentose, light blue base. The sepals are bluntly lanceolate and densely appressed-hairy. The appendages are sharply triangular, lanceolate, and twice the length of the hidden calyx tube. It is similar to *C. aucheri* but differs by having smaller flowers and shortened, spatulate leaves. Propagation is by seed sown in autumn or spring, or by cuttings taken in spring. Plant it in a sunny scree, crevice, or trough with excellent drainage.

Campanula alpina, the alpine bellflower, comes from Austria, Bulgaria, and Italy, where it grows in alpine meadows at around 1250–2000 M and usually occurs on lime-free soil. It makes rosettes of dark green, occasionally wooly, linear-lanceolate leaves. Stems are 10–20 CM tall, with many pale to dark blue, tubular, hairy flowers in May–June. It sets a fair amount of seed, and some nice selected forms can be grown from this. Although it is reputed to be perennial, I have never found it so and grow it as a monocarp or biennial. Be prepared to replace it after flowering, with plants grown from seed sown in autumn or spring. It is suitable for the rock garden, trough, or as a pot plant in the alpine house.

Campanula alpina, Bulgaria.

Photo by Ann Borrill

Short white form of
Campanula alpina,
Bulgaria.

Photo by Ann Borrill

Campanula alsinoides comes from the northwestern Himalaya, where it grows at around 2460–3075 M. From a woody rootstock grow several thin, hairy, zigzag stems to 10 CM tall. Stem leaves are small, oval-ovate, softly hairy on both surfaces, and faintly dentate. Small, erect, whitish, tubular-campanulate flowers to 1.5 CM long are on thin peduncles to 2.5 CM long that grow from the leaf axils. The flowers have wide, well-rounded lobes and pink-purple veining. This species is more interesting than spectacular and although occasionally perennial is best treated as an annual. It is similar to *C. samarkandensis* in growth and flower size. Propagation is by seed, plenty of which is set every year, sown in autumn or spring. Grow it in a trough or rock crevice and sow seed every year to keep it going.

Campanula andrewsii (synonym *C. rupestris* subsp. *andrewsii*) grows in limestone rock crevices in the southern Greek Peloponnese. It makes tufts of soft grey-green, oval-obovate leaves that are densely hirsute, crenate, and have a sharp apex. The blue-lilac, tubular flowers are 2–3.5 CM long, erect, and in short racemes on long decumbent stems. This species is very near to *C. celsii* and like that species is monocarpic or biennial. Propagate by seed sown in spring. In the rock garden or trough, grow it in a sunny crevice with protection from winter wet if possible. It can also be grown as a pot plant in the alpine house.

Campanula anomala comes from the Kabardino-Balkaria, a mountainous area in the northern Caucasus, where it grows in limestone crevices on gravelly substrates and rocky slopes. It is a large, prostrate plant. From a thick, short taproot covered with dead leaf remnants, it makes dense mounds of deep green, lanceolate-spatulate leaves that taper to petioles with hairs on the lower margins. Thin stems 10–15 CM tall have sublinear leaves and solitary, dark violet-blue, widely campanulate, glabrous flowers 4–5 CM long. It can be found growing with the white-flowered *Dryas caucasica*. Propagate by seed sown in autumn or spring. Grow it in a sunny trough or in the alpine house.

Campanula anomala, Mt. Fisht.

Photo by Vojtěch Holubec

Campanula ardonensis is a narrow endemic of Severo-Osetinsky Zapovednik, in Russia's Republic of North Ossetia–Alania in the mountains of the central Caucasus, where it grows in limestone rock crevices. It makes tufts of deep green, oblanceolate-spatulate leaves to 5 CM long. Ascending to erect stems 10–15 CM long have solitary, pendant, purple-blue, campanulate flowers with well-reflexed lobes. This species is often included with the *C. tridentata* complex, but judging from photographs there is a definite difference. Propagation is by seed sown in autumn or spring. It is best grown in a crevice in a trough, or in the alpine house.

Campanula ardonensis.

Photo by Vojtěch Holubec

Campanula argaea comes from Turkey, where it grows in calcareous and schistose rock crevices at around 800–2300 M. It makes rosettes of basal leaves that are oblong-spatulate, sinuate, 3.2–7 CM long on short, broad petioles. Ascending to erect stems, 20–40 CM long and sometimes branched, are densely leafy at the base and have lavender, narrowly campanulate flowers to 1.3 CM long in clusters of three to seven, sometimes forming a spike. As it is monocarpic or biennial it must be kept going by sowing seed in autumn or spring. In the rock garden, grow it in sunny, dry rock crevices with protection against winter wet.

Campanula argentea grows in crevices in the mountains of Armenia. It makes masses of tiny, flat rosettes of linear-obovate to spatulate, glaucous, sinuate leaves to 2.5 CM long. Stems to 7.5 CM tall are shortly branched and have a few oblong, glaucous, entire leaves and one to three erect, velvety-blue flowers on short pedicels. Propagate by seed sown in autumn. Grow it in a trough or in the alpine house.

Campanula argyrotricha comes from the Himalaya, where it grows on rocky slopes at 3000–4700 M. It forms low mounds to 20 CM across with tufts of tiny, ovate, dentate, silvery green, softly hairy leaves. The thread-like stems are decumbent, trailing, and to 7.5–15 CM long. The powder blue, tubular flowers with well-reflexed lobes are 1–1.7 CM long, solitary or in small clusters, nearly pendant, and on long, thin pedicels. They bloom from midsummer until early autumn. Propagation is by seed sown in autumn or spring. This is a choice species for warm, protected crevices or troughs, or for the alpine house in a shady position. It is not long-lived but sets plenty of seed and will self-sow.

Campanula aristata ranges from Afghanistan to Bhutan and the Hengduan Mountains of southwestern China, where it grows in grassland and alpine meadows at 3500–4500 M. From a thick taproot it makes basal tufts of elliptic, almost entire leaves to 3.5 CM long, with petioles at least as long again. The numerous thin, erect stems are 7.5–30 CM tall, with narrowly linear, sessile leaves. The small, solitary, often pendant, infundibular, pale blue flowers are 5–10 MM long and have five short, acute lobes. Propagate by seed sown in autumn or spring. In the United Kingdom this species is unlikely to be hardy outside and is best grown as an alpine house plant in a gritty, humus-rich compost.

Campanula arvatica.

Photo by Robert Rolfe

Campanula arvatica comes from the Picos de Europa in northwestern Spain, where it grows among limestone rocks. It is tufted, making small clumps with a vigorous, creeping rootstock. The small, bright green, cordate, dentate leaves are on long petioles. The slender, ascending to prostrate stems are 7.5–10 CM long and hold upward-facing, star-like, violet to pale blue flowers, each to 2.5 CM across and appearing June–September.

Propagation is easy by dividing the plant from spring onward and replanting. A large plant can be divided into a great many small pieces that soon grow into plants of reasonable size. This is best carried out at least every couple of years to keep the plant's vigour. *Campanula arvatica* is one of those happy-go-lucky campanulas that in cultivation adapts to life anywhere in the rock garden. Tumbling down over rocks like a blue waterfall, making a mat on a flat surface, growing from a crevice or in a piece of tufa—as long as its position is well drained, it is contented.

Campanula arvatica var. *alba* is like the usual form of the species but with white flowers. It is just as easy in the garden as the usual form and makes a nice foil when planted beside it. It also makes a very good pot plant in the alpine house, when in June or July it covers itself with white stars. It is reputed to be short-lived but in my experience has been as vigorous and long-lived as the common form of the species.

Campanula arvatica
var. *alba*

Campanula atlantis grows at around 2800–3100 M among limestone rocks in the Atlas Mountains of Morocco. It has a woody, branching rootstock with basal rosettes of long, lanceolate to spatulate, grey-green, hirsute leaves. Flowering stems are prostrate to ascending, 5–15 CM long, each with a solitary, openly campanulate, pale violet flower with darker veins. Propagation is by seed sown in autumn or spring, or by division in spring. Grow it in the rock garden or trough in a sunny, dry rock crevice with protection against winter wet, or in the alpine house.

Campanula aucheri (synonyms *C. froedinii*, *C. pallidiflora*) comes from the central regions of the Caucasus, Balkan Peninsula, Turkey, and northern Iran at around 1800–4200 M, growing from meadows up to screes, talus slopes, and in rock crevices. From a brown, thick, branched taproot with overwintering buds it makes dense mats, tufts, or clumps of lanceolate-spatulate, roughly pubescent, partially dentate leaves 1–5 CM long on short petioles. Thin, ascending stems 5–15 CM tall have sessile, spatulate leaves, becoming lanceolate near the top of the stem. Solitary, erect, blue to violet-blue, campanulate flowers are to 3 CM wide and to 4 CM long, with a white or light blue base. Propagation is by seed sown in autumn, with many plants flowering the following summer. This is an excellent caespitose plant for the rock garden and is closely related to *C. tridentata*. Grow it in a sunny rock crevice or scree, or as a pot plant in the alpine house using a gritty compost.

Campanula autraniana comes from Mt. Fisht in the western Caucasus, where it grows in dry, stony grassland and on limestone rocks in tight crevices at 1500–2867 M. When it is found growing among rocks in woodland, the stems are more lax or appear to hang, whereas in the alpine zone the stems are erect and compact. From a thin, long, branched root it makes dense tufts or rosettes of shiny, cordate-acuminate, finely dentate leaves on long petioles. The slender, few-branched, ascending stems are 5–25 CM long, with a few narrow leaves and one to three tubular-campanulate, deep violet-purple flowers 2–3 CM long and with a white base. This plant dies back late in the year, overwintering with a few resting buds. Propagate by seed sown in autumn or spring, or by cuttings taken in spring. It is a beautiful species and if grown outside needs to be planted in a tight crevice in a partial sunny site. It makes a good pot plant for the alpine house and for exhibition. If grown in tufa, it makes a lovely compact plant.

Low-altitude form of
Campanula autraniana
in forest conditions.

Photo by Vojtěch Holubec

High-altitude form of
Campanula autraniana.

Photo by Vojtěch Holubec

Campanula barbata,
Switzerland.

Photo by Ann Borrill

Campanula barbata comes from the European Alps and Norway, where it grows in subalpine meadows, rocky areas, and open woodland. From a deep taproot it forms basal rosettes of pale green, hairy, lanceolate-oblanceolate, occasionally undulate leaves. Unbranched and practically leafless stems 10–30 CM tall grow from each rosette. Campanulate, lavender or milky blue flowers are 2–3 CM long, have a fringe of long white hairs around and inside the petal lobes, and hang in pendant clusters at the tips of the stems in early summer. This species gets its common name, bearded bellflower, from the fringe of hairs at the mouth of the flowers. It is a biennial or short-lived perennial, and in cultivation seed should be sown every year to keep it going. However, self-sown seedlings usually appear, so that may be unnecessary. It prefers a well-drained soil as excessive moisture will surely shorten its life even further. It is an excellent plant for the rock garden or alpine house.

Campanula bayerniana comes from the Caucasus, Armenia, and northern Iran, inhabiting the rocky alpine and subalpine regions at 1845–3100 M, where it grows in tight crevices on limestone. It is a prostrate species and makes rosettes of small, reniform or ovate-cordate, dentate leaves to 2 CM long growing on long petioles from a branched, creeping rootstock. Wiry, erect, branched, prostrate to ascending stems are 5–15 CM long and have numerous leaf-like bracts. The medium to dark blue, terminal, upward-facing, infundibular flowers are to 2 CM long, glabrous outside, barbate within, have flared lobes, and are on short pedicels. Propagation is by seed, which it sets quite freely, sown in autumn or spring, or by division in spring. Cuttings can be taken from fresh growth in spring. In cultivation it requires a gritty lime-free soil and placement in full sun. It makes an excellent pot plant for the alpine house and was awarded an RHS Certificate of Preliminary Commendation in June 1985. It grows well in tufa, remaining compact.

Campanula bellidifolia (synonym. *C. tridentata* var. *bellidifolia*) is endemic to the central Caucasus in the Terek River area, where it grows in rock crevices in the subalpine and alpine zones. It is a low, prostrate plant that from a branching root system makes rosettes of subglabrous, ovate-orbicular, dentate leaves on long petioles. Thin, ascending stems 10–15 CM high have leaves similar in shape but smaller than the basal rosette, and solitary, violet-blue, campanulate flowers with a densely hairy base. Early in the season the buds are covered with many remnants of dead leaves and petioles. The sepals are glabrous and bluntly lanceolate, the appendages lanceolate and longer than tube. This species is often included within the *C. tridentata* complex. Propagation is by seed sown in autumn or spring, or by cuttings taken in spring. Grow it in a sunny scree, in a crevice in a trough, or in the alpine house.

Campanula bellidifolia.

Photo by Robert Rolfe

Campanula bessenginica comes from the central Caucasus (Russia), where it grows in acidic rocks at around 2500 M. From a taproot it makes compact tufts or mounds of broadly linear, dark green leaves. Wiry stems to 12.5 CM tall have many large, violet, campanulate flowers 3–4 CM long. Propagation is by seed sown in autumn or spring, or by cuttings taken in spring. This is a first-rate campanula for a sunny trough or the alpine house.

Campanula betulifolia (sometimes misspelt *C. betulaefolia*) comes from Armenia, Turkey, and the Caucasus, where it grows in limestone and volcanic rock crevices at 250–2280 M. It makes a woody rootstock with tufts of thick, glossy, pale to deep green, cuneate, dentate leaves with long petioles. The decumbent to ascending, brittle stems are 10–20 CM long and have pale pink to white, tubular flowers to 3 CM long. The buds are usually pink to red. Propagation is by seed, which is set quite freely, and some very good compact plants can be grown this way. Cuttings of new growth in spring can also be taken. This species is quite perennial in the rock garden, although it dies back to the rootstock during winter, and you have to be careful that slugs or snails do not chew off the new spring growth. Some nice specimens have been exhibited at AGS shows.

Campanula betulifolia

Campanula biebersteiniana (synonyms *C. tridens*, *C. tridens* var. *barbata*, *C. tridentata* var. *barbata*, *C. tridentata* var. *rupestris*) comes from the Caucasus, where it grows in pastures and screes at 2000–4000 M. From a thick, short taproot it makes rosettes of spatulate, glabrous or glabrate leaves to 5 CM long that have three dents on the rounded end and taper to a short petiole. The ascending to erect, glabrous or glabrate stems are 5–10 CM tall and have oblanceolate-linear leaves and light to dark blue, widely campanulate, solitary flowers 3–4 CM long, with lobes cut to a quarter of the corolla length. *Campanula biebersteiniana* differs from *C. tridentata* by having larger flowers that are campanulate rather than infundibular, and by having wider sepals that are blunt and covered with interlocked hairs rather than ciliate. There are ecological differences as well: *C. tridentata* grows nearly always in turf, while *C. biebersteiniana* is often found on screes.

Campanula bornmuelleri comes from southeastern Turkey, where it grows at 2350–3500 M in granite and limestone crevices. It makes dense tufts of obovate-spatulate and crenate leaves 5–20 MM long. Stems 3–10 CM tall have leaves that are ovate and much smaller. The rich violet-purple flowers are terminal, campanulate, upward-facing, and to 1.5 CM long. It is a summer-flowering species. Although it is rare in cultivation, a seed collection in Turkey by Jim McPhail and John Watson (*McP. & W. 5813*) made during the late 1970s produced many good plants that are still in cultivation. Propagation is by seed, division, or cuttings in spring. Although this species is best cultivated in the alpine house using a very gritty compost, it can also be grown successfully outdoors if situated in a vertical crevice or a deep, lean scree. It is reportedly resistant to heat and drought.

Campanula buseri (synonyms *Diosphaera tubulosa*, *Trachelium tubulosum*) comes from western Syria and Turkey, where it grows among rocks at 1000–1300 M. It makes tufts of lanceolate-obovate, grey-green leaves 1.5–3 CM long. The many ascending to erect stems 10–25 CM high have corymbs of 6–15 infundibular, creamy white flowers to 8 MM long. Propagation is by seed sown in autumn or spring, and it is suggested that this be done every year, as this species is usually biennial and sometimes even monocarpic. Probably best grown as an alpine house specimen.

Campanula calaminthifolia grows in rocky areas of Crete, mainland Greece, and the eastern Mediterranean islands. It makes basal rosettes of small, orbiculate, sharply dentate, greyish green leaves on petioles. Trailing to decumbent stems are 10–15 CM long and very brittle. The white to blue axillary or terminal flowers are to 1 CM long. This campanula is very similar to *C. sartorii* and is often confused with that species. It should be treated as a short-lived perennial, with seed sown every year in autumn or spring. It resents winter wet and if grown in the open garden should be placed in sunny, dry rock crevices with some protection in winter. Care should be exercised when handling the plant or weeding nearby due to its brittle stems. In the alpine house it should be grown in a very gritty compost.

Campanula cana comes from the temperate Himalaya, India, and Sichuan, Guizhou, and Yunnan provinces (China), where it grows in rock crevices at 1845–2465 M. It makes dense tufts of finely serrate, lanceolate leaves. Decumbent stems are 15–25 CM long and have many small, sessile, sublanceolate, acute, and denticulate leaves that are softly hairy above and ash grey below. The large, terminal, solitary, purple-blue flowers are broadly infundibular and have sharply reflexed lobes that are hairy on the outside. Propagation is by seed sown in autumn or spring, or by division of the running rootstock in spring. It is a short-lived perennial and is best grown as an annual in the alpine house. Crook (1951) likens it to *C. cashmeriana* and questions whether it can be regarded as a distinct species. Unfortunately I have not had an opportunity to grow both species side by side for comparison.

Campanula candida comes from Iran, where it grows at around 1850 M in shady limestone rock fissures. It makes tufts of obovate to spatulate, partially serrate leaves to 3.5 CM long, with petioles approximately as long, forming cushions. Many erect, unbranched stems to 15 CM tall have large, solitary, terminal, infundibular, white to bright blue flowers in the axils of the upper leaves, blooming in autumn. The flowers are to 2 CM long, with lobes divided for half the corolla length. Stem leaves are ovate, crenate, and on short petioles, and are more prevalent at the top of the stem. Propagation is by seed sown in autumn or spring, or by cuttings taken in spring. Grow it in a trough or the alpine house.

Campanula carnica (synonym *C. linifolia*) is wide-ranging throughout the European Alps, from the Pyrenees to the Carpathians, growing above 2155 M. It makes basal tufts of small, deep green, reniform-cordate leaves on long petioles, with many decumbent to ascending or erect stems 15–35 CM tall. The stem leaves are sessile, linear-lanceolate, and ciliate, with the lower leaves occasionally dentate. The pale to rich purple-blue, campanulate flowers are 1.5–2.5 CM long and from one to six on very thin, short pedicels. In overall appearance it is not unlike *C. rotundifolia* and can quite often be mistaken for that species. Propagation is by seed sown in autumn or spring, or by division in spring. It is easy to grow in the rock garden or trough.

Campanula carpatha is restricted to the island of Karpathos, where it grows at low altitude in the fairly shady crevices of limestone cliffs and rocky areas. It is tufted to clump-forming and to 30 CM across. The thick, dark grey-green, spatulate leaves to 7.5 CM long are hairy and sharply toothed. The stems are to 20 CM tall, and the stem leaves are smaller than the basal leaves but just as hairy and toothed. The rich blue to violet-blue, tubular flowers are to 3.8 CM long and have

Campanula carpatha

Campanula carpatha
var. *alba*

flared lobes. This species was introduced into cultivation by Peter Davis in 1950 and was quickly lost to cultivation, but a reintroduction was made by H. and I. Barton in 1983. Although some authorities consider *C. tubulosa* to be a synonym for *C. carpatha*, I have described *C. tubulosa* separately, as there is a definite difference. *Campanula carpatha* is also often confused with *C. carpatica* due to the similarity of their names. *Campanula carpatha* var. *alba* is a white-flowering form that makes a wonderful pot plant.

Propagation of *Campanula carpatha* is by seed sown in autumn or spring, or by cuttings taken in spring. Although variety *alba* is reluctant to set seed, cuttings taken from fresh growth in February–March usually root within six weeks. In *C. carpatha*, the stems carrying the tufts of leaves are quite brittle, so you must treat them gently when removing dead leaves or taking cuttings. This is a superb plant for pot work and is guaranteed to flower well over a long period. When the flowers have finished, give the plant a trim; this should ensure a repeat blooming later in the year, even into winter. Although reputed to be biennial or even monocarpic, this campanula can be kept going for several years as long as it is kept fairly dry over winter. Dead leaves should also be removed to prevent botrytis.

Campanula carpatica was introduced as long ago as 1774 but is still often confused with *C. carpatha*, although it grows some distance away in the Carpathian Mountains. It has a low-growing, spreading habit from a central rootstock, forming tufts that gradually increase in size as the plant grows, with clumps to 45 CM across. Leaves are medium green, ovate-orbicular, sharply serrate, and on long petioles. The wide-open, saucer-shaped flowers to 4 CM across are large for the size of the plant and come in every shade of white, lavender, blue, purple, and violet. They are produced terminally on wiry, erect, slightly branching stems. Propagate by seed sown in autumn or spring. This species does well in sunny or slightly shady but not excessively wet sites and in a rich, well-drained soil. It is a very useful garden plant, doing as well in the front of a border as it does in a rock garden, and blooms throughout summer. It has been used extensively in hybridisation for florist campanulas sold in pots and baskets.

Many cultivars of this species are offered in the trade, among them 'Blue Clips', to 20 CM tall, with lavender-blue flowers; 'Bressingham White', to 15 CM tall, with extra large white flowers; 'Flora Plena', with blue double flowers; 'Hannah', to 10 CM tall, with small white flowers; 'Isabel', to 25 CM tall, with wide, almost flat, deep blue flowers; 'Pelviformis', a dwarf compact form; 'Riverslea', to 30 CM tall,

Campanula carpatica

Double form of
Campanula carpatica.

Photo by Harold McBride

with large purple-blue flowers; 'Turbinata' (synonym *Campanula turbinata*), to 15 cm tall, with only one violet flower per stem and with hairy leaves; and 'White Clips', to 20 cm tall, a beautiful form with pure white saucers to 6 cm wide.

Campanula cashmeriana (synonym *C. evolvulacea*) is a lovely, delicate-looking, saxatile species from the Himalaya, where it inhabits rock crevices and cliffs up to 3692 m. It makes tufts of leaves growing from a woody rootstock, with erect to procumbent, wiry, brittle, branched, zigzag stems to 15 cm long. Leaves are to 1.9 cm long, alternate, elliptic, slightly toothed, and pointed at the end. The underside is grey and the upper side pale green, the whole leaf covered with tiny hairs. The solitary pale blue or blue-grey flowers are 2–2.5 cm long and hang down from each branch. Seed is dust-like and freely set. However, self-sown seedlings quite often appear adjacent to the mother plant and can be potted up to grow on to maturity.

 Campanula cashmeriana is deciduous and prone to rotting off in a wet winter if grown outside, although in the alpine house there will be some evidence of foliage. Nevertheless, it is a long-blooming species and well worth growing, usually remaining in flower from late summer well into October or even November in mild weather. If planted in a crevice it sometimes comes through the winter. From experience, it is better to treat it as an annual if growing it outside, and sow

Campanula cashmeriana

seed every spring. If growing it as a pot plant, cut the stems back to half their height in late spring, which will force the plant to send up more stems and produce more blooms. It makes a lovely exhibition plant for the autumn shows if three to five plants are potted together and then continually cut back as soon as buds are showing, to make bushy plants. Obviously, the final cut back has to be estimated correctly so the plant will be in bloom for the shows.

Campanula celsii (synonyms *C. ephesia*, *C. tomentosa*) comes from southeastern Greece, where it grows in rocky areas, its beautiful silvery grey, hairy foliage forming compact plants to 15 CM across. It makes tufts of spatulate-lyrate basal leaves with ovate, crenate, terminal leaflets. The flexible, ascending, branched stems grow to 30 CM tall, each holding several tubular, wide open, lilac-blue flowers, to 3 CM long, which bloom in summer. Propagate by seed sown in autumn or spring. This is another of the lovely biennial species that grow in Greece, but in cultivation it needs to be grown in full sun in a limey, well-drained site such as a dry wall. It is probably best in an alpine house, though, as it resents excessive moisture.

Campanula cenisia is a very high alpine plant growing in the western European Alps, especially Mont Cenis, above 2500 M, where it runs around in the cracks and crevices on granite rocky ridges and in moist acid screes. It forms a mat to 7.5 CM across made up of small rosettes of tiny, bright green, glabrous, obovate leaves growing at the end of thin underground runners. Slate blue, erect, stellate flowers appear June–July and are solitary on a short stem that rises from the centre of each rosette. Propagation is by seed, if available, or by careful division in spring. Like many choice campanulas, this species is prone to aphid attacks.

It is a very difficult species to grow, requiring an acid compost of almost all grit, plenty of moisture during spring and summer (avoiding a hot position), and an almost dry winter. If you are growing it in a pot, a few pieces of slate wedged in the compost will help it run as in nature. I remember seeing a lovely 15 CM pot of this species at an AGS show in 1987. The grower, Joy Hulme, said that she stood the pot in a saucer of water during its growing season. I can vouch for this method of cultivation. Having acquired three plants from a German nurseryman, I grew them on in the original compost of almost pure grit to the flowering stage, at which point I repotted them all into one pot containing an equal mix of John Innes compost number 1 and granite chippings. Within two weeks several stems died back and the plants looked very sickly. Remembering Joy's method, I stood the pot in a saucer and continually topped up the saucer with water. The plants soon perked up and are now growing well, with a lot of increased basal growth and growth from the remaining stems.

It has been recorded that a white form received an RHS Award of Merit in 1914 by a person whose surname was Tucker.

Campanula cenisia.

Photo by Franz Hadacek

Campanula cespitosa (sometimes misspelt *C. caespitosa*) grows in the Italian Alps at 600–2400 M, forming taprooted mats among rocks and in screes. It makes tufts of short, thin stems that have tiny, ovate-spatulate, slightly crenate leaves. The stems eventually grow to 15–30 CM tall, with linear-lanceolate, glabrous, slightly serrate leaves to 3 CM long, and have many lavender-blue flowers in sparse, secund racemes during summer. The flowers are bulbous, heavily veined, and to 1.5 CM long and 1 CM wide, with the mouth slightly constricted. Like *C. zoysii*, this species has a flower that cannot be confused with any other. It is beautifully curved—even sexy, some might say. There have been arguments in the past about this plant, some saying that if it is taprooted it cannot send out underground side shoots. However, like *Silene hookeri*, it does have a central taproot, but fibrous-rooted side pieces pop up around the plant.

Campanula cespitosa

Propagation is by seed sown in autumn or spring, or by removal of rooted side shoots in spring. In the garden it needs a sunny spot and a dry rock crevice, or maybe a trough, where I find it grows well. If possible, give it some protection against winter wet. The old flowering stems die back by autumn and can be cut back to the basal rosettes. It makes a nice pot specimen for the alpine house, requiring a gritty, well-drained compost; unfortunately, though, the stems tend to flop all over the place due to the weight of the flowers, so I suggest growing it outside for most of spring to prevent the stems being drawn up.

Campanula chamissonis (synonyms *C. dasyantha*, *C. pilosa*) ranges from the Aleutian Islands of Alaska to Siberia and Japan, growing in sandy, gravelly soils at around 2800 M. It is a rhizomatous species that forms clumps or colonies to 30 CM across from rosettes of serrate, spatulate-oblanceolate, light green leaves that are 2–4.5 CM long. The decumbent to erect stems grow 5–15 CM long, with solitary, pendant, blue, campanulate to tubular flowers, 3–4.5 CM long, that are heavily veined and very white-hairy inside, especially on the petal lobes. It is a very floriferous species and blooms in early summer and sometimes again in autumn. Propagation is by division in spring. This species grows well in the rock garden if the soil is fertile and well-drained and the site is in full to partial sun, but it will not tolerate wet soil. Although it spreads slowly, it does not become invasive. It also makes a very good pot plant for the alpine house.

Campanula chamissonis.

Photo by Cliff Booker

Flower of *Campanula chamissonis* 'Oyobeni'

Campanula chamissonis 'Oyobeni' has stems that grow 10–15 CM tall. It is more floriferous than the usual form of the species, with blue flowers that have a pronounced striping, very much like a gentian flower.

Campanula choruhensis comes from Tortum and Kargapazari Dag in Turkey, where it inhabits rotten schist and volcanic rock crevices at elevations around 2500 M, although the first collection was made at a lower altitude, 2000 M. It was named after the dominant river of the region and loves a cool northern exposure. It makes tufts of cordate, serrate, deep green, hairy leaves to 5 CM long. Plants vary in growth habit: some have a number of fairly short stems branching off and hanging down, carrying clusters of as many as six flowers, while others grow upright, with the bells massed together in a huge bunch. The flowers are white, sometimes flushed with pink or occasionally pink overall, and are to 4.5 CM across, blooming in May–July in the United Kingdom but later in the wild. The stems are very brittle, breaking easily if mishandled when repotting or planting in the garden.

This species was first described by Gwen Kelaidis (1993), who added that it was "sensational," and I have to agree. Her seed had been collected and introduced by Josef Halda, and my original plants were grown from that seed. A year later another Czech seed collector, Vojtěch Holubec, also listed this species, and so it became one of the best campanula introductions in recent years. At the AGS Summer Show South in 1997, both my plant and one grown by another member of the Wiltshire AGS group were awarded a Certificate of Preliminary Commendation by the RHS Joint Rock Garden Plant Committee. Propagation is straightforward by seed, which is quite abundantly set most years. Seed-grown plants vary in growth habit from upright to drooping, and leaf size may also vary; nevertheless, so far all my seed-sown mature plants have the large flowers of their parents. If you have a particularly nice specimen that you want to duplicate, you can take cuttings in spring when the new shoots are growing vigorously.

Campanula choruhensis grows well in a range of soils despite the rigors of its native habitat, and although it looks good in a pot, in the rock garden its downward-hanging flowers tend to be spoilt by dragging on the ground. It is a wonderful species and is easy to grow, almost as easy as the closely related *C. betulifolia*, with which it will hybridise if grown in close proximity. After it flowers in May or June, the stems gradually die back to a central rootstock, and during winter, a plant growing outside will look quite bare. In the alpine house, however, plants usually have a few green leaves showing. Slugs will attack and eat the fresh shoots in spring. Red spider mite can be a big problem if this species is grown in the alpine house, the leaves becoming very mottled.

Campanula choruhensis in a rock garden.

Photo by Zdeněk Zvolánek

Rose-coloured form of *Campanula choruhensis.*

Photo by Zdeněk Zvolánek

Campanula choziatowskyi comes from the Caucasus (Armenia), where it grows on cliffs and rocky slopes. From a creeping rootstock it makes tufts or clumps of small, thick, denticulate leaves. The numerous flexible, branching stems are to 30 CM or occasionally to 60 CM tall and carry many deep azure blue, tubular flowers with a pale blue stripe at the base. This plant is unusual in that the calyx flares outward, giving the effect of a blue cup sitting in a green saucer. Propagate by seed sown in autumn or spring. Plants usually flower in the second year after sowing. In the rock garden it needs sunny scree conditions.

Campanula ciliata (synonym *C. tridentata* var. *ciliata*) comes from the central Caucasus, where it grows on rocky slopes at around 3200–3600 M. It makes rosettes of lanceolate, glabrous, ciliate leaves. Each rosette produces a single stem with a solitary pale blue flower to 2 CM across and with dark blue points on the petals. Propagation is by seed sown in autumn or spring. It makes a nice compact plant in a sunny trough.

Campanula cochlearifolia (synonyms *C. bellardii*, *C. pumila*, *C. pusilla*) grows throughout the European Alps and along with *C. carpatica* must be the most popular of all dwarf campanulas. It quickly forms clumps or mats, spreading by its thin rhizomes running underground. Leaves are small, shiny green, orbicular-

Campanula cochlearifolia, Valle de Pineta, Pyrenees.

Photo by Harold Bevington

ovate or cordate, and slightly serrate. Stems to 10 CM tall and slightly branching carry many small bells in colours ranging from blue to lavender and a clear white. It is no wonder the common names are fairy thimbles or fairy bells. *Campanula cochlearifolia* var. *alba* is a white form.

Campanula cochlearifolia var. *alba*

Campanula cochlearifolia 'Elizabeth Oliver'

Campanula cochlearifolia 'Baby Bell' has small round bells, and *C. cochlearifolia* 'Lilacina' has rosy lilac bells. Both were found by Clarence Elliott in the 1930s one afternoon on the Galibier Pass, above the Lautaret, but are now probably lost to cultivation.

Campanula cochlearifolia 'Elizabeth Oliver' has double powder blue flowers, and *C. cochlearifolia* 'R. B. Loder' is almost identical. Lewis and Lynch (1998) suggest that they are one and the same plant, since, although 'R. B. Loder' had an RHS Award of Merit in 1922, no authority for 'Elizabeth Oliver' has been traced. However, the New Ornamentals Society (2003) states that 'Elizabeth Oliver' was found in a garden in Nottingham, England, about 1972. Other research suggests that they are two separate clones. Gardeners who grow both cultivars tell me that 'R. B. Loder' is less vigorous and blooms a couple of weeks later than 'Elizabeth Oliver'.

Campanula cochlearifolia 'Miranda' was discovered by Reginald Farrer and has fat, pale lavender bells on short stems. Clarence Elliott (1936) wrote that "Farrer let himself go at the top of his voice, and rather at the expense of all other pusillas, but 'Miranda' comes as near to living up to a Farrer description as a mortal plant could."

Campanula cochlearifolia 'Miss Willmott' is a vigorous clone with masses of shining lavender-blue bells that have a luminous quality about them. It dates back to the early 20th century, and Clarence Elliott (1936) states that the Miss Willmott for whom it is named claimed to have discovered it on the Rhône Glacier in the Swiss Alps.

Other popular cultivars are the china blue 'Blue Tit', pale blue 'Cambridge Blue', and silver-blue 'Silver Bells'.

Propagation is easy: just divide a clump or pull a piece off and replant from spring through summer. It is one of those campanulas that will grow anywhere, at the front of the rock garden, in troughs, screes, walls, between paving slabs—in fact, anywhere you want to plant something and just leave it to run around. Although some people consider it a menace because of its spreading capabilities, most gardeners are happy to let it do its own thing.

Campanula collina ranges from the Caucasus to Armenia and Turkey, where it grows in meadows and on rocky soils at 1600–2300 M. It is clump-forming, increasing quickly by rhizomes. Basal leaves are hairy, ovate-cordate to oblong or lanceolate, crenate, 5–10 CM long, 2–3 CM wide, and on petioles equally as long. Stems are 15–35 CM tall, occasionally more. The pendant, infundibular-campanulate, violet to rich purple-blue flowers are one to several on a stem, to 3 CM long, and hirsute inside. Propagation is by seed sown in autumn or spring, or by division in spring. Grow it in a sunny, moist spot in the border and it will increase very quickly. Farrer (1918) described this species as one of the most gorgeous campanulas we have. It is one of the most adaptable and worthwhile Turkish species for the open garden in the United Kingdom, but I do not recommend planting it in the rock garden, as it is likely to be invasive. It is a completely deciduous species over winter, so be careful when digging the ground during this period.

Campanula conferta comes from Turkey and Iraq, where it grows on rocky slopes at 1550–3300 M. From a short, thick taproot it makes crowded basal rosettes of pubescent, spatulate-oblanceolate, serrate leaves 2.5–5 CM long that are on short petioles. Prostrate to ascending, hairy stems grow to 25 CM tall and have a number of ovate-acute leaves. Lavender, infundibular flowers, to 1 CM long, are in clusters of three to five in the leaf axils and have exserted, trifid styles. Propagate by seed sown in winter or spring. In the garden it needs a warm spot with protection from winter wet. It is also suitable for alpine house cultivation.

Campanula coriacea

Campanula coriacea is endemic to Adilcevaz (Bitlis) and Van castle (old Van city) in eastern Turkey, where it grows on calcareous rocks and in crevices at 1500–2600 M. It makes dense tufts of spatulate, thick, pubescent, crenate leaves to 3.5 CM long and 1.3 CM wide. The ascending to erect, occasionally branched stems are 5–15 CM tall and have solitary, infundibular, lilac flowers to 2 CM long that are widely flared at the lobes. This is a very attractive species and can often be seen on the show bench. Propagation is by seed sown in autumn or spring, or by division in spring. Grow it in a sunny trough or in the alpine house using a gritty compost. It goes dormant over winter, looking quite dead.

Campanula crispa is a rare species from the Caucasus, Georgia, and Armenia that grows in rock fissures and volcanic shale at 1500–2100 M. It makes rosettes of shiny, ovate-cordate, crenate-dentate leaves to 7.5 CM on long petioles. The erect, unbranched stems are 30–50 CM tall, with racemes of broadly campanulate, blue to white flowers to 2.5 CM across that are deeply cut into ovate-acute lobes. It is closely related to *C. rupestris* and like that species is a monocarp, biennial, or short-lived perennial. Propagation is by seed sown in autumn or spring. It is likely to be very difficult to grow, and I suggest alpine house treatment where a close eye can be kept on the plant.

Campanula cymbalaria (synonym *C. billardieri*) comes from Turkey and Lebanon, where it grows in shady rock fissures at 1000–2700 M. From a branched, caudex-like root it makes rosettes of ovate-reniform, broadly crenate leaves on long petioles, and the flexible, decumbent stems are 20–30 CM long. The violet-blue, upright, broadly campanulate flowers are to 1.5 CM across and have distinctive spreading lobes, giving them a starry appearance. Propagation is by seed sown in autumn or spring. This plant can be grown in shady, humus-rich rock crevices, but as it is short-lived, it might be best placed in an alpine house.

Campanula davisii comes from Turkey, where it grows among limestone rocks at 800–2000 M. It makes basal tufts of ovate-cordate, serrate leaves to 6.5 CM long, with thin, erect to spreading stems 15–25 CM tall. Stem leaves are ovate and smaller than the basal leaves. The cylindrical, lavender flowers are 1–1.5 CM long and in racemes. The whole plant is softly hirsute. Propagation is by seed sown in autumn or spring, or by division in spring. Grow it in a sunny scree or trough with protection from winter wet, or as an alpine house plant.

Campanula dichotoma is an annual that grows in the Mediterranean region. It gets its specific name from the dichotomous growth of the hairy stems, which are 7.5–15 CM tall and have oblong, entire, sessile leaves. The lilac-blue, tubular-campanulate, pendant flowers are to 2 CM long and are terminal as well as being held singly in the leaf axils on short pedicels. The short lobes are not reflexed. Propagation is by seed sown in autumn or spring. Although this species is an annual, it can still make a pleasant patch of blue and is used mainly as a filler after the spring bulbs have finished.

Campanula divaricata, the southern harebell, comes from the southeastern United States, from Maryland to Georgia, where it grows in part to full shade in dry rocky or wooded areas. It makes clumps of basal rosettes with dark green, narrowly oblong or linear-lanceolate, coarsely and sharply serrate leaves that are pointed at both ends and 2.5–7.5 CM long. The slender, much-branched, almost leafless stems grow to 60 CM tall, with large, loose clusters of small, pale blue-violet, campanulate flowers, to 8 MM long, hanging from horizontal branches in early autumn. Each flower has a long, protruding style almost twice the length of the corolla. It is a beautiful and elegant species. Propagation is by seed sown in autumn or spring. It makes a lovely patch of colour in the shady garden in early autumn and looks best in a large garden where it can be grown in drifts.

Campanula dolomitica comes from the Caucasus, where it grows in stony, sub-alpine meadows and limestone rock fissures. It makes tufts of hairy, slightly crenate, reniform or orbicular-cordate leaves on long petioles. Stems are 35–60 CM tall and have similar leaves. The few broadly infundibular white flowers are 3–5 CM long, lobed to a third of their length, bearded at the edges, and are either terminal or in the upper leaf axils. This species is reputed to be a near relation of *C. alliariifolia* but is not very similar in appearance. Propagation is by seed sown in autumn or spring. It is a good garden plant for the sunny border but a little too big for the average rock garden.

Campanula drabifolia is an annual species that comes from southern Greece and the Aegean region, where it grows in dry, stony places. It has a number of short, erect to ascending, dichotomously branched, slightly hairy stems that have sessile, elliptic-oblong, coarsely dentate leaves. The erect, blue to violet-blue, campanulate flowers have a white throat, are to 1.6 CM long, and are on short pedicels. This species is similar to *C. erinus* but with larger flowers and pedicels. Propagation is by seed sown in autumn or spring. This is another of the attractive dwarf annual species, and like *C. dichotoma* it can be used as groundcover once the spring bulbs have died down.

Campanula dzaaku is endemic to the western end of the Russian Caucasus, where it is found growing in north-facing limestone crevices and on boulders at 2000–3000 M. From a slender taproot it makes tufts of dark green, leathery, linear-lanceolate to spatulate, dentate leaves 4 CM long and 4 MM wide. Thin stems 4–12 CM tall have few small, linear leaves and solitary, terminal, infundibular, light to mid-blue flowers 2.5–4 CM long and 1.5 CM wide. Mature plants eventually form a mat or loose cushion. This species was named for a young Abkhaz girl named Dzaku. There is also a striking white form that is probably not in cultivation yet. Like many other campanulas from this region, almost all stocks presently in cultivation can be traced back to Czech introductions made in 1996. Vojtěch Holubec collected *C. dzaaku* several times on Mt. Fisht. It is a beautiful and elegant species that deserves to be grown far more than it is. Propagation is by seed sown in autumn or spring, or by cuttings taken in spring. Grow it in a crevice in a trough or as a pot plant in the alpine house. It grows well in tufa and makes an excellent exhibition plant but unfortunately is still rarely seen on the show bench. It dies back to resting buds over winter.

Campanula dzaaku.

Photo by Vojtěch Holubec

Campanula elatines comes from the Cottian Alps in northwestern Italy, where it grows on hot cliffs and walls. From a thick rootstock it makes a number of basal rosettes of small leaves that are rounded to broadly ovate, cordate at the base, and sharply crenate, on long petioles. Brittle, procumbent stems are to 15 CM long, branching at the ends, and are covered with masses of violet-blue, occasionally white, stellate flowers to 1 CM across. The whole plant can be glabrous or softly grey-hairy. This species is often confused with *C. elatinoides*, which is coarser and more vigorous. Propagation is by seed sown in spring or autumn, or by cuttings taken from fresh growth in spring. This species is ideally situated above a hot rock that it can fall over or in a warm, well-drained crevice, where it will bloom all through summer. It does not like winter wet and often rots off if the drainage is not perfect. This is more likely to happen if the form with hairy foliage is grown. It can also be grown in the alpine house.

Campanula elatines

Campanula elatinoides comes from just one area in the Italian Maritime Alps, and although it is closely related to *C. garganica*, it is more like a vigorous form of *C. elatines*. It makes tufts of thick, broadly ovate-cordate, sharply dentate, grey-green, hairy leaves on long petioles. The many decumbent, ground-hugging, leafy stems are to 15 CM long, holding clusters of small, stellate, purple-blue flowers. The flowers are on short pedicels growing from leaf axils the length of the procumbent stems. Propagation is by seed sown in autumn and spring. Division is easily carried out in spring, and cuttings can also be taken successfully at that time. It is a fine, easy rock garden plant that makes a mound absolutely covered with blue stars during summer.

Campanula elatinoides

Campanula elegantissima is quite a rare plant and comes from the Caucasus. Procumbent stems grow 10–15 CM long, with numerous blue flowers that are 2–3 CM long. It is related to *C. choziatowskyi*. Propagation is by seed sown in autumn or spring. Grow it in a sunny scree, trough, or alpine house.

Campanula erinus is another annual from the Mediterranean region, where it grows on limestone rocks and walls. It makes basal tufts of obovate to ovate, dentate leaves on short petioles. Thin, erect, dichotomously branched stems make a small bush to 15 CM tall, with sessile leaves similar in shape to the basal tufts. Small, white to pale mauve, tubular flowers 3–5 MM long are terminal, axillary, and almost sessile. The whole foliage is softly hairy. A bright blue form has also been recorded. Propagation is by seed sown in autumn or spring. Although this species may be of some interest to an enthusiast if seed could be obtained, Crook (1951) considers that it is not worth space in the garden.

Campanula excisa comes from a very restricted area in the southwestern and south-central Alps, where it runs around in acid screes and rocky areas. It makes clumps of small basal leaves that are orbicular-cordate and serrate. These die off before flowering. Thin, erect, wiry stems grow from underground rhizomes to 10 CM tall. The stem leaves are linear-lanceolate, entire, and grow to 1.5 CM long. Flowers are tubular, dark blue, pendant, and in my experience solitary, although other growers occasionally report more. They are to 1.5 CM long and 1.5 CM wide. What makes this species individual is the unusual flower shape. The lobes are pointed, pleated down the centre, and curve outward, but at the base there appears to be a hole punched out between each lobe. This gives the plant its specific name and also has the effect of making each lobe look like an arrowhead.

Propagation is by seed sown in autumn or spring, or by removal of pieces of rooted stems in spring. *Campanula excisa* is one of the classics for the rock garden but is a bit of a traveller and loves moving to new ground each year. After dying down over winter, it usually emerges in spring in a different place. Plant it in a granite scree area in semi-shade or sun if you can ensure it will not dry out. I have lost plants in the past when conditions were much too dry. Although it appears occasionally on the show bench, this species does not like growing in a pot. It will die away unless repotted into new compost every spring, and even then it doesn't always make it.

Close-up flower of
Campanula excisa

Campanula excisa.

Photo by Panayoti Kelaidis

Campanula fenestrellata (synonym *C. garganica* subsp. *fenestrellata*) comes from Serbia and Montenegro, and Albania, where it grows in limestone rock crevices. It is in the same group as *C. garganica*, *C. elatines*, and *C. elatinoides* but unlike those species does not have completely procumbent stems. In makes neat mounds of small, bright green, glabrous, heavily dentate, ovate, cordate leaves on petioles. Stems to 15 CM long carry masses of stellate, bright blue flowers to 2 CM across on pedicels that lift them above the foliage. The whole plant is like a more compact *C. garganica*. Propagation is by seed sown in autumn or spring, or by removal of rooted pieces or cuttings in spring. This is another fine species for the rock garden, where it should be grown in full sun or partial shade.

Campanula filicaulis (synonyms *C. antiatlantica*, *C. maroccana*, *C. reboundiana*) comes from Algeria and Morocco, where it inhabits open woodland and shady, rocky places at 800–3300 M. It makes basal tufts of dull green, ovate-oblong leaves that form rosettes from a fleshy rootstock. Thin, flexible, ground-hugging stems with few leaves grow out to 40 CM and have panicles of a few pale blue, infundibular flowers whose spreading, narrow lobes give them a star-like appearance. Propagate by seed sown in autumn or spring, or by cuttings taken in spring. It will probably not be hardy in United Kingdom gardens and will do better in the alpine house.

Campanula formanekiana is a monocarpic species that comes from Greece and Macedonia, where it grows in rock crevices or vertical fissures on steep limestone cliffs. It makes a solitary, flat rosette of ovate, crinkly, grey, downy leaves 15–20 CM across. In time, from the centre arises an erect, rigid, leafy stem 20–60 CM tall bearing white or lilac-blue, campanulate flowers 5–6 CM long with broadly flared lobes. The flowers are usually solitary on pedicels growing from the leaf axils and are very much like small Canterbury bells. The stem leaves are spatulate, sinuate, and serrate. Decumbent stems also grow from the base and have flowers at the tips. A well-flowered plant can look like a pyramid of bloom. Propagation is by seed sown in autumn or spring. The frost hardiness of this species is doubtful, but do not be put off growing it because of that, or because it is monocarpic. It does take a couple of years to build up to maturity, but it is beautiful, long-blooming, and makes a wonderful pot plant for the alpine house, where you can enjoy its beauty close up. Just make sure to grow it in a deep pot.

Campanula fragilis comes from central and southern Italy, particularly the Naples area, where its habitat is coastal limestone rocks in partial shade. From a woody rootstock it sends up tufts of deep green, ovate, crenate leaves that may be intensely hairy, causing the leaf to have a grey appearance. The leaves gradually become smaller as the flowering season progresses. Stems are numerous, branched, and prostrate, to 45 CM, with mid-blue, campanulate flowers 3–4 CM in diameter that have a darker ring at the base, and well-spread lobes. The style is very prominent and extends beyond the lobes. Flowers bloom July–August. This plant is a close relation of *C. isophylla. Campanula fragilis* subsp. *cavolinii* is a form from the Apennines that has ovate-cordate, serrate leaves and flowers 2.5–3 CM wide.

Propagation is by seed sown in autumn or spring, or by cuttings taken in spring, although I have had success with autumn cuttings as well. Rooted side shoots may also be detached during the growing season and potted up. The stems are quite brittle, though, hence the specific name, and the plants have to be handled carefully when taking cuttings. It is usually cultivated as an alpine house plant but will succeed outside if you can find a warm limestone crevice. One reference even suggests it might be best in a hanging basket, but I have yet to try that myself.

Campanula fragilis

Campanula fruticulosa (synonym *Tracheliopsis fruticulosa*) comes from Turkey, where it grows in rocky areas in the mountains. It is very similar to *C. buseri*, the main difference being that the stems of *C. fruticulosa* have long, soft hairs and are very fragile. It also has broader and serrate leaves. Propagate by seed sown in autumn or spring. It is not long-lived and is best grown as an alpine house specimen.

Campanula garganica is a widely distributed and variable species throughout southeastern Italy and western Greece, where it grows among shady rocks and has been in cultivation since 1832. It forms clumps or tufts of bright green basal leaves that are orbicular-cordate, mildly serrate, and to 1.3 CM wide on long petioles. The prostrate to decumbent stems are branched and 10–15 CM long. The stem leaves have decreasing petiole length as they progress up the stems. The blue, stellate flowers are to 2 CM across, have a white centre, and are held upright on short pedicels. Occasionally there are white flowers. The plant can be glabrous or slightly hairy. T. C. Mansfield (1942) was enamoured by this floriferous species, whose flowers he described as "little blue starfish spread over the plant in that profusion with which starfish multiply. The plant itself is like a many-pointed starfish."

Campanula garganica 'Blue Diamond' is very like the usual form of the species in size and habit, but the corolla has a paler base, and when the stellate flower is seen fully opened it appears similar to a pale blue five-sided diamond.

Campanula garganica 'Dickson's Gold' is a cultivar with foliage very different from the more common form of the species and is a further example of why we should collect and sow our own campanula seed. It was raised by Stan Dickson of Newcastle, who found a golden-leaved form among the seedlings produced from a batch of *C. garganica* seed in the spring of 1974. He grew it on for four years, not realising its potential. Eventually he consulted A. J. Robinson, formerly of Greencourt Nursery, Kent, who propagated and distributed it under the name *C. garganica* 'Dickson's Gold'. The rest is history. It makes a neat mound of rich golden foliage to 10 CM high that grabs your eye and contrasts beautifully with the lavender-blue, stellate flowers. However, in my experience it is slow to establish and is nowhere near as robust as the usual form of the species, but it will put up with any amount of ill treatment in the garden.

Campanula garganica var. *hirsuta* is a densely grey-hairy form that has the same long flowering period as the common form of the species.

Campanula garganica 'W. H. Paine' has rich blue flowers, much deeper than those of the common form of the species, with white centres. A stunning plant that when well grown can conceal all foliage beneath the flowers.

Propagation of *Campanula garganica* is by seed sown in autumn or spring, or by cuttings or division in spring. It produces a lot of rooted shoots from the base, and these can be detached in spring, potted up, and grown on to make mature plants the following year. This species is one of the easiest and most widely grown in gardens. It starts blooming in early summer and carries on until the frost, and does well either in the sunny rock garden or in pots and troughs.

Campanula garganica 'W. H. Paine'

Campanula glomerata (synonym *C. stenosiphon*) is widespread throughout Europe, including the United Kingdom, where it grows in meadows and semi-dry turf on stony, calcareous soil. It makes clumps very quickly, increasing by slender rhizomes. The rough, pubescent basal leaves are ovate-lanceolate, cordate or sub-cordate, crenate, and on long petioles, often dying back at flowering time. Stiff, erect stems grow to 60 CM tall and have lanceolate leaves on shorter petioles. The campanulate, deep blue to violet flowers are 2.5–3.5 CM long and in small clusters at the stem leaf axils. They are also in dense terminal clusters at the top of the

Campanula glomerata,
French Alps.

Photo by Harold Bevington

stem, resulting in the common name of clustered bellflower. Although Will Ingwersen (1978) dismissed this species as being "of no real garden value," it is a well-known and popular campanula for the border and can be obtained at garden centres.

Campanula glomerata var. alba is a white form that grows 45–60 CM tall and also comes under a variety of cultivar names, such as 'Schneekrone', 'Snow Flake', and 'Snow Queen'. Campanula glomerata 'Caroline' is shell pink to lavender and grows 6–10 CM tall. Campanula glomerata 'Joan Elliott' is an early-blooming cultivar that was introduced by the late Joe Elliott, well-known nurseryman and founder of Broadwell Nursery in the Cotswolds. He named it for his wife. It has a crop of basal leaves with erect stems of large, blue, clustered flowers reaching about 40–45 CM. 'Purple Pixie', 'Acaulis', and 'Nana' are three well-known dwarf forms of C. glomerata. Although forms with double flowers have occasionally cropped up, they have not made much difference to the appearance of the plant; the flower heads are already tightly clustered, so the effect is lost.

Propagation is by seed sown in autumn or spring, or by division in spring. Campanula glomerata spreads quickly, so dividing it each year helps to keep it in check. It is easy to grow in the garden border in sun or semi-shade and can bloom for a long time, from May onward, attracting butterflies and, in certain parts of the world, hummingbirds. It is popular as a cut flower and is grown commercially for that purpose.

Campanula grossheimii comes from the Caucasus, where it grows on limestone screes. It makes tufts of deep green, ovate, crenulate leaves. Branched stems to 15 CM have ovate, crenulate leaves to 5 CM long on short pedicels, and large, terminal, violet-blue, campanulate flowers. Propagation is by seed sown in autumn or spring, or by division in spring. Plant it in a sunny crevice in a trough or grow it as a pot plant in the alpine house. It is a charming species and deserves to be more widely grown.

Campanula hagielia comes from Turkey, especially the southwest coast and Baba Mountain, where it grows on limestone cliffs up to 300 M. It makes basal rosettes of ovate-cordate, semi-lyrate, crenate leaves to 20 CM or more long on petioles. The several erect, occasionally wavy stems to 30 CM have leaves similar to the basal tufts. The erect, blue to violet-blue, broadly campanulate flowers are to 2 CM long, have reflexed lobes, and are in clusters. They are very elegant, like a

Campanula hagielia,
Priene, Turkey.

Photo by Panayoti Kelaidis

smaller version of *C. medium*. This species is a biennial or short-lived perennial. Propagation is by seed sown in autumn or spring. Grow it in a warm spot in the rock garden and propagate it every year.

Campanula hakkiarica comes from Turkey, where it inhabits limestone cliffs, crevices, and gorges at 1750–3200 M. It was discovered by Peter Davis and Oleg Polunin in August 1954 when they were visiting Cilo Dag in southeastern Turkey and was later named after Hakkâri Province. Since then it has been found to the north in Van Province. It makes basal tufts of shiny, dark green, spatulate-obovate and oblanceolate, dentate leaves to 3 CM long. The many ascending stems to 10 CM tall each have up to six slate blue to violet-blue, narrow, infundibular flowers 2–3 CM long that are more or less erect on slender pedicels. It makes a very tight, tufted mound to 12.5 CM across, although plants in cultivation have grown as large as 20 CM across. It blooms June–August. Propagation is by seed sown in autumn or spring, or by cuttings taken in spring. Rooted pieces can also be removed from the edge of the plant in spring. This species makes a good trough or pot plant when grown in gritty compost or in tufa, but beware of slugs if growing it outside, and some protection from winter wet is also advisable. It is an excellent species to grow as a pot plant in the alpine house and is often seen on the show bench. Occasionally in cultivation the stems grow out of character and tend to fall over.

Campanula hawkinsiana is a beautiful species that inhabits the steep and unstable schist and serpentine screes and rocks of northern Greece and Albania at around 1700 M. It makes low mounds of small, green, rounded and scalloped leaves that grow from a central rootstock. The ascending to erect, thin, wiry stems are 7.5–15 CM long and have solitary, terminal, rich deep purple, bowl-shaped flowers to 1.5 CM in diameter that turn up at the tips and are darker at the petal base. The pollen is so bright that the flowers appear to have golden stamens, giving the flower a bright yellow eye. It is in bloom throughout summer. A good form exists that was grown from seed collected from the 1999 AGS Macedonia and Epiros Seed Expedition under the collection number *MESE 515*. Propagation is by seed sown in autumn or spring. Although quite a spectacular rarity, and a must for the sunny rock garden and scree, this species is short-lived and must be kept going annually by seed, which it sets freely. It often self-sows, especially in the alpine house, where it will pop up in neighbouring pots.

Campanula hakkiarica

Campanula hawkinsiana

Campanula hedgei comes from Turkey, where it grows in limestone and volcanic rock crevices at around 2100–2900 M. It makes tufts of broadly ovate, slightly dentate leaves 5–20 MM long, and the whole plant is pubescent to hirsute. Slender, procumbent stems 5–20 CM long have lavender-blue, narrowly campanulate flowers in lax panicles in summer. Propagation is by seed sown in autumn or spring. Grow it in sunny, dry rock crevices or poor soil, but give it some protection against winter wet. It can also be grown as a pot plant in the alpine house.

Campanula hercegovina comes from Bosnia and Herzegovina, where it grows in limestone crevices and cliffs. It makes tufts of green, ovate-cordate, serrate basal leaves from a short, woody rhizome. Slender, branched, decumbent stems 10–20 CM long have many rich lilac, campanulate flowers to 2 CM long with flared lobes. It blooms from late May to June and sometimes continues sporadically into autumn. *Campanula hercegovina* slowly forms a clump, never becoming invasive. It grows well in the rock garden or trough in a gritty soil, where it dies down during the winter and reappears in late spring. In an alpine house or cold frame, a few green stems linger throughout the winter. It is a very easy plant to grow, either in an alpine bed or trough. It was introduced into cultivation many years ago by Walter Ingwersen.

Flowers of *Campanula hercegovina* 'Nana'

Campanula hercegovina 'Nana' is much more compact than the more common form of the species and is an absolute gem for a trough or as an exhibition plant. The flowers are small, campanulate, and deep lilac, like those of the usual form, and borne on slender, branched, decumbent stems 7–10 CM long. Well-grown plants in the alpine house can make a mound to 33 CM across.

Occasionally seed is set, and this can be sown during autumn, but if you collect seed from your own garden plants you may end up with hybrids. On the one occasion I found seed, the resultant four plants were each different from one another and from the mother plant. Cuttings can be taken from new growth in spring or increased by division, pulling the plant apart and potting up the rooted pieces. In the nursery I grow half a dozen plants in plastic pots and use them for propagation stock rather than continually digging up the garden specimen. In this way I can divide the stock plants at least three times in one year.

Campanula herminii ranges from the Sierra Nevada of southern Spain into Portugal, where it grows on stony slopes at 1900–3000 M. It makes loose tufts of orbicular-ovate, softly crenate to entire leaves on long petioles that form rosettes. The ascending to erect stems, 10–15 CM long, are occasionally branched, and the few stem leaves are lanceolate-linear, the upper ones sessile. The blue, broad, infundibular flowers are 1–2 CM long, with spreading lobes, and are produced in a few flowered panicles. This plant spreads by a creeping woody rhizome. Propagation is by seed sown in autumn or spring, or by division in spring. It is a short-lived perennial, occasionally only an annual, and is best kept going by seed each year. It makes a good trough plant.

Campanula heterophylla comes from Crete and the Cyclades Islands, where it grows in rock crevices. It makes tufts of smooth, light green, oblong-lanceolate basal leaves to 4 CM long on short petioles. The numerous decumbent, unbranched stems to 20 CM grow out from the tufts and have small, orbicular, nearly sessile leaves to 1.2 CM long. The mauve-blue, erect, infundibular, sessile flowers are to 1.5 CM long and 2 CM wide, have spreading lobes, are dense throughout three-quarters the length of the stem, and bloom over a long period. It is a beautiful species and is unusually hardy, bearing in mind its native habitat. Crook (1951) noted that one of his plants survived temperatures between −14°C and −17°C in Southport, United Kingdom, during the winter of 1944–1945. However, winters like that in the United Kingdom are a thing of the past. Propagation of

Campanula heterophylla

Campanula hierapetrae

C. heterophylla is by seed sown in autumn or spring, which, as with many campanulas, will produce plants that have quite a variation in colour and flower size. Grow it in a sunny crevice in the rock garden with plenty of chippings around the crown and some protection from winter wet. It has very brittle stems, so be careful with where it is planted (out of the wind) and when you collect seed. This species also makes a lovely alpine house plant.

Campanula hieracioides is a perennial species that comes from the western region of the Caucasus, where it grows in the gorge of the Gega River and in mountain meadows. From short rhizomes it makes tufts of leaves on long petioles. Many mostly unbranched stems are slightly geniculate and grow 20–30 CM tall, with sessile, ovate-lanceolate, serrate leaves. The blue flowers are 2.5–3.5 CM long and in large racemes. Propagate by seed sown in autumn or spring. This is a deciduous species and grows best in partial shade in the rock garden or as a pot plant in the alpine house.

Campanula hierapetrae is an endemic of Afendis Kavousi in eastern Crete, where it inhabits limestone rock faces at 1000–1450 M. From a central crown come many thin, brittle, unbranched, prostrate stems to 10 CM long with ovate to almost orbicular leaves. The many upright, lilac-blue bells are 1.2–1.5 CM long and have exserted styles. Crook (1951) considered it to be a small form of *C. calaminthifolia*. Propagation is by seed sown in autumn or spring. If growing it in the garden, plant it in a trough but with protection from winter wet. It can also be grown in the alpine house, where it will self-seed in its own pot.

Campanula humillima comes from the Zagros Mountains, Iran, where it grows at around 3700 M in crevices of tufa-like limestone, often close to and among plants of *Dionysia khuzistanica*. It is a tiny caespitose plant that makes tufts of light green, glabrous, orbicular-cordate leaves 3–5 MM wide that have up to seven angular teeth and are on long, thin petioles. The several smooth, loosely branched stems grow 2–4 CM tall, each with up to three small, white, tubular flowers that have violet- to blue-tipped, flared lobes and are on thin pedicels. Propagate by seed sown in autumn or spring. This species is best grown as an alpine house plant in a very gritty compost.

Campanula hypopolia.

Photo by Robert Rolfe

Campanula hypopolia is endemic to the Caucasus, where it grows in rock fissures from subalpine to alpine level. It is a deciduous, tufted plant. The linear to lanceolate, serrate leaves are to 6.5 CM long and 4 MM wide and have a central groove running from base to tip that gives the appearance of a fold in the leaf. The leaves are dark green on the upper surface and silvery-haired on the underside. Stems grow from the tufts to 12.5 CM high and terminate in panicles of light blue to lilac, tubular, campanulate flowers to 2.5 CM long and 2 CM wide. The lobes are deeply cut to almost half the length of the flower. Propagate by seed sown in autumn or spring, or by cuttings taken in spring. This beautiful species makes a fine pot plant, especially for exhibition, but it does require a deep pot. In the garden grow it in full sun and give it a deep root run.

Campanula incanescens (synonym *C. fedtschenkiana*) comes from Iran and Iraq, where it grows in rock crevices and screes in montane to subalpine areas. It makes tufts of small, grey, pubescent, oval leaves on short petioles. The numerous thin, fragile, branched stems grow 5–20 CM tall and have small, infundibular, violet-blue flowers, either solitary or in few-flowered corymbs. This species is very much like *C. quercetorum*. Grow it in a sunny crevice in a trough, or in the alpine house. Propagation is by seed sown in autumn or spring, or by cuttings taken in spring.

Campanula incurva (synonym *C. leutwinii*) comes from eastern Greece, where it grows among shrubs and in rocky places. It makes rosettes of ovate-cordate, crenate, yellow-green leaves on long petioles. The ascending to decumbent stems are to 30 CM or more and have large, beautifully formed, ice blue, campanulate flowers 4–5 CM long, in racemes or panicles. Its buds are just as nice, described by one nursery as looking like "rosy-tipped, Turkish turbans" (Annie's Annuals 2005). In flower it is like a smaller but bushier *C. medium*, Canterbury bells, but even out of flower the low, tight foliage rosette is attractive and evergreen. Propagation is by seed sown in autumn or spring. There are various opinions on the longevity of this species: some say it is perennial, others say biennial or even monocarpic. I suggest you treat it as monocarpic and sow seed each year; in this way you will not be disappointed. Grow it in a rich, well-drained soil in full sun.

Campanula incurva 'Blue Ice' is quite spectacular, growing to 30 CM and smothered throughout summer with masses of flowers with glistening blue and white tinges. It is best planted at the front of a rock garden or border.

Campanula involucrata comes from Turkey, Iraq and Iran, where it grows in open forests and on rocky slopes and screes. It makes rosettes of obovate-obtuse, crenulate, slightly downy leaves to 5 CM long, with petioles to 4 CM long. The erect to ascending stems are 20–30 CM long, with oblong-lanceolate, sessile leaves to 2 CM long. Blue, infundibular flowers are to 1.5 CM long, lobed to half their length, and in dense terminal clusters. Propagation is by seed sown in autumn or spring, or by division in spring. Grow it in a sunny scree or as a pot plant in the alpine house.

Campanula isaurica (synonym *C. ermenekensis*) comes from Turkey, where it grows on limestone rocks at 1800–2200 M. It makes tufts of green, spatulate leaves with brittle, erect, grey, lanate stems to 20 CM. The pale blue, campanulate flowers are 2.5–3 CM long and in short, lax racemes. This species is very much like *C. leucosiphon* but with a different leaf shape. Propagation is by seed sown in autumn or spring. It is best grown as an alpine house plant in a very gritty compost.

Campanula isophylla, commonly known as Italian bellflower or falling stars, comes from northwestern Italy, where it grows in coastal limestone rock crevices near Savona. From a woody rootstock come many soft stems to 25 CM long, with long-stemmed, oval to cordate leaves that are occasionally slightly hairy. The large, blue, lavender-blue, or white flowers are stellate and held in erect, loose clusters. There are a number of cultivars. 'Mayi' is greyish blue with darker tips, 'Alba' is white, 'Orion' has large flowers with a whitish centre, and 'Vega' has deep blue flowers. There are also double forms.

Propagate by seed sown in autumn or spring. Seed that will produce plants with a mixture of colours is available from commercial seed lists. It is best to treat this species as an annual or half-hardy perennial and keep it going by seed, cuttings, or division in spring. It cannot really be classed as winter-hardy if planted in the rock garden, even though in mild winters it can come through unscathed. It is very easy to grow and is probably more suited to window boxes or hanging baskets, although in the rock garden it can make a fine hanging or trailing plant. Grow it in a hanging basket with fuchsias and geraniums.

Campanula isophylla is occasionally found in gardens or nurseries mislabelled as *C.* 'Mollis' or *C. isophylla* 'Mollis'. There is a distinct difference in the shape of the leaves between *C. isophylla* and *C. mollis*, however, and the mature seed capsules of *C. mollis* are fully pendant.

Campanula jaubertiana is a limestone dweller from the screes and rock crevices of the Aragonese Mountains of the central Pyrenees at 700–2000 m, and in isolated sites on the high southern slopes of the foothills of the Spanish Pyrenees. It shares these limestone rocks with *C. cochlearifolia*, but although these species grow so close together, they never appear to hybridise. *Campanula jaubertiana* is tufted and makes thick mats, growing from rhizomes, with basal leaves that are ovate and serrate and on petioles longer than the leaf. The densely hairy stems grow 5–12.5 cm tall, with a few oblong-lanceolate, mildly serrate stem leaves and narrow, solitary, intense violet-blue, tubular, pendant flowers 8–12 mm long on short pedicels. It is a lovely, free-flowering, vigorous species. Although described as long ago as 1868, it was first photographed by Harold Bevington in June 1980 and reintroduced into cultivation by Harold and Winifred Bevington in about 1990. In the wild *C. jaubertiana* normally flowers from July to August, but in cultivation it blooms about a month earlier.

A plant thought to be *Campanula jaubertiana* was found growing at one station in Andorra and was tentatively identified as *C. jaubertiana* subsp. *andorrana*. Further examination of this form, however, leads me to suspect it is a hybrid with *C. cochlearifolia*. It makes basal tufts of orbicular, serrate leaves with stems to

Campanula jaubertiana.
Photo by Harold Bevington

Campanula jaubertiana
subsp. *andorrana,*
probably a hybrid with
C. cochlearifolia

Campanula kemulariae
in a rock garden.

Photo by Zdeněk Zvolánek

12.5 CM tall that have lanceolate-ovate, serrate leaves. The deep blue, campanulate flowers to 1.5 CM long and 1 CM wide are in racemes.

Propagation of *Campanula jaubertiana* is by seed sown in autumn or spring, or by cuttings taken in spring. It can also be increased very quickly by division as long as you exercise some care. Early in spring dig it up or remove it from its pot, and using scissors, cut off any piece of stem that has a root on it. Carefully pot the pieces up, and by late spring they will be growing well. You should never be without this jewel.

Cultivation is straightforward, whether growing this plant in a scree, raised bed, or trough with very gritty soil and some shade on hot summer days. It also thrives in pots and in the United Kingdom is often exhibited at summer shows. As it loves to run, top-dress the pot with at least 3.5 CM of grit. In winter, outdoor plants usually disappear below ground level, but those in the alpine house show some green foliage and start into growth earlier. With alpine house specimens, it is best to clip over the stems in autumn, removing the spent flower heads and any stems that appear dead. Slugs are the worst problem it encounters.

Campanula kemulariae comes from the Caucasus. It is very similar to *C. raddeana* and indeed has been merged into this species in Oganesian's "Synopsis of Caucasian Campanulaceae" (1995). This makes sense, as everyone I have spoken to during research has told me that they have never been able to tell the two species apart. This is another of the Caucasian campanulas related to *C. choziatowskyi*.

Campanula kirpicznikovii comes from the central Caucasus (Russia), where it grows in cracks and crevices of vertical limestone rocks at around 1300 M. It is a beautiful member of the *C. betulifolia* group. It makes tufts of dark green, dentate leaves with leafy stems 15–30 CM tall that carry yellowish buds that open to extremely big, creamy white flowers. Propagation is by seed sown in autumn or spring. Grow it in a sunny limestone crevice or scree, or in a trough where it can hang over the side.

Campanula kolakovskyi comes from the Transcaucasus and is endemic to Georgia (Abkhazia), where it grows in rock fissures in the forest zone. It makes basal rosettes of glossy, deep green, ovate, dentate leaves on short petioles. Erect to ascending stems 15–20 CM tall have two to three lavender-violet, campanulate flowers with lobes deeply cut to more than half the length of the corolla. Propagate by seed sown in autumn or spring. This species is very rare in cultivation and when available should be grown in the alpine house.

Campanula kolenatiana is a monocarpic or biennial species that comes from the subalpine regions of the Caucasus, where it grows among shady rocks. It makes tufts of thick, smooth, ovate-obtuse, cordate, crenate leaves on long petioles. Stiff, ascending to erect stems are to 20 CM tall and occasionally branched from the base. Stem leaves are few, oblong, and sessile. Each branch carries a few broadly campanulate, glabrous, violet-blue, pendant flowers that are to 2.5 CM long, with well-reflexed lobes that are hairy inside, held in one-sided racemes. In broad outline it resembles *C. sarmatica*. Propagation is by seed sown in autumn or spring. In the garden it needs a shady, humus-rich spot among rock crevices. It also makes a good alpine house plant when grown in a gritty, humus-rich compost.

Campanula komarovii comes from the northwestern Caucasus, mainly along the Black Sea coast between the cities of Gelendzhik and Novorossiysk, where it grows in dry meadows and on limestone slopes. Although a short-lived perennial, it is very attractive and can easily be raised from seed each year. From a woody rootstock it makes basal rosettes of long, spatulate leaves on narrow petioles. Leafy, branched, ascendant, pubescent stems grow to 50 CM tall, occasionally more, with leaves that are sessile, lanceolate, pubescent, and to 4 CM long and 1.5 CM wide. The large, bright blue to deep violet, campanulate flowers are to 5 CM long and on pedicels, have acute reflexed lobes, and start to bloom in early summer. Propagate by seed sown in autumn or spring. Grow it in full sun and a dry position in the large rock garden or perennial border, as it hates damp conditions and will quickly rot off. The large flowers and long blooming period make it an attractive addition to the garden.

Campanula kryophila (synonyms *C. ardonensis* var. *kryophila*, *C. saxifraga* var. *leptorhiza*, *C. tridentata* var. *saxifraga*) is endemic to the high mountains of northern Ossetia in the central Caucasus, where it grows at 2100–3400 M in alpine volcanic screes and rocks near melting snow. From a thin, branched root system it makes rosettes of orbicular-ovate, nearly glabrous leaves to 1 CM long, with several small dents on the tip, on long, thin petioles. Very thin, ascending stems 4–10 CM long have several small, lanceolate leaves on petioles that are shorter than those on the basal leaves, and carry solitary, narrow, campanulate, light blue flowers with the lobes cut back a third. The base of the flower is glabrous. The sepals are sharp, linear-lanceolate, and the appendages sharply lanceolate, longer than the tube. This species is related to *C. ardonensis* and *C. bellidifolia* and differs only by having linear stem leaves and a glabrous flower bottom. Propagation is by seed sown in autumn or spring, or by division or cuttings in spring. Grow it in a fine scree, a trough, or the alpine house, but it does require a cool spot.

Campanula kryophila, Mt. Elbrus, Georgia.

Photo by Vojtěch Holubec

Campanula laciniata comes from mainland Greece, Crete, and Karpathos, growing at sea level in limestone fissures. From a thick rootstock below and above the ground come large basal rosettes of light green, broadly obovate, laciniate leaves to 15 CM long and diminishing to winged petioles. The stout, erect, smooth stems are to 50 CM tall or more and have leaves that are smaller, ovate-lanceolate, and sessile. Lavender-blue, broadly or flatly campanulate flowers to 5 CM across have distinct white centres and are in loose terminal panicles of one to three per peduncle. Joseph Pitton de Tournefort, the discoverer of this species, described it as "the fairest campanula in all of Greece," and in 1938 Peter Davis wrote that it was "one of the finest monocarpic species" he knew (Archibald and Archibald 1993–1994). Nicholas Turland (1993) observed that "it forms rather small plants with thick leaves when growing on exposed cliffs facing the sea but reaches its full size in shady gorges sheltered from the elements." Propagation is by seed sown in autumn or spring. This species is probably not hardy in the garden and is best cultivated in the alpine house, although it may be a little too large for some alpine house owners.

Campanula lanata (synonym *C. velutina*) is a monocarpic or biennial species that comes from northern Greece, Bulgaria, and Serbia and Montenegro, where it grows in rock crevices, sending its roots deep down into the rocks. It makes basal tufts of grey-tomentose, ovate-cordate leaves on long petioles. Stems grow 30–60 CM tall, with the upper leaves almost sessile. The pale yellow to cream or pale pink, broadly campanulate, terminal flowers are to 2.5 CM long and grow from the leaf axils or on short pedicels. The corolla lobes are bearded, with long hairs inside. When the main stem has almost reached its height for flowering, it sends out stiff stems from the base, holding many terminal upturned flowers, giving the plant a pyramid shape. This species is very much like *C. medium*, Canterbury bells. Propagation is by seed sown in autumn or spring. Grow it at the front of a warm, sheltered wall or in the alpine house. It needs protection from winter wet if planted outside.

Campanula lanceolata is extremely similar to *C. rhomboidalis*, and Crook (1951) considers the two to be indistinguishable. However, after comparing paintings of these species (Jaume Saint-Hilaire 1828–1833), I can find one difference: the leaves of *C. lanceolata* are entire.

Campanula lasiocarpa (synonym *C. algida*), despite having the common name of Alaska bluebell, grows not only in Alaska but also further south as far as the Cascade and Olympic mountain ranges of central and western Washington. It also grows in the screes of high mountains and cold areas of northern Japan, where the whole plant is slightly larger than in North America. This species inhabits rocky alpine slopes and ridges, thriving in scree areas, and blooms July–August. It is a tufted plant making basal rosettes of spatulate-oblanceolate, serrate leaves. Although the teeth are few, they are sharply pointed and turned inward, similar to a holly leaf. Stems grow 5–12.5 CM tall, with lanceolate stem leaves. The violet-blue to deep blue, campanulate flowers are 2.5–3.5 CM long, solitary, and more or less upward-facing, with deeply cut lobes. There appear to

Campanula lasiocarpa,
Kantishna Hills, Alaska.

Photo by Carolyn Parker

be two forms: a high-alpine form, which is very compact, and a form found growing at lower altitudes, which makes a larger, looser plant and usually flowers in the first years from seed.

Campanula lasiocarpa 'Talkeetna' is a high-alpine form that was found at the western end of the Talkeetna Mountains in Alaska by Rick Lupp, who also gave it its cultivar name. It is very condensed and makes a prostrate mat of tiny rosettes sparsely studded with large blue cups on 1–2 CM stems. A very good dark blue form has also been found on Council Mine Road, Nome, Alaska, where it grows on dry rock humus.

Propagation of *Campanula lasiocarpa* is by seed sown in autumn or spring, or by division in spring. I have found that 'Talkeetna' is more difficult to increase than the more common form of the species. Although it is propagated by division of the rooted pieces as with other campanulas, the matted roots are very near the surface and extremely tightly entwined. Consequently it is not easy to pull rooted pieces away, and great care must be taken to prevent damage to the root system. Once potted up, the rooted pieces should be placed in a shady frame. Dieback will occur occasionally, but once they are happy they will grow away very quickly.

Campanula lasiocarpa is fairly difficult in cultivation, dying back naturally over winter and more often than not failing to reappear the following spring. It requires an acid, moisture-retaining, gritty compost and space to run around. If you are successful in your growing technique it will make a very good plant for a trough, for exhibition, or just as an alpine house specimen. 'Talkeetna', in spite of all my efforts, is impossible to keep going in my garden due to the high level of winter wet and humidity. In areas of winter rainfall, therefore, it must be grown in the alpine house and kept just moist over winter. From spring through autumn it does require a fair amount of water to grow well and can be placed outside in partial shade.

Campanula ledebouriana comes from Turkey, where it inhabits limestone and basalt rocks and blooms in late summer. It makes tufts of oblanceolate-linear, dark green, slightly felted, mildly dentate basal leaves to 5 CM long that are heavily grooved down the middle as if partially folded. Many ascending to erect, branched stems to 10 CM tall carry pale blue, solitary, campanulate flowers with rounded lobes that curl back to half the length of the corolla, giving a star-like appearance when seen head on. It looks completely dead during winter and comes into growth in late spring. In the late 1970s the well-known seed collector

John Watson issued a list of seed from his Turkey expedition, and plants grown by myself under the collector's number *McP. & W. 5805* turned out to be absolute gems, one gaining a Certificate of Merit at an AGS show.

Campanula ledebouriana subsp. *pulvinata* (synonym *C. pulvinaris*) grows in the Sevan Range of the Lesser Caucasus in central Armenia at around 2200–3200 M, where it makes a tight mound 8 CM across of ash grey to silvery leaves. This sub-species blooms in early summer, with very large violet flowers that are similar in shape to those of the more common form of the species, on stems 4–7.5 CM tall. It was described in a seed collector's list in 1991–1992 as "a little-known cushion campanula." Although this may be true, subspecies *pulvinata* certainly deserves to be better known, and I recommend keeping a good lookout for seed. It must be one of the best cushion campanulas I have ever grown.

Propagation of both species and subspecies is by seed sown in autumn or spring, or by cuttings taken in spring. Both can be grown in a gritty limestone bed in the rock garden, in a trough, or as an alpine house specimen.

Campanula leucosiphon comes from the Taurus Mountains of Turkey, where it grows on shady limestone rocks and in cave entrances at 900–1550 M. It makes small mats of grey, lanate, ovate-orbicular, coarsely dentate leaves 1–2 CM long that are on petioles. The ascending, fragile stems are occasionally branched, grow 10–20 CM long, and have sessile, triangular-ovate leaves. White, narrowly tubular, softly hairy flowers to 1.5 CM long broaden at the mouth and are in short, lax racemes. Propagate by seed sown in autumn or spring, or by division in spring. In the rock garden it needs a sunny, dry rock crevice and protection against winter wet. In the alpine house it needs a sunny position and a compost that is well drained.

Campanula lingulata (synonyms *C. capitata*, *C. cichoracea*) is a biennial species that ranges from Italy and the Balkan Peninsula to western Turkey, where it grows on limestone cliffs, rocky slopes, scrub, and in dry stony places. It makes tufts of hirsute, oblong-spatulate, crenate basal leaves, 1–3 CM long, narrowing toward the base but sessile. Erect, hirsute stems 30–40 CM tall have oblong to lanceolate, sessile leaves. The narrowly infundibular flowers are to 2 CM long and have violet to deep blue lobes, gradually becoming pale blue to white toward the calyx. They are held in terminal clusters of five to seven. Crook (1951) reported a very dwarf form from Bulgaria with procumbent stems not exceeding 10 CM tall and with smaller heads of flowers, but I do not think it is cultivation. Propagate by seed sown in autumn or spring. Plant it in a sunny, dry spot. It can sulk if the location is not right, but once happy it is long-blooming and very showy. Seed must be collected each year, however, to keep it going.

Campanula loefflingii (synonym *C. pyrenaica*) is an annual species from Spain, Portugal, and northwestern Africa, where it grows in sandy places. It makes a basal tuft of small, ovate-spatulate, dentate leaves on small petioles. Many thin, branched stems have sessile, lanceolate leaves and grow to 10 CM high. The erect, bright violet-blue flowers are to 1 CM across, have a white base, and are on thin pedicels that grow from the leaf axils. The wide-spreading lobes give a starry appearance to the flowers. Propagation is by seed sown in autumn or spring, and since it is an annual, it is suggested that seed be sown in situ, just scattering it where you want the plants to grow. It is a very pretty species and will make nice clumps. Its flowering period is not very long, but it can take over from where the spring bulbs left off if sown in the same place.

Campanula lourica come from Iran in the Chalus River, Kandovan, and Elborz areas at 2300 M, where it grows in limestone crevices. It is a tiny caespitose species that makes tight mats of small rosettes of lanceolate, tomentose, entire leaves

4–6 mm long. Thin, decumbent stems 3–6 cm long have a few leaves and three to four blue, campanulate flowers on long, hair-like pedicels. Propagation is by seed sown in autumn or spring. This is not a very spectacular species but would be at home in a trough with winter protection.

Campanula lusitanica comes from sandy soils in Spain and Portugal. Although Crook (1951) lumped it into *C. loefflingii*, it appears to have a specific rank, as seed has been sold, rating it a perennial, in a well-known commercial seed list. It is tufted, with decumbent to ascending stems that are branched in the same way as those of *C. loefflingii* but that grow to 30 cm. The starry, purple flowers are 1–2 cm across and cover the plants, blooming over a long period. Propagation is by seed sown in autumn or spring. Although this species is listed as a perennial, I feel that it should be treated as at least half-hardy, given that seed distributors give its hardiness zones as 8–9. Cultivation is as for *C. loefflingii*.

Campanula lyrata ranges from Turkey to Greece, where it grows among rocks and on limestone cliffs and banks at around 1700 m. It makes a rosette or clumps of rosettes of tomentose, alternate, lyrate or oblong-ovate to cordate, crenate basal leaves to 7.5 cm long on petioles. Ascending to erect, single- or many-branched stems are to 50 cm tall, with a few small, sessile, obovate, crenate leaves. The erect, violet-blue, cylindrical to narrowly infundibular flowers are to 2.5 cm long and in one-sided panicles that bloom April–July. Propagation is by seed sown in autumn or spring. When introduced into cultivation in 1797 it was considered to be perennial and tender. However, experience has shown that it is monocarpic or biennial, and if grown in the garden it must have protection from winter rains or it will easily rot off. Cultivation in the alpine house will give it a better chance.

Campanula macrorhiza (synonyms *C. kahenae*, *C. rotundifolia* subsp. *macrorhiza*) comes from southeastern France, Corsica, and northwestern Italy, where it is found in rock crevices, usually on cliffs. From a thick rootstock it makes tufts of round, cordate, dentate leaves on small petioles. The several ascending to erect stems, occasionally branched, grow 12–20 cm tall, with small, ovate-acute leaves on short petioles near the base and sessile, linear-lanceolate leaves higher up. The numerous erect, rich violet, openly campanulate flowers with spreading lobes are carried on long, thin pedicels and cover the plant in summer. It is in effect like a small *C. rotundifolia*. Propagation is by seed sown in autumn or spring. This species is perfect in a trough or crevice.

Campanula macrostyla is a very attractive and unusual annual species that is endemic to Turkey, where it grows in rocky places. It makes an erect, bushy plant 20–25 CM tall, with branching stems that have small, ovate-lanceolate, sessile, mildly serrate leaves. The erect, bowl-shaped, solitary flowers are 5–6 CM across, white with purple veining on the exterior, and dull purple and hairy within. The lobes are broad, short, and pointed. The long, protruding style, which gives this species its name, is brown and spindle-shaped before the stigma becomes tripartite. The unusual shape of the flower can be described as looking like an upside-down umbrella or a satellite dish. Propagation is by seed sown as soon as it is ripe, as late-sown seed is likely to lie dormant for a year before germinating. Self-sown seeds can also take a year to germinate.

Campanula mairei is endemic to slopes of the Atlas Mountains of Morocco. It differs from *C. herminii* only by having more flexible stems and smaller, narrower flowers. Propagation is by seed sown in autumn or spring. Although *C. herminii* is considered an annual, I have found that *C. mairei* is quite perennial, lasting many years as a pot plant in an alpine house.

Campanula makaschvilii comes from the Caucasus. It makes tufts of greyish green, ovate-cordate leaves on petioles to 15 CM. Arching to erect, slightly hairy stems 25–60 CM tall bear similar leaves but on shorter petioles and are branched in the upper half. The white, pink-flushed, campanulate flowers to 2.5 CM long have flared lobes and are on short pedicels. It resembles a smaller and less hairy *C. alliariifolia*. Propagation is by seed sown in autumn or spring, or by division in spring. It is suitable for the larger rock garden or border in sun to light shade and is long-lived.

Campanula malicitiana comes from southeastern Spain, where it grows in rocky limestone crevices. It makes clusters of rosettes of small, oval-spatulate, tomentose leaves. Thin, prostrate, brittle stems grow to 15 CM and have a few leaves similar in shape to the basal rosette. Small, light blue, erect, campanulate flowers that have a white throat and wide reflexed lobes are freely produced on short peduncles all along the stems. Propagation is by seed sown in autumn or spring. This species is a long-lived perennial and should be grown in well-drained soil with some protection from winter wet.

Campanula marchesettii comes from Slovenia, Croatia, and the central Apennines, where it grows in rocky areas. Thin, spindly stems grow to 60 CM, with many linear leaves mostly on the lower half. Five to eight, pendant, pale lilac-purple, campanulate flowers on short peduncles grow from the top quarter of the stems. This species is closely related to *C. rotundifolia*. Propagation is by seed sown in autumn or spring. Rarely seen in cultivation, it needs a gritty soil and positioning in full sun.

Campanula massalskyi comes from the Transcaucasus and Turkey, where it grows in rocky areas. From a thick perennial root it forms low, soft grey tufts of tomentose, ovate-rotund leaves on short petioles to 15 CM across. Trailing or spreading stems are 5–7.5 CM long, with small, ovate-cordate, undulate, dentate leaves on short petioles, the upper surface bright green and the lower surface tomentose. The few white to soft pink or pale blue, tubular flowers with flared lobes are terminal or axillary and on long pedicels. It blooms over a long period. Propagation is by seed sown in autumn or spring. This is a choice campanula that requires careful cultivation in a rock garden, scree, or trough with protection from winter wet, or in the alpine house.

Campanula medium, the well-known Canterbury bells, really needs no description. It is a useful and colourful biennial species for the border. Propagation is by seed sown in autumn or spring. It comes in a variety of colours and in double forms, and seed can be purchased from all the large commercial seed merchants.

Campanula mirabilis is a monocarpic but beautiful species that comes from the western Caucasus, in the valley of the Bzyb River, where it grows on rocky limestone slopes. From a thick, deep taproot it makes congested rosettes of dark green, leathery, oblong-spatulate leaves to 20 CM across. Branched stems 20–35 CM tall have alternate, sessile leaves similar to those at the base. Pale lilac or blue, broadly and fully campanulate flowers to 5 CM across, with fully reflexed lobes, are from one to four on short peduncles from each leaf axil. Forms with white flowers and yellow-margined leaves are known. It normally flowers in the wild after two to three years of vegetative growth, although in cultivation it can flower the year after sowing. This species was considered the "Queen of the Abkhazian flora" by A. Albov, a specialist in the Caucasian flora and the describer of the species (Missouri Botanical Garden 1995–2005, "Ornamental Plants in Their Natural Habitats: Georgia"). Propagation is by seed sown in autumn or spring. In cultivation it prefers a somewhat shaded crevice on limestone-derived, well-drained soil and suffers when exposed to direct sunlight. It needs protection from winter wet and can also suffer in spring from late frosts. In the wild it blooms August–September, occasionally into October, and a well-grown plant in cultivation can produce around 450–460 flowers.

Campanula modesta comes from south-central China, eastern and western Himalaya, Nepal, and Tibet. It is very similar to *C. aristata*, differing only in that it is more erect, 5–10 CM tall, and smaller in foliage and flower size. The calyx segments are also shorter. Propagation is by seed sown in autumn or spring. Like *C. aristata*, it is probably not hardy in the United Kingdom and is best grown in the alpine house.

Campanula moesiaca comes from the Balkan Peninsula, where it grows in subalpine meadows. It is biennial and in the first year makes large rosettes of oblong, hairy, serrate leaves. In the second year, erect, pubescent stems grow 30–40 CM tall topped with dense terminal clusters of lilac-blue, narrow, campanulate flowers 2.5–4 CM long. Smaller clusters grow from the leaf axils up the stem. This species resembles *C. glomerata* in overall appearance. Propagation is by seed sown in autumn or spring. Grow it in the rock garden with protection from winter wet.

Campanula mollis comes from southern and southwestern Spain and the western Mediterranean, where it grows in limestone rock crevices. It makes tufts of velvety, obovate-spatulate, subsinuate basal leaves to 4 CM long, covered with silvery white hairs, and on short petioles. Fragile, decumbent to ascending stems to 15 CM long have smaller, elliptic-orbicular, sessile leaves that become smaller near the end of the stems. Erect, campanulate flowers are pale blue to lavender and lilac, with a white throat and nerves outlined in a deeper blue, and are 1.5–2.5 CM long and 1.5 CM across. They are on long pedicels near the end of the stems.

The plants occasionally found in gardens or nurseries as *Campanula* 'Mollis' or *C. isophylla* 'Mollis' have been mislabelled. Both are forms of *C. isophylla*. There is a distinct difference in the shape of the leaves between *C. mollis* and

Campanula mollis, Sierras de Cazorla, Spain.

Photo by Panayoti Kelaidis

C. isophylla, plus the mature seed capsules of *C. mollis* are fully pendant. Be aware of this when you obtain a plant under this name, and examine it closely if you want the true species.

Propagation is by seed sown in autumn or spring. This species is best cultivated in the alpine house or, if grown outside, in a dry, well-drained spot in full sun.

Campanula morettiana is a choice species that grows in partially shady limestone cliff areas of the Dolomites. The *Convention on the Conservation of European Wildlife and Natural Habitats* lists it as a strictly protected flora species. It makes tufts of small, broadly ovate, toothed leaves that are felted with grey hairs. Ascending to decumbent stems to 7.5 CM have small leaves that are almost circular. The solitary, broadly infundibular, violet-blue flowers are 2.5–3.2 CM long and have broad, reflexed lobes. There is a small tuft of hairs at the end of each lobe.

Campanula morettiana var. *alba* is a white form but has many variations in flower size and vigour, as it crops up now and again in seedlings grown from a batch of seed collected from the more common form of the species.

Propagation of the usual form of the species is by seed, which is occasionally set in cultivation, sown in autumn or spring. It usually takes at least a year before germination takes place. The seed is very fine, so be extra careful in sowing it or you will have so many seedlings growing in a small pot that they will rot off. You

Campanula morettiana

Campanula morettiana
var. *alba*

can also increase the blue or white forms by carefully removing rooted side shoots as soon into the growing season as possible. This will enable the small plants to get a good root system going before winter. Even so, be prepared for casualties the following year. Cuttings can be rooted in spring.

Campanula morettiana grows well if planted in tufa in a trough, but beware of slugs if the trough is kept outside. It also makes a beautiful specimen in the alpine house if grown in a gritty compost but should be treated with a systemic pesticide early to combat red spider mite. The problem with growing this species is that it dies down over winter and does not always come into growth the following year. Letting the plant dry out during winter is the main cause of this, although excessive moisture in early spring before it has come into growth properly can also kill it. Be sure to remove the dead leaves and stems as early as possible, because this will encourage grey mould and eventually kill the plant. If you sow your seed too thickly and find that the seedlings are tightly packed and difficult to prick out individually, prick them out in small clumps and let them grow on for a while before splitting them up individually or into smaller clumps. This of course applies to all batches of seedlings if you find them too crowded.

Campanula myrtifolia (synonyms *Tracheliopsis myrtifolia, Trachelium myrtifolia, Trachelium tauricum*) is endemic to southern Turkey, where it grows at 1000–2100 M in rock fissures and vertical limestone rock faces. It is woody-based

Campanula myrtifolia 'Helmi'

and makes tufts of ovate, sessile leaves to 7 MM long. Decumbent to ascending, leafy stems are to 3 CM long. The two to five lavender or occasionally white flowers are narrowly infundibular, upward-pointing, to 6 MM long, with short lobes, and in terminal corymbs. The whole plant is softly hairy throughout and rarely exceeds 5 CM in height. This is a beautiful, compact dwarf species that is a joy to grow. Propagation is by seed sown in autumn or spring, or by cuttings taken in spring or autumn from old flowered-out stems. Grow it in a sunny, dry rock crevice or trough with protection against winter wet, or in the alpine house in a shallow pan. A magnificent plant appeared on the show bench in 2003 exhibited by a Dr. M. and Mrs. A. Sheader and received an AGS Certificate of Merit. In June 2005 this same plant—now ten years old, in a 36 CM pan, and with the cultivar name 'Helmi' (Finnish for "pearl")—was awarded an RHS Certificate of Preliminary Commendation.

Campanula ochroleuca (synonyms *C. alliariifolia* var. *cordata*, *C. alliariifolia* subsp. *ochroleuca*) is endemic to the Caucasus, where it grows on rocks and in crevices, screes, and grass at subalpine levels, 1300–1800 M. From a thick, branched rootstock it makes rosettes of deltoid-cordate, irregularly crenate-dentate, reticulate leaves 5–12 CM long on short petioles. Thick, erect stems 10–30 CM tall are occasionally branched in the upper part. The pale yellowish, pendant, open, campanulate flowers, to 3 CM long, are ciliate, with lobes cut to a third of the corolla length, and are on short peduncles growing from the upper leaf axils. The whole plant is tomentose. Propagation is by seed sown in autumn or spring, or by cuttings taken in spring. It is best grown in a sunny scree or crevice, but it can become weedy.

Campanula oligosperma comes from Turkey, where it grows in alpine meadows and serpentine screes up to 1950 M. From a thick rootstock it makes basal tufts of oblong-linear leaves to 5 CM long that narrow to a long petiole. Stems grow 15–30 CM tall and have thick, oval, sessile leaves. The blue-violet, narrowly campanulate flowers are to 2 CM long. Propagation is by seed sown in autumn or spring. Grow it in a sunny scree bed or in the alpine house.

Campanula olympica (synonym *C. hemschinica*) comes from Turkey and the Caucasus, where it grows from alpine meadows to forests. It makes rosettes of obovate-elliptic, crenate leaves on long petioles. The several erect, unbranched

Campanula olympica,
northeastern Turkey.

Photo by Ann Borrill

stems to 30 CM have oblong-lanceolate, sessile leaves, and the three to five terminal, erect, violet-blue, campanulate-infundibular flowers with well-reflexed lobes are on short pedicels. It is a short-lived perennial or possibly a biennial. This plant should not be confused with *C. rotundifolia* 'Olympica', which comes from the Olympic Mountains, Washington State, United States. Propagation is by seed sown in autumn or spring, or by division of the stolons in spring. Plant it in a warm gritty site in the rock garden and collect and sow seed each year as an insurance.

Campanula oreadum comes from eastern Greece, where it grows among mountain rocks and in crevices. It makes basal tufts or rosettes of deep green, faintly hairy, oblong-spatulate leaves to 1.3 CM wide and to 3.2 CM long on petioles. The ascending to erect, thin, hairy stems are to 10 CM tall, with a few oblong leaves to 2 CM long. Solitary, campanulate, light blue to rich violet-purple flowers are to 3.5 CM long and 2.5 CM wide, have flared lobes, and are on one to five peduncles. The flowers are faintly hairy inside, giving the appearance of small cobwebs. Propagation is by seed or rooted side shoots in spring. Plant it in a sunny limestone crevice in the rock garden or in a trough.

Campanula oreadum.

Photo by Panayoti Kelaidis

Campanula orphanidea comes from southern Bulgaria and northeastern Greece, where it grows in crevices of limestone rocks. It makes rosettes of grey, hairy, lanceolate, slightly undulate leaves on long petioles. It has an erect central stem to 15 CM or more and many other shorter decumbent stems that spread out from the base. Stem leaves are hairy, strap-shaped, and sessile. The erect, deep violet-purple, campanulate flowers are to 2.5 CM long and somewhat pinched just behind the flared rectangular lobes. This biennial or monocarpic species is beautiful and, although short-lived, is well worth growing as a pot plant in the alpine house. Propagation is by seed sown in autumn or spring. Plants in cultivation usually set plenty of seed, so it is fairly easy to keep this species going. If you grow it in the rock garden, give it a warm spot and make sure it has protection from winter wet. In the alpine house, which is the best place to grow it, use a pot deep enough to take the long taproot.

Campanula pallida (synonym *C. colorata*) ranges from Afghanistan to northeastern Pakistan, Nepal, and southwestern China, growing at 600–4500 M, often on banks and walls, and occasionally in cultivated places. It is tufted, with many-branched, decumbent to erect stems 15–50 CM long, with lanceolate-elliptic, pubescent, sessile leaves 2–3 CM long. The pale lilac-purple flowers are to 1.5 CM long. Propagation is by seed sown in autumn or spring. In the rock garden it needs a humus-rich, well-drained, sunny spot.

Campanula paradoxa is endemic to Georgia (Abkhazia), where it grows in calcareous rock fissures in the lower forest belt. It makes tufts of deep green, spatulate, dentate leaves to 7.5 CM long on short petioles. Stems to 15 CM carry panicles of creamy pink, campanulate flowers to 1.5 CM long that have well-reflexed, blunt lobes. It is a fairly recent discovery, being first described by Alfred Alekseevich Kolakovsky in 1976. Propagation is by seed sown in autumn or spring. This is a nice species for the alpine house.

Campanula parryi grows in a large number of states across the western United States, inhabiting moist, subalpine and low alpine meadows at 1525–3700 M. From a mass of slender underground rhizomes it makes dense, tufted mats of strap-shaped, coarsely dentate leaves with thin, decumbent to erect stems to 20 CM long that have similar leaves. The large, violet-purple to blue, infundibular, star-like flowers are upward-facing and one to three on long pedicels from the leaf axils.

Campanula parryi.

Photo by Panayoti Kelaidis

Campanula parryi var. *idahoensis* inhabits rocky subalpine meadows at 1970 M near Wenatchee in Washington State. Its stems are shorter than those of *C. parryi*, up to 10 CM long, and carry solitary, erect, purple-blue, campanulate flowers. Like the usual form of the species, it spreads by underground runners.

Propagation of *Campanula parryi* is by seed sown in autumn or spring, or by careful division of the runners in spring. It prefers light or medium, well-drained soil and sun or partial shade, and is quite happy growing and slowly spreading in a scree bed. After dying down in winter, it causes a slight worry until it appears again the following spring, but generally this is a nice, easy campanula for the rock garden.

Campanula patula is a short-lived, usually biennial species that grows throughout Europe, including Great Britain, inhabiting grassy meadows, shady woods, and hedge banks to 1600 M. During the first year it makes tight rosettes of smooth, oblong-lanceolate, dentate, sessile leaves. In the second year, erect, slender, branched stems grow to 50 CM or more and have leaves that are sessile, oval, and dentate, becoming linear higher up the stem. Flowers are numerous, violet to pale blue or purple-blue, occasionally white, erect, stellate, and to 2.5 CM in

Campanula patula,
Bulgaria.

Photo by Ann Borrill

diameter, in loose panicles. Propagate by seed sown in autumn or spring. Although this species is a biennial and rather tall for the small rock garden, it is well worth growing in the border for its beautiful flowers.

Campanula patula subsp. *abietina* (synonym *C. abietina*) comes from rocky ridges or montane grassland, pastures, and wood margins in the Carpathian Alps and Balkan Peninsula. It makes compact rosettes of bright green, narrow leaves that are finely crenate and eventually form wide mats that spread by short stolons. Many erect, wiry stems 20–40 cm tall have a few lanceolate leaves and bear solitary, erect, reddish purple, open, stellate flowers, to 2 cm in diameter, during June. This is a short-lived perennial. Propagation is by seed sown in autumn or spring, or by division, and it should be replanted every couple of years to keep it going. It is evergreen and makes an excellent edging, container, or rock garden plant. It does well in bright shade.

Campanula pelviformis is endemic to Crete, especially in the Samaria Gorge, a well-known national park. It is a close relation to *C. medium*, Canterbury bells, and likewise is biennial. It makes a basal rosette of greyish green, rough, ovate-acute, serrate leaves. The several hairy, decumbent to ascending and erect stems grow to 30 cm and have leaves similar to the basal rosette but sessile. The lilac-blue, widely campanulate flowers with broad, reflexed lobes are single in the leaf axils and in terminal clusters of up to three. This species must not be confused with *C. carpatica* 'Pelviformis', which is a dwarf, compact form of *C. carpatica*. Propagation of *C. pelviformis* is by seed sown in autumn or spring. However, it is a rare plant and seed will never be freely available. It can be grown in the same way as *C. medium* in the flower border.

Campanula perpusilla comes from the central Zagros Mountains of Iran, specifically the Bazoft Valley, between Aligoudarz and Shoulabad, and the Kuhrang Valley, where it makes mats to 3 cm high in limestone crevices and nestles against the rocks. It grows in association with other chasmophytes, like *Dionysia haussknechtii*, *D. heterotricha*, and *Viola pachyrrhiza*. The stem leaves are orbicular-ovate or cordate, wider than long, have up to ten angular teeth, and are on long, thin petioles. The pale violet, infundibular flowers are to 7 mm across and deeply cut into acute lobes. They have a stigma that varies in colour from nearly white to nearly black.

Campanula persica (synonyms *Asyneuma persicum*, *C. aspera*) comes from Iraq, Iran, and Turkey, where it grows on rocky slopes at 2200–2500 M. It is tufted, with erect to arcuate stems 20–60 CM long. Lanceolate lower leaves are to 8 CM long and taper to a petiole 3–5 CM long. The many upper leaves are linear-lanceolate and subsessile. The blue, erect, infundibular flowers are to 1 CM long, 1 CM wide, and in spikes. Propagation is by seed sown in autumn or spring, or by division of the rhizomes in spring. In the garden this plant needs a well-drained, warm crevice with protection from winter wet. Although it can be grown in the alpine house, it will need a large pot and may be a little ungainly when grown alongside some of the dwarf species.

Campanula persicifolia is widely distributed throughout southern Europe, where it grows in light subalpine woodland and shady places. It makes large clumps of rosettes of long, smooth, oblong-lanceolate, serrate leaves that taper to a petiole, and erect, unbranched stems that grow to 90 CM. The blue or white, campanulate flowers are 1.5 CM long and erect or pendant, in racemes growing from the leaf axils. This form of the species is much too big for the rock garden but is included here so that comparison can be made with its lovely dwarf variant, variety *planiflora.*

    Campanula persicifolia var. *planiflora* (synonym *C. nitida*, *C. planiflora*) makes tight rosettes of dark green, oblanceolate, crenate, undulate, sessile leaves. Stiff, erect stems to 25 CM tall have the same foliage as the basal rosettes to midway up the stem. Deep blue, saucer-shaped flowers to 5 CM wide, with protruding styles, are in terminal racemes. *Campanula persicifolia* var. *planiflora* f. *alba* is a superb form with glistening white flowers.

    Propagation is by seed sown in autumn or spring, although seedlings from the white form are likely to turn out blue. Division in spring can also be successful. Variety *planiflora* is a lovely and striking plant for the rock garden but does require protection from slugs. I have also lost it by rotting off from winter wet. It makes an excellent pot plant in the alpine house and for the show bench.

Campanula petraea comes from the rocks of the southern European Alps. It forms thick trunks with tufts of rough, hairy, ovate-lanceolate, crenate-dentate leaves to 5 CM long that are on thin petioles to 2.5 CM long. The leaves are green above and grey below. Stiff, erect to ascending stems grow to 30 CM long, with a few sessile, linear-lanceolate, acute leaves. The stems terminate in a cluster of

Campanula persicifolia
var. *planiflora*

Campanula persicifolia
var. *planiflora* f. *alba*

small, dirty yellow or dirty white, campanulate flowers. Occasionally, smaller clusters of flowers grow in the upper leaf axils. Candolle (1830) considered this to be an attractive plant that had been unjustifiably overlooked, but Farrer (1918) described it as "a species of great ugliness." If seed of this rare species was readily available, many of us could judge for ourselves.

Campanula petrophila comes from the Caucasus, where it grows on damp rocks and in cool rock crevices at 1845–3600 M. It forms loose mats of very thin stems with small, broadly ovate basal leaves that are occasionally serrate. Prostrate stems to 10 CM long have obovate, sessile leaves. The large purple-blue flowers are mainly solitary but can be up to five, terminal, upward-facing, and campanulate, with reflexed lobes and bearded margins. Sometimes the flowers are cup-like when the lobes are well reflexed. This is not one of those beautiful plants that flower once and die with no possibility of propagation. It can be easily propagated by seed sown in autumn or spring. However, seed is rarely available, and I have succeeded in propagating this lovely species by careful division. If dug up or removed from the pot, the tangled mass of roots can be teased apart after being washed off. Each rooted piece can be cut away from the mat and potted up to grow on. If you do this in spring, you will have a small potful by autumn.

This species came to my notice many years ago while browsing over a nurseryman's sales table. I spotted a campanula that I did not recognise but that looked promising, and anything unknown is worth a try. This has turned out to be another wonderful species for the garden. It grows well outside in a trough, gritty alpine bed, or sand bed, making a wonderful tight and compact plant. Some cover from winter wet is suggested. If you grow *Campanula petrophila* under glass, be careful to give it full light and a gritty compost or you will find that the stems elongate and the charming compactness is lost. As always, there has to be a downside, and once again it's the slug problem. Nevertheless, *C. petrophila* increases quickly enough to keep itself going in several places around the garden, and it is certainly worth the trouble.

Campanula petrophila

Campanula piperi comes from the Olympic Mountains, Washington State, United States, where it grows at an elevation of 1690–2000 m in rocky, subalpine slopes and screes. There, the slender rhizomes happily run around underground, emerging to form prostrate, compact, tufted rosettes of shiny, dark green, spatulate, serrate leaves. Stems 2.5–8 cm tall have upward-facing, lavender to deep blue or purple-blue, flattish, stellate flowers that are 2–3 cm in diameter. They bloom July–August in the wild, earlier in cultivation.

Campanula piperi,
Olympic Mountains,
Washington.

Photo by Dick Redfield,
courtesy of the North
American Rock Garden
Society

There is great variation in flower form and colour among the many selections of this species. Some of the best cultivars have been named by Rick Lupp of Mt. Tahoma Nursery and by Steve Doonan and Phil Pearson of Grand Ridge Nursery (both of Washington). *Campanula piperi* in any of its forms is an outstanding species and well worth the effort it takes to cultivate it. 'Marmot Pass' is a cultivar with blue flowers that open flat, with just a blush of lavender to the edge. 'Mt. Tahoma' has a dense, compact habit and a reliable bloom of rich lavender-blue. 'Townsend Violet' has lovely, soft violet blooms with contrasting deep blue stigmas.

Campanula piperi var. *sovereigniana*, described in 1973 (Woodward) as "a white form which tantalizes because of the prominent maroon stamens in such dramatic contrast," inhabited Deer Park, in western Washington State, at that time. Two more white forms were introduced in the mid-1990s, both more vigorous than the usual form of the species, and both make lovely pot plants for exhibition. The first, 'Townsend Ridge', blooms all summer, with brilliant white flowers shaped like those of *C. piperi*. It was introduced into cultivation by Grand Ridge Nursery. The other, 'Snowdrift', was found by Roger Whitlock of Victoria, Canada, in the Olympics. It is just as vigorous as 'Townsend Ridge' and has beautiful white blooms that open quite flat.

Propagation of the more common form of the species is by seed sown in autumn or spring, or by division in spring or summer. I have never found seed on my white forms. Nevertheless, seed may be set on white forms in the wild, but the resultant plants are most likely to turn out blue.

Campanula piperi, in both blue and white forms, delights in gritty granite conditions, and despite reports that it does not flower well, I have never found this to be a problem. The rosettes become brown in winter and some parts look dead, but be very careful not to start pulling these brown stems and leaves off willy-nilly. Although some of these parts will in fact be dead, a lot of the brown stems will be alive. Any obvious dead foliage can be removed, but otherwise be patient and wait until growth restarts in early spring. Use scissors and a great deal of care when cutting away the dead parts. If you cut away a stem and then spot a white milky substance oozing from the cut, you will know you have blundered. In the open garden it is susceptible to fungal blights.

This species makes a lovely alpine house plant for exhibition and requires a gritty compost, with at least the top 5 cm being pure grit. This will encourage it to run around and become a large plant quickly.

Campanula piperi
'Townsend Violet'

Campanula piperi
'Townsend Ridge'

Campanula portenschlagiana (synonym *C. muralis*), commonly known as dalmatian bellflower, comes from Serbia and Montenegro, Bosnia and Herzegovina, and Croatia, where it grows on limestone cliffs, usually at low altitude. It makes clumps of small, bright green, glabrous, cordate, heavily dentate leaves to 5 cm in diameter. Procumbent stems are 12.5–25 cm long, with numerous leaves, and grow from the rosettes. Shorter stems branch from the main stems and carry panicles of upward-facing, lilac-blue, campanulate flowers to 2.5 cm wide and 2.5 cm long, with oblong, reflexed lobes. Flowers are on short pedicels and cover the plant in summer. As the rosettes get larger they grow into one another, eventually making a large, tight mat 15–20 cm high and 50 cm across. *Campanula portenschlagiana* 'Resholdt's Variety' is much the same as the more common form of the species but has larger, better-coloured flowers and is less invasive.

Propagation is easy. Dig up clumps of stems in spring, bury them in pots of compost, and keep them shaded. They will die back a little but will soon start growing again, and within a month or so you will have new plants. This is one of the most popular campanulas and among the easiest to grow—so easy in fact that it can become a menace if grown in rich soil. This can be forgiven, however, so wonderful is the show of bloom throughout summer and well into autumn. It is suitable for a dry, shady wall or the rock garden. Grow 'Resholdt's Variety' if you want a less invasive plant.

Campanula portenschlagiana 'Resholdt's Variety'

Campanula poscharskyana comes from Serbia and Montenegro, Bosnia and Herzegovina, and Croatia, where it grows in stony places. It was introduced into cultivation in 1933 by Walter Ingwersen and was given an RHS Award of Merit the same year. It makes rosettes of bright green, cordate, dentate leaves to 3.5 CM wide on long petioles. The rosettes quickly form mats with thick rooting stems running around in any crevice they can find. Stems to 30 CM long have bright green, cordate, dentate leaves to 2.5 CM across, with axillary racemes of lavender-blue, starry flowers that are to 1.5 CM wide and cover the plant for weeks in summer. The whole plant is mildly hairy. Although an extremely attractive plant, it is very invasive. In fact, Will Ingwersen (1978) described his father's introduction as "rampagious," and Crook (1951) said that "this species in many ways resembles *C. garganica* but is a stronger and more rampant grower." If you want a campanula that will flower over a long period but will also invade every crook and cranny in your paved area, rock garden, or wall, seed itself in any other empty crack it can find, and prove almost impossible to eradicate, then this one is for you. If not, then give it a wide berth. Propagate by digging up rooted pieces of stem and potting up anytime during the growing season. No cultivation instructions are necessary, as it will grow practically anywhere.

Campanula postii (synonyms *C. amana*, *C. shepherdii*, *Diosphaera postii*, *Trachelium postii*) comes from Turkey, Iraq, and Syria, where it grows among limestone rocks and cliffs at around 700–2000 M. It makes tufts of spatulate basal leaves that soon die off. The wooly, ascending to erect stems are 15–30 CM long, with obovate stem leaves 2.5–5 CM long that are slightly serrate and white-pubescent underneath. The many white, infundibular flowers are to 1.5 CM long and in loose or dense corymbs, blooming in late summer. Propagate by seed sown in spring or by division. In the rock garden it needs a sunny, dry rock crevice and protection against winter wet. It can also be grown as a pot plant in the alpine house.

Campanula prenanthoides ranges from northern California, where it grows in mixed coniferous woodland in the Sierra Nevada, to Oregon at up to 1845 M. It makes tufts of small, oblong-ovate to lanceolate, slightly downy, mildly serrate leaves on short petioles. Erect stems are 15–45 CM tall, with leaves similar to the basal leaves but sessile. The bright blue, pendant, campanulate flowers with flared lobes are on short pedicels in many-flowered, terminal racemes. The flowers have a style that protrudes way beyond the corolla in an unusual shape similar to

C. scouleri, to which *C. prenanthoides* is related. Propagation is by seed sown in autumn or spring, or by division in spring. This is a good species for dry shade, although it may not be hardy in the United Kingdom.

Campanula propinqua is an annual species that comes from the Syrian desert, Turkey, northwestern Iran, and Transcaucasia, where it grows in sandy soil on steppes and slopes at around 1800 M. The erect, dichotomously branching stems grow to 30 CM tall, with alternate, spatulate to oblong-lanceolate, sessile leaves to 3 CM long and 1 CM wide. The pale to dark violet, infundibular flowers are to 1.5 CM long, with well-reflexed lobes, and are solitary, terminal, and on short peduncles. Blooming commences in April. Propagate by sowing seed in autumn or spring. This species is very likely to be a half-hardy annual and should be treated as such, using it as colourful groundcover during summer.

Campanula psilostachya (synonym *Asyneuma psilostachya*) comes from Turkey, where it grows at 700–2000 M among limestone rocks in open forest and scrub. It makes basal rosettes of ovate-cordate, crenate, roughly hairy leaves to 3 CM long on petioles to 5 CM long. Unbranched stems to 50 CM or more carry violet to light blue, broadly infundibular flowers to 6 MM long and 10 MM across in long, dense spikes. The style is noticeably exserted. It is monocarpic or occasionally a short-lived perennial. Propagation is by seed sown in autumn or spring. Research indicates that this species is probably not in cultivation, but if it was it would possibly require a warm crevice. It would also be suitable for the alpine house, although some growers might find it too tall for their liking.

Campanula ptarmicifolia comes from Turkey, where it grows at 1700–2900 M on limestone rocks and screes. From a thick, woody root it makes dense rosettes of oblong-spatulate, ciliate leaves to 4 CM long on long petioles. Erect to ascending, unbranched stems 10–30 CM long have cylindrical flowers to 2 CM long and 1 CM wide in small, lax spikes. It is a biennial or possibly a short-lived perennial. Propagation is by seed sown in autumn or spring. In the rock garden grow it in a warm, sunny crevice or trough. Collect and sow seed each year to keep it going.

Campanula pulla comes from the eastern European Alps, where it grows in alpine meadows, stony slopes, and screes at 1500–2200 M, usually but not always on limestone. It makes a mat of small rosettes of small, ovate, glossy leaves on short petioles. Stems with a few ovate, sessile leaves grow 5–15 CM tall from almost every rosette. The solitary, terminal, pendant, deep purple-blue, campanulate flowers are to 2 CM long. This plant quickly increases by rhizomes. It is considered by many to have the darkest blue flowers in the genus. They certainly are dark, causing problems when photographing the plant by not reflecting much light. *Campanula pulla* var. *alba* is a nice white form. Propagation is by seed sown in autumn or spring, or by division in spring.

Campanula pulla is one of the great favourites among growers of alpine plants and can grow in shade as well as sun, but it must not be allowed to dry out or it will die. Although in some soils it can spread very quickly and become a menace, in most soils it needs digging up, splitting, and replanting every couple of years or so; otherwise it will exhaust the soil and die away. It makes a fine pot plant in the alpine house but needs repotting every year.

Campanula pulla, Col de Larche, Italy.

Photo by Harold Bevington

Campanula punctata (synonym *C. takesimana*) comes from Japan, where it grows on grassy mountain slopes at low altitudes. The large basal leaves are ovate-cordate, hirsute, and on long petioles. Erect stems, to 30 CM or more in a vigorous form, have similar leaves that are mainly sessile. The beautiful, terminal, pendant, campanulate flowers are to 5 CM long and creamy white or creamy yellow, with

Campanula punctata
'Bowl of Cherries'

Dwarf form of
Campanula punctata

rose-purple stains and darker purple freckles inside. The calyx lobes are triangular, with the tip of the triangle extending almost halfway down the corolla. Propagation is by seed or division in spring. This is a very vigorous species and seems to prefer sandy soil. When happy it will make clumps and eventually form colonies. I have tried growing it many times in my clay soil, but it does not like it.

Quite recently I was given a lovely dwarf form of this species that appeared in the garden of a friend. It makes basal clumps of deep green, ovate-cordate, hirsute leaves to 3.2 CM long and to 2.2 CM wide on petioles to 7 CM long. Stem leaves are sessile or on short petioles. Stems to 9 CM tall have flowers that are campanulate, to 4 CM long and 2 CM wide, cream, purple-flecked on the outside, and heavily spotted purple on the inside. The flowers are on short peduncles. It is a good plant for the rock garden, and although like the larger forms it has a tendency to spread, it is much slower and more manageable.

Campanula punctata var. *hondoensis* comes from the mountains of Honshū and has darker, less spotted flowers that are larger and more ungainly than those of the more common form of the species.

As with many of the popular herbaceous perennials, a number of good cultivars are available. 'Alba' has creamy white flowers, freckled reddish purple. 'Alba Nana' is shorter. 'Bowl of Cherries' grows to 25 CM tall and has beautiful deep red flowers to 4.5 CM long. It is a very good plant for outside pot culture. 'Cherry Bells' is deep red and very compact, just 30–45 CM tall. 'Flashing Lights' has variegated green and white foliage set with large, pendulous, lavender-pink flowers. A vigorous plant, it blooms all summer if deadheaded, and grows to 60 CM tall. 'Pantaloons' has light purple flowers shaped in a double "hose-in-hose" (having one perfect corolla inside another). It is vigorous and grows 30–45 CM tall. 'Pink Chimes' is very compact at 37.5 CM tall, perfect for the border, and easy to grow in containers without falling over. It has prolific repeat flowering if the old stems are removed. 'Plum Wine' is a combination of red winter leaves, or wine-darkened summer leaves, and huge rose-purple blooms. It is easy to grow, with the usual spreading habit, and 37.5 CM tall. 'Rubiflora' is 30–40 CM tall and has flowers that are creamy white to deep purple-pink with intense crimson freckles.

Campanula quercetorum comes from the shady limestone gorges of Turkey, growing among trees and scrub. It makes dense rosettes of elliptic, coarsely dentate leaves 1–2 CM long on petioles of about the same length. Thin, ascending stems 10–20 CM tall have violet-blue, narrowly campanulate flowers to 1.5 CM long in panicles. The whole plant is shortly setose. Propagation is by seed sown in autumn or spring. Grow it in a sunny crevice with protection from winter wet, or in the alpine house.

Campanula radchensis comes from the Transcaucasus (Racha-Lechkhumu) and is endemic to Georgia, where it grows on cliffs and in rocky places. From a fibrous root it makes mounds to 10 CM tall, with star-like blue flowers that have rounded lobe tips and corollas that are white at the base. Propagation is by seed sown in autumn or spring, or by cuttings taken in very early spring. This makes a lovely pot plant for the alpine house.

Campanula raddeana (synonym *C. brotheri*) is endemic to Georgia, where it grows in rocks of the middle mountain belt at around 1230 M. It makes tufts of stiff, glossy, cordate, serrate leaves to 5 CM wide on long, hairless petioles. The erect, wiry, stiff stems are multibranched and grow 20–30 CM tall from each rosette, although the weight of the flowers may cause them to bend a little. The stem leaves are on short, winged, toothed petioles. The pendant, lavender-blue, campanulate flowers are to 2 CM long and 3 CM wide, in racemes of up to 15, and the corolla is lobed to about a third of its length, with reflexed lobes. The style is like a bell clapper and is as long as or longer than the corolla. It has orange-toned pollen. *Campanula kemulariae* is very similar and has been merged into *C. raddeana* in Oganesian's "Synopsis of Caucasian Campanulaceae" (1995). Propagation is by seed sown in autumn or spring, or by division in spring. It is an easy plant to grow in a wide variety of soils, even preferring poor soil. It is surprisingly shade-tolerant but because of its strong running habit is best kept away from delicate plants. Grow it where you need to fill gaps or where it can tumble down over walls and rocks.

Campanula radicosa is endemic to Mt. Parnassus, Greece, where it ranges in habitat from meadows to limestone rocks, growing at 1700–2400 M. It makes rosettes of oblong-spatulate, mildly serrate leaves that gradually reduce to a petiole. A number of prostrate stems to 5 CM long grow from the rosettes and have several small, orbicular, sessile leaves. Small, bright violet, infundibular, sessile flowers with a white eye are in short, terminal racemes. It is a rare plant and probably not yet widespread in cultivation. Propagation is by seed sown in autumn or spring. Grow it in a sunny or partly shady scree.

Campanula radula comes from eastern Turkey, northern Iraq, and Armenia, where it grows in shady, humid limestone or volcanic crevices at around 1800–2400 M. From a thick rhizome it makes basal tufts of thick, ovate-cordate, dentate leaves 2.5–5 CM long on short petioles. The numerous ascending to erect, sometimes flexuous stems are 7–45 CM tall. The lower stem leaves are thick, ovate-spatulate, and on short petioles, while the upper leaves are sessile, broadly ovate, elliptic-orbicular, with crisped-undulate to irregularly dentate margins, and gradually decrease in size. The dark to light blue, occasionally milky white, narrowly campanulate flowers are 1.5–3 CM long, tomentose-hispid outside, and in clusters of one to seven on erect pedicels. The pedicels are densely tomentose-hispidulous. This campanula greatly resembles *C. coriacea*, a species with which it has been confused on many occasions during expeditions to Turkey. Propagation is by seed sown in autumn or spring. It should be suitable for a shady crevice in the rock garden with protection from winter wet. I have not seen seed available for this species, however, and therefore have no experience growing it.

Campanula raineri grows on limestone cliffs in the Bergamo region of northern Italy and into Switzerland, and is a beautiful, dwarf, saxatile plant. From a woody rootstock it makes tufts of small, greyish green, ovate-obovate, finely dentate, subsessile or sessile leaves with soft, hairy margins. Erect stems grow 5–7.5 CM tall, with narrow, crenate-serrate leaves. The mostly solitary, large, erect flowers vary in colour from dark blue to lavender-blue and have a dark blue, almost black spot at the base of the petals. They can also vary in shape, especially in seed-grown plants, from campanulate with reflexed, rounded lobes to broadly infundibular with pointed lobes. *Campanula raineri* 'Gothenburg Form' is a good example of this variation. Raised at Gothenburg Botanical Garden, this outstanding form is very distinctive, with large, shallow (almost saucer-shaped), milky blue flowers. It has been exhibited at AGS shows.

There is a lovely white form, *Campanula raineri* var. *alba*, that appears on the show bench occasionally, but like many rare forms it is much more difficult to keep in cultivation. Similar to the more common form of the species, the flowers vary in shape from campanulate to infundibular. Also recorded is a form known as *C. raineri* var. *hirsuta* that has fully hairy leaves, but I have never seen it.

Campanula raineri increases by underground runners and is deciduous, dying down completely during winter. Propagation is by seed sown in autumn or spring, but since seed offered in exchanges quite often turns out to be

Campanula raineri,
Grigna septentrionale,
northern Italy.

Photo by Zdeněk Zvolánek

Campanula raineri
'Gothenburg Form'.

Photo by Robert Rolfe

Campanula raineri
var. *alba.*

Photo by Paul Ranson

C. 'Pseudoraineri', it is recommended that you purchase wild-collected seed from commercial seed lists. It can also be propagated by division in spring or summer, or by cuttings in spring. Grow it in a limestone scree or in a trough, but beware of slugs, as they love this plant. It makes a superb pot plant for the alpine house when grown in a gritty compost and repotted every year. However, in a dry atmosphere, red spider mite can easily cause the leaves to be terribly mottled in the summer, unless the problem is kept under control.

Campanula ramosissima (synonym *C. loreyi*) is a lovely annual species from the Balkan Peninsula, where it grows in alpine meadows and rocky places. It makes erect mounds with oval, entire, sessile leaves on many-branched stems 15–30 CM tall. The lilac-blue, stellate flowers have a white eye, rounded and prominently veined lobes, and are to 2.5 CM or more across. Propagation is by seed sown in autumn or spring where you want this plant to flower, or treat it as a half-hardy annual and sow it in spring, pricking out seedlings when ready. Although an annual, it is a very pretty species and is a useful and colourful addition to the border during summer. 'Meteora' is a selected form that grows to 25 CM and appears in commercial seed lists.

Campanula ramosissima.

Photo by Panayoti Kelaidis

Campanula recta is an attractive species from the Pyrenees and the mountains of southern France. It is very like *C. rhomboidalis* and *C. serrata*, the only difference being that *C. recta* has leaves that are pubescent on both surfaces and entire. Propagation is by seed sown in autumn or spring. Grow it at the rear of the rock garden or in a sunny border.

Campanula rhomboidalis comes from the southwestern and central European Alps, where it grows in alpine meadows. It makes basal tufts of ovate, acute, crenate leaves on long, thin petioles. The several erect stems are 20–60 CM tall, with broadly ovate, smooth or hairy, sessile leaves that are pubescent on the underside. The pendant, campanulate, purple-blue flowers are to 2.2 CM long, with short unreflexed lobes, and form loose racemes on short pedicels. This species is very similar to *C. serrata*. Propagation is by seed sown in autumn or spring, or by division of the underground runners in spring. It is best grown in a border or in the wild garden, as it likes the company of other plants and can spread there without too much trouble.

Campanula rigidipila is a perennial species from the mountains of Ethiopia. It makes tufts of elliptic-lanceolate or obovate, slightly dentate, sessile leaves to 2.5 CM long from a woody rootstock. The erect to ascending, bristly-haired stem is branched from the base and grows to 30 CM tall. The blue, campanulate, pendant flowers are to 1.2 CM wide and carried on short peduncles on the top half of the stem. Propagation is by seed sown in autumn or spring. This is a plant for the rear of a rock garden or in a sunny border.

Campanula rotundifolia is the well-known bluebell of Scotland and is circumboreal in distribution, growing in a range of moist or dry habitats around the northern hemisphere in Europe, Asia, and North America. These vary from sand dunes to cliffs, rocky outcrops, grassy slopes or grassy wayside edges, roadsides, and even open fields from lower mountain slopes up to alpine zones. One of this plant's favourite haunts is among gravel and rocks above the water line of rivers and streams, where it can often be found growing in large clumps. It forms tufts of crenate, orbicular-cordate basal leaves with erect stems 10–50 CM tall, although plants to 80 CM have been recorded, and this height should be expected under garden conditions. Each stem has several erect or nodding, blue, campanulate, short-lobed flowers that bloom June–October. The stem leaves are lanceolate-linear and to 7.5 CM long. The specific name *rotundifolia* refers to the rounded leaves of the basal rosettes, which often disappear before the plant flowers, leaving just the stem leaves. *Campanula rotundifolia* spreads by slender underground rhizomes and can easily make a colony 90 CM across.

Campanula rotundifolia var. *alaskana* (synonyms *C. alaskana*, *C. latisepala*) ranges from British Columbia to Alaska. It differs from the more common form of the species in that its stem leaves are narrowly to broadly ovate and its flowers are usually solitary, but research shows that it is no more than a coastal race of the usual form, replacing it along all but the southern coast of British Columbia. In fact many taxonomists (Scoggan 1978–1979, Shetler 1963, and Welsh 1974, for example) do not recognise any infraspecific taxa within this species.

Campanula 'Alaskana' is a cultivar name given to a large form of *C. rotundifolia* that grows to 50 CM tall. It was most likely collected in Alaska or grown from seed collected from plants growing in that state.

Campanula rotundifolia subsp. *arctica* 'Mt. Jotunheimen' was collected in Norway on Mt. Jotunheimen by Henrick Zetterlund and introduced into the United States by Grand Ridge Nursery. It makes a prostrate mound of tiny, linear, tightly packed leaves and circling stems that grow to 5 CM tall. The blue, campanulate flowers are to 1.2 CM long. This is a lovely dwarf form and, as Rick Lupp once exclaimed, "a plant of incredible cuteness!"

Campanula rotundifolia

Campanula rotundifolia
subsp. *arctica*
'Mt. Jotunheimen'

Campanula rotundifolia 'Mingan' is an arctic dwarf form. As René Giguère, curator of the alpine garden at the Montreal Botanical Garden, Canada, informed me in 2004, this plant was collected by members of the botanical garden at the Mingan Archipelago, Quebec, in 1986. It was not named as a cultivar by them, however, but was probably named by a nurseryman with whom they exchange plants. "Taxonomically," says Giguère, "as far as we are concerned, this plant is *C. rotundifolia*." It grows 2–8 CM tall and is usually medium blue. Although it is claimed (Van der Werff 1999) to be the only dwarf polymorphic form of *C. rotundifolia* that grows vigorously in the garden and keeps its dwarf habit, I know from experience that 'Mt. Jotunheimen' does just the same. Comparing the two plants using photographs, there does not appear to be any difference. It would be nice to see both plants flowering side by side, however, in order to compare them.

Campanula rotundifolia 'Ned's White' is an excellent white cultivar discovered by Ned Lowry on Mt. Townsend, Washington State, United States, and named after him. This has very large, cup-shaped, white flowers on 20 CM stems. When planted out in one of my alpine beds it grew happily side by side with *C. parryi* for two years before succumbing to the damp winter. Although reputed to be quite vigorous, it did not increase quite as quickly for me as did the blue form. Seed from this cultivar has produced a number of plants that have come true, with the majority having large white flowers.

Campanula rotundifolia 'Olympica' is a form that was found growing in the Olympic Mountains, Washington State, United States. It grows to 30 CM tall, with blue, campanulate flowers to 2 CM long.

Propagation of *Campanula rotundifolia* is best by seed sown in autumn or spring. This species easily hybridises, and depending on other *Campanula* species growing in the locality where seed was collected, seed-grown plants can vary in height, flower size, and colour. This will give a wide range to select from. I have raised a number of beautiful dwarf forms, especially seed collected from *C. rotundifolia* subsp. *arctica* 'Mt. Jotunheimen'. In cultivation the usual form of the species is very suitable for the rock garden, while the dwarf forms can make good trough or alpine house plants.

Campanula rupestris (synonym *C. anchusiflora*) comes from southern and central Greece, where it grows in dry limestone rock crevices and on roadsides. From a thick taproot it makes rosettes of grey-pubescent, ovate or orbicular, dentate, and irregularly lyrate leaves, with the terminal lobe being the largest. The stems grow to 25 CM long and are many, with the central stem erect and the others ascending to decumbent. The basal and lower stem leaves are on petioles, while the upper ones are ovate and sessile. The lilac-blue, erect, tubular, campanulate flowers are to 1.5 CM long and have widely flared lobes. They are carried in few-flowered racemes both terminal and in the leaf axils. This is a monocarpic or biennial species that comes in the same group as *C. andrewsii* and *C. celsii*, species that are easily confused with one another. Propagation is by seed sown in autumn or spring. Grow it in a sunny, dry rock crevice with protection against winter wet. It also makes a good alpine house plant and is quite regularly seen on the show bench.

Campanula rupestris.

Photo by Panayoti Kelaidis

Campanula rupicola comes from the Peloponnese, Giona, and Parnassus in southern and central Greece, where it grows on limestone cliffs and rock communities above 1500 M. It makes tufts of small ovate, dentate basal leaves that are slightly hairy and on comparatively long petioles. Thin, decumbent stems grow to 12.5 CM long and have a few small leaves on short petioles. The many erect, deep violet-blue to purple-blue, narrowly campanulate, broad-lobed flowers are to 3.2 CM long. A good specimen can be totally covered with flowers so that no leaves can be seen. This is a beautiful but difficult plant to cultivate due to its tendency to collapse for no apparent reason (as I know only too well). Nevertheless, it is a species with which to persevere, as it is so rewarding when it flowers. Propagation is by seed sown in autumn or spring, or by cuttings taken in spring. Grow it in a warm, sunny crevice or in the alpine house, where it makes a lovely exhibition plant. Due to its tendency to collapse, I suggest propagating it and keeping small plants available for replacements.

Campanula rupicola.

Photo by Robert Rolfe

Campanula ruprechtii comes from the western Caucasus (Russia) at around 1800–2000 M, where it grows in limestone crevices. It makes tufts of elliptic, undulate, crenate leaves 5–10 CM long. Branched stems are 10–45 CM tall, with few leaves, and carry five to seven light blue to purple, infundibular, pendant or erect flowers on long peduncles. Propagation is by seed sown in autumn or spring, although seed of this species is rarely offered in lists. In the rock garden it will require a sunny crevice with protection from winter wet. It also makes a good alpine house plant.

Campanula samarkandensis (sometimes misspelt *C. samarkadensis*) was described as new to cultivation by Josef Halda in his 1991–1992 seed catalogue, and plants that I grow can be traced back to those raised from seed under the collection number *JJH918057*. It inhabits limestone crevices in Tajikistan at around 2400–2700 M. It is a tiny, tufted species growing from a central rootstock, with thread-like, decumbent to erect stems 2.5–7.5 CM long, holding tiny, grey, ovate leaves to 1 CM long. The tiny, tubular, pale pink flowers are 10 MM long and 8 MM wide, with dark pink veins. Although not long-lived, it sets plenty of seed. Propagation is by seed sown in autumn or spring. The seed is very fine and dust-like, and the plant quite often will self-sow in adjacent pots or soil. Be careful not to sow the seed too thickly or you will have a lot of trouble separating the seedlings. Seedlings grow fast and usually bloom the same year as germination. This is a suitable species for trough culture; in a rock garden it will be lost due to its diminutive size.

Campanula samarkandensis

Campanula sarmatica (synonyms *C. albiflora*, *C. betonicaefolia*, *C. brotherorum*, *C. commutata*, *C. gummifera*) is endemic to the northern Caucasus, Transcaucasus, Georgia (Shiga Kartli, Mtiuleti, Tush-Pshav-Khevsureti), and Azerbaijan, where it inhabits rocky places in the subalpine belt, 1300–2100 M. From a partially woody taproot with underground stolons it makes basal rosettes of wrinkled, pubescent, oblong-ovate to cordate, doubly crenate leaves to 15 CM long and 6.3 CM wide on long, winged petioles. In many cases the petioles are longer than the leaves. Hairy, suberect, unbranched stems 10–45 cm tall have a few hairy leaves to 3.3 cm long, similar to those at the base but sessile and narrower. The pale blue, occasionally white, campanulate flowers have very barbate, flared lobes and are to 3 cm long and 4 cm across, on five to seven short peduncles up the stem, with one at the very top. At first glance some people might consider this is a coarse and unattractive species. I did initially, but after a close look into those flowers, I loved it. It is a beautiful plant. This species is closely related to *C. collina* and is similar to it in habit (although some reference books suggest it is related to *C. alliariifolia*), and although it has a different flower colour it is just as hardy and perennial. Propagation is by seed sown in autumn or spring. Plenty of seed is set, so you should have no trouble in keeping it going in the garden. It blooms a year after germination. Grow it in a sunny or semi-shaded site in a large rock garden or border, but keep a keen eye out for slugs, as they can strip the leaves in no time.

Campanula sarmatica

Campanula sartorii is a short-lived perennial or monocarp that comes from Greece, where it grows in rocky places. From a taproot it makes tufts of orbicular or reniform-cordate, mildly crenate, slightly hairy leaves on short petioles, the leaves withering at flowering time. Wiry, brittle, prostrate to decumbent, occasionally branched stems have a few small leaves and grow 10–15 cm long. The numerous erect, white to pale pink, infundibular flowers have flared lobes, are to 1 CM long and 1.2 CM across, and grow singly in the leaf axils or on short pedicels along the stems. This species is often confused with *C. calaminthifolia*, as they are so much alike. Propagation is from seed sown in autumn or spring; however, quite often self-sown seedlings will appear alongside the dead plant. This is a beautiful species for a trough, in spite of it being a monocarp. Keep it going by seed each year.

Campanula saxatilis is relatively rare in the wild, reportedly growing in only four areas near the western end of Crete and the Aegean Islands at altitudes to 300 M, where it is found in limestone crevices on cliffs, forming compact clumps that mould themselves to the cliff face. From a thick taproot it makes rosettes of thick, glossy green, spatulate-oblanceolate, entire or crenate-serrate leaves. From spring onward, a number of decumbent to prostrate stems grow to 20 CM long from the rosettes; these are quite brittle and will break if roughly handled. Stem leaves are few, small, sessile, and oblong or linear-oblong. The stems follow the contours of the rock and carry many pale blue, narrowly campanulate flowers, which are 1.4–2.5 CM long, have a darker-coloured stripe to each of the flared lobes, and are in clusters of three to five on short pedicels. Propagation is by seed sown in autumn or spring. Cultivation is best in the alpine house, as it resents winter wet. Success has also been achieved by growing it in pieces of tufa set in a sunny trough with overhead protection in winter, although it may not be too hardy in temperatures below −8°c. It makes a fine exhibition plant, but watch out for slugs and red spider mite in the alpine house.

Campanula saxifraga comes from the northern Caucasus, where it grows at subalpine to alpine levels in rock crevices and on pockets of boulders. From a thick, branched root it makes rosettes of glabrous, lanceolate-spatulate basal leaves to 7 CM long. Ascending to erect stems 5–10 CM tall have linear-lanceolate, sessile leaves to 3 CM long and deep purple-blue, pendant to erect, solitary, campanulate flowers 2–3 CM long, with a subglabrous, white or light blue base. This is another species often included in the *C. tridentata* group, but as with *C. ardonensis*, I feel it is different enough to be described separately. Propagation is by seed sown in autumn or spring. If grown in the rock garden it needs a sunny, tight crevice and protection from slugs and snails. It also makes a fine pot plant for the alpine house. It dies down completely to untidy brown rosettes over winter.

Campanula saxifraga.

Photo by Harold McBride

Campanula scabrella, the rough harebell, is from the United States, ranging from Washington State to California, Montana, and Idaho, where it grows in screes and rocks in dry, exposed sites at subalpine to alpine levels. It makes dense rosettes of spatulate-oblanceolate, grey-blue leaves 2–5 CM long at the end of stolons that roam through the sunny and occasionally shifting screes, eventually forming small colonies. Stems to 12 CM tall have one to six upward-facing, grey-blue to violet, stellate flowers to 2.5 CM across, and the whole plant is covered with minute, spreading hairs.

Propagation is easily carried out by seed sown in autumn or spring. The stolons that run around underground are not really suitable for propagation purposes, but it has been found that plants that have been grown in a pot for a couple of years can be vegetatively propagated by treating the short stolons as cuttings. However, this is not a quick way to build a stock.

Campanula scabrella is among the more challenging North American species but is not impossible to grow and is worth the extra care required in cultivation, particularly as it is breathtaking in full flower. Trying to simulate the soil conditions for this species is very difficult, and to keep it in character it has to be grown hard in full sun. Any form of shelter, such as the alpine house, and its stems become a little lankier. This means that if grown as a pot plant, it has to spend a

Campanula scabrella,
Burnt Mountain,
eastern Cascades,
United States

lot of time outdoors during the growing season. Growing it in a trough makes things a little easier. When I do grow it in a pot, I use the same gritty compost I use for *Campanula piperi* and *C. shetleri* and give it as much sun as possible, but it still has stems of 7–8 CM. There is no way that I will be able to grow and flower it as I have seen on Burnt Mountain in the eastern Cascades.

Rick Lupp, proprietor of Mt. Tahoma Nursery in Graham, Washington State, United States, has found that he can keep this species in character with stems of less than 2.5 CM when grown very lean. He once commented, "I grow it in a large trough with *Penstemon caespitosa* var. *deserti-picti*, which looks great. I have not improved the original lean mix for about six years now, and both plants just seem to get better and better. I do give it a very weak feeding every once in a while, though."

Campanula scheuchzeri (synonym *C. linifolia*) is widely distributed throughout the southern and central European Alps, inhabiting the higher rocky pastures above 2155 M, where it gradually forms large colonies. If given just a cursory glance it can easily be mistaken for *C. rotundifolia*. It makes loose tufts of reniform-cordate, crenate basal leaves on long petioles that are withered at flowering time. Ascending to erect stems are 10–25 CM tall, with sessile, linear to narrowly lanceolate leaves. The pale to deep purple-blue, rarely white, campanulate flowers are 1.9–2.5 CM long with spreading lobes and are up to six per stem on long, hair-like pedicels. Some botanists consider *C. scheuchzeri* to be no more than a subspecies of *C. rotundifolia*, the main distinguishing features being that *C. scheuchzeri* has a great many more and larger flowers, and that these open from nodding buds, while the buds of *C. rotundifolia* are erect. Propagate by seed sown in autumn or spring, or by division of the rhizomes in spring. Cultivation is the same as for *C. rotundifolia*. It is happy in the rock garden or trough.

Campanula scouleri grows in mountain woodlands and north-facing talus slopes from Alaska to California. It makes rosettes of orbicular, serrate leaves. Thin, branched stems are 10–38 CM tall and have many leaves similar to those at the base but becoming gradually more linear up the stem. The infundibular, white to pinkish lavender flowers are in loose panicles and have strongly reflexed lobes that reveal styles shaped like baseball bats. Sometimes the stems are so weak that the entire plant tends to bend over when in full bloom, but nevertheless it is a very attractive and delicate species. Propagation is by seed sown in autumn or spring, but it is a vigorous plant and can easily be divided in spring. It needs a real spartan diet to remain compact but is suitable for the rock garden or a large trough.

Campanula scouleri

Campanula seraglio comes from Sarigol in eastern Turkey, where it grows in crevices on cliffs at around 1200 M. It is the most recent addition to the *C. betulifolia* group, which includes *C. choruhensis*, *C. kirpicznikovii*, and *C. troegerae*, and like those species, it does not disappoint the grower. It makes tufts of thick, densely pubescent, ovate-cordate, crenate leaves on short petioles, similar to *C. troegerae*. Stems to 7.5 CM tall have pure white, occasionally pink flowers that are 2.5–3.5 CM across, with wide, flaring, recurved lobes. Propagation is by seed sown in autumn or spring. Grow it in a trough with some protection from winter wet, or as a pot plant in the alpine house. It will make a very good exhibition plant.

Campanula serrata comes from Slovakia, where it grows in moist meadows and pastureland at around 1200 M and gradually forms clumps. It makes tufts of orbicular to ovate, crenate leaves that wither by flowering time. Erect stems grow 20–40 CM tall, with many ovate to narrowly lanceolate, serrate leaves. The blue, pendant, campanulate flowers are 1.5–2 CM long and in few-flowered racemes. It is very similar to *C. recta* but without the entire leaves. Propagation is by seed sown in autumn or spring, or by division in spring. Grow it at the back of a large rock garden or in the border, where it will slowly increase.

Campanula shetleri grows in the Mt. Shasta and Trinity Mountains area of California at 1540–2155 M, usually in places that offer some shade, tucking itself into the crevices of north-facing granite cliffs where it can grow upside down like a *Dionysia* plant. It forms dense rosettes of spatulate, sharply serrate, dark green leaves and loves a cool, moist root run, needed for the woody rhizomes. Stems grow 5–7 CM tall, with small, bowl-shaped flowers ranging from white to pale or darker grey-blue, to a lovely deep blue. It is often described as a compact version of *C. piperi*, but I think it is much more delicate and attractive, and is worth every effort required to grow it. It makes a great trough plant or can be treated as a pot plant with alpine house or cold frame protection in the winter.

Propagation is by seed sown in autumn or spring, or by division in spring or summer. It is worthwhile propagating it from seed and selecting the forms with the best colour. Collect seed from these and then grow it again from second-generation seed. I now have a number of nice compact plants with deep blue flowers. You just have to keep hunting for the right colour. If you have a good clone, you can remove rooted pieces from around the edge of the plant in spring as soon as the plant is in full growth, or dig it up and divide it.

Campanula shetleri is among the most beautiful North American campanulas I have grown. I tried growing it several times outside in a scree bed alongside other North American alpines, but as soon as the cold rains arrived it rotted off; it was, however, quite happy during the summer period. Now I prefer to grow it in a pot or trough with a gritty compost and a topdressing of at least 5 CM of grit. Similar to *C. piperi*, it loves these conditions and runs around, popping up at the edges of the pot throughout summer. During autumn and winter the green rosettes become brown around the edges just like those of *C. piperi* and like that species should be kept in control by judicious use of scissors. The flower stems also die back and can be removed with a gentle tug in spring. If the stems don't come away easily, use scissors to cut them off.

Campanula shetleri,
Castle Lake, California.

Photo by Phyllis Gustafson

Campanula sibirica is a biennial species that ranges from eastern Europe to Siberia, where it grows on rocky slopes and in mountain pine forests. It makes basal tufts of obovate to spatulate, crenate leaves on petioles. Erect stems grow 30–45 CM tall, with violet-blue, erect to pendant, infundibular flowers 2–2.5 CM long on short peduncles growing from the leaf axils. The whole plant is covered with coarse, stiff hairs. Propagation is by seed sown in autumn or spring. Grow this species in the border, but propagate by seed every year to keep it going.

Campanula spatulata (synonym *C. spathulata*) comes from Greece, where it grows in mountain pastures and grassland at an altitude of 1700–2500 M. From a thick, tuberous root it makes basal tufts of oblanceolate, crenate, occasionally papillose leaves on thin petioles. Erect stems to 30 CM tall or more have elliptic-obovate or ovate, sessile leaves. The blue, erect, broadly infundibular flowers are to 4 CM wide, have prominent arching lobes, are solitary on long peduncles, and bloom over a long period.

Campanula spatulata subsp. *filicaulis* is endemic to Crete and has stems to 25 CM tall, with the middle stem leaves on petioles and the solitary flowers on long peduncles. *Campanula spatulata* var. *guiseppii* has trailing stems and flowers that are wider than those of the common form of the species. *Campanula spatulata* subsp. *spruneriana* (synonym *C. spruneriana*) grows at low elevations, 400–1100 M. Its stems are to 50 CM tall, with lanceolate stem leaves at the middle. There are two to five pale blue flowers per stem, and the flowers are larger than those of the usual form of the species.

Propagation is by seed sown in autumn or spring, or by division in spring. This species is not long-lived and should be propagated every year. Grow it in a warm, sunny spot in the rock garden or border and give it protection from winter wet.

Campanula speciosa comes from the Pyrenees in Spain and France, growing on steep, stony limestone slopes and in dried-up riverbeds, where it sows itself around. At first glance this species looks like a compact form of *C. medium*, Canterbury bells. It makes large, flat basal rosettes of hairy, linear-lanceolate, sessile leaves with crenate, undulate margins. Leafy stems 30–50 CM tall carry white to purple-blue, rounded, campanulate-tubular flowers to 3 CM long held singly on long peduncles all the way up the leafy stem, forming a loose pyramidal raceme. There is some argument over whether this species is a monocarp or a short-lived perennial, but as it is easily grown from seed sown in autumn or spring, there should be no reason to lose it. However, it can succumb to winter wet if grown in too rich a soil, so it is best to mix in plenty of grit before planting. A wide range of forms can be expected from seed-grown plants. Grow it in the larger rock garden or in a warm, sunny border.

Campanula spicata is a biennial that ranges from the eastern Pyrenees to the central Italian mountains. From a thick, fleshy taproot it makes loose rosettes of

Campanula speciosa,
Port del Comte, Spain.

Photo by Harold Bevington

oblong-lanceolate, undulate, slightly dentate leaves. Thick stems grow in the second year to 70 CM tall, with many hispid, linear leaves reducing almost to bracts near the top. The lilac to purple, infundibular, sessile flowers to 2 CM long have deeply cut lobes and are in clusters of one to three up the stem, making stiff, open spikes. Although quite attractive, it is not a very choice species and overall is a bit too large for the rock garden. However, to promote new growth you should emulate the local goats in the wild by cutting the stem back at around 30 CM before the plant flowers. This results in many more flowering stems and a much better display. Propagation is by seed sown in autumn or spring. Plant in the border.

Campanula stefanoffii comes from Bulgaria and is a very close relative of *C. stevenii*. It makes neat rosettes from which erect, slender, occasionally branched stems grow 15–30 CM tall. Stem leaves are few, small, spatulate, and entire on short petioles. The large, erect, white, infundibular flowers have pointed lobes and are solitary and terminal. Propagation is by seed sown in autumn or spring. Grow it in a rock garden, trough, or alpine house.

Campanula stevenii comes from the Caucasus and Turkey, where it grows in mountain pastures and stony slopes at 1800–3075 M. It is closely allied to *C. patula* subsp. abietina. It makes close mats and clumps of smooth, bright green, obovate,

Campanula stevenii var. *beauverdiana* (collection number *JJH919083*)

crenate leaves on long petioles. The thin, erect stems are 15–45 CM tall and carry erect, lavender-blue, infundibular flowers to 2.5 CM long, with long, flared lobes that give them a starry appearance. Flowers are either solitary or in a few-flowered raceme. A white form has been recorded. Propagation is by seed sown in autumn or spring, or by division in spring. This species tends to be short-lived if not regularly divided and replanted in fresh soil, but during its life it rewards the gardener with masses of flowers. This is a nice plant for the front of the rock garden or for a trough.

Campanula stevenii var. *beauverdiana* comes from Turkey and Armenia, where it grows at around 3100 M, making dense tufts of bright green, serrate leaves. The many stems are 7–12 CM tall, with large, dark violet flowers. A form introduced by Josef Halda in 1991 under the collection number *JJH919083* is like a dwarf *C. collina* and makes a wonderful exhibition or trough plant. Propagation is by seed sown in spring or autumn, or by division in spring. If divided every couple of years, it will retain its vigour. Grow it in a trough or as a pot plant in the alpine house. It dies down over winter, and care must be taken not to overwater it during that period.

Campanula strigillosa (synonym *Asyneuma strigillosum*) comes from Turkey, where it grows among limestone and serpentine rocks at 1300–1800 M. It makes tufts of linear-lanceolate, entire, grey-setose, sessile basal leaves that are 1–2.5 CM long. The many ascending to erect stems, 20–30 CM tall, have pale blue to violet-blue, broadly infundibular flowers in narrow panicles. Propagation is by seed sown in autumn or spring. Grow it in a sunny crevice in the rock garden with protection from winter wet, or in the alpine house.

Campanula suanetica comes from the Transcaucasus, Georgia (Svaneti, where it is endemic) at around 1800 M, growing on limestone crevices in forests and gorges from the middle mountain to the subalpine level. It is a deciduous species that in spring makes basal rosettes of deep green, reniform or ovate-cordate, dentate leaves to 5 CM long and to 2.2 CM wide on petioles as long as, or occasionally longer than, the leaf. They have prominent veins. Stems to 18 CM tall have dentate, oblanceolate-ovate leaves that are much narrower than the basal leaves and on short petioles. The solitary, terminal, erect, deep purple-blue, campanulate flowers are to 2 CM long, have flared lobes, and are on several pedicels per stem. Propagation is by seed sown in autumn or spring, or by division in spring, which is easily undertaken. This lovely species will grow well in a sunny spot in the rock garden. However, since it can become a menace, spreading vigorously by underground runners, it should be grown either as a pot plant in the alpine house or in its own container in the garden.

Campanula telephioides comes from Turkey, where it grows at 2300–2740 M in short, dry grassland. It makes dense basal rosettes of ciliate, oblong-spatulate, crenate-serrate leaves 1–3 CM long that gradually narrow to petioles. Procumbent stems to 15 CM long have ovate, sessile leaves and small, violet-blue, subsessile, narrowly campanulate flowers to 8 MM long that are almost hidden in the leaf axils. Propagation is by seed sown in autumn or spring, or by division in spring. Grow it in the rock garden or trough.

Campanula teucrioides (synonym *C. bipinnatifida*) comes from Turkey, where it grows at 1600–2100 M in schistose screes and outcrops. It makes low, dense cushions from tufts of greyish green, ovate, pinnatifid, cuneate, undulate leaves 5–15 MM long and sessile or on petioles. Prostrate stems 2–5 CM long have few leaves, smaller than the basal tufts. The erect, lilac to violet-blue, narrowly infundibular flowers are to 1 CM long and solitary or in small clusters of two to five at the end of the stem. This is a very attractive campanula, and a particularly fine form was introduced from Turkey in 1977 by Jim McPhail and John Watson under the collector's number *McP. & W. 5861*. Propagation is by seed sown in autumn or spring. This is a choice species for growing in a trough or in a tight crevice in the rock garden. It has appeared on the show bench a number of times in the summer shows and makes an excellent exhibition plant.

Campanula thessala (synonym *C. pelia*) comes from central Greece, where it grows among rocks and on steep limestone cliffs. It makes basal tufts of densely grey-green, hairy, pinnatifid to pinnatisect leaves to 10 CM long, with the terminal lobe being the largest. The many flexible, prostrate to decumbent stems to 15 CM or more have small, oblong-obovate, sessile leaves. The pale violet-blue, tubular, narrowly infundibular, upward-facing flowers are 1.5–2.2 CM long, have short acute lobes, and are in loose racemes on short pedicels. In 1999 the AGS Macedonia and Epiros Seed Expedition brought back seed collected in the Tembi Gorge in central Greece and distributed it under the collection number *MESE 311*. Plants raised from this seed have since graced the show bench, one gaining a Farrer

Medal in June 2003. Propagation is by seed, plenty of which is set, sown in autumn or spring. This species is a short-lived perennial or monocarp and is best raised every year. Although it will grow in a warm, well-drained spot or dry wall, it is much better if grown as an alpine house plant. By removing the buds when they first show, and by giving the plant supplementary doses of early-season high-potash liquid fertiliser in its early years, you can build up your plant to give a one-time huge explosion of bloom.

Campanula thessala, a Farrer Medal–winning plant.

Photo by Jon Evans

Campanula thyrsoides (synonym *C. macrorhiza* var. *thyrsoides*), the yellow bell-flower, comes from the Jura mountains, European Alps, and Balkans, growing at 900–2700 M in subalpine meadows and limestone rocky areas. It makes rosettes of many long, oblong-lanceolate, undulate, entire, pale green leaves. Thick, erect stems to 40 CM have many sessile, straw yellow, narrow, campanulate flowers to 2.5 CM long carried in dense terminal spikes. The flowers are lobed to a third of their length. Stem leaves are linear-lanceolate. The whole plant is rough and covered with stiff hairs. Although this isn't an elegant plant, see it in the wild and you cannot help feeling that it makes a statement. It is biennial or monocarpic and best grown in a humus-rich, sunny spot as a feature or architectural plant that can be replaced every year. Propagation is by seed sown in autumn or spring.

Campanula thyrsoides in a mountain pasture.

Photo by Ann Borrill

Campanula thyrsoides subsp. *carniolica* comes from the eastern European Alps and mountains of Serbia and Montenegro. It grows to 60 CM and has spikes of flowers less crowded than those of the more common form of the species.

Campanula tommasiniana comes from Mala Ucka, Croatia, where it grows in rocky beech woods. From a thick rootstock it forms clumps of small, ovate basal leaves that die back in winter. Wiry, branching stems 15–20 CM tall have small, linear-lanceolate, serrate leaves and carry many small, blue, pendant, narrowly campanulate-tubular flowers that have pointed, reflexed lobes. With well-grown plants, the stems arch under the weight of the flowers. Propagation is by seed sown in autumn or spring, or by cuttings taken in spring. This species is a good perennial for the sunny or semi-shaded rock garden. It also makes a nice pot plant for the alpine house or for exhibition.

Campanula tommasiniana

Campanula topaliana comes from southern Greece, where it grows on limestone. From a taproot it makes basal rosettes of small, silky, grey-haired, lyrate leaves. Unbranched stems grow 20–40 CM tall, with many blue to violet-blue, tubular, campanulate flowers, with widely flared lobes, to 1 CM long and 2.5 CM across. There is a darker median line along each lobe that enhances the flower. It is very similar to *C. rupestris* and like that species is either a monocarp or a short-lived perennial. Propagation is by seed sown in autumn or spring. Although it can be grown in a warm, dry area in the rock garden, its tendency to rot off over winter makes it a candidate for the alpine house. Grow it in a pot containing a gritty, limy (tufa, if possible) compost. *Campanula topaliana* subsp. *delphica* is a form from Delphi, Greece, with flowers 1–1.2 CM long.

Campanula trachyphylla comes from Turkey, where it grows among rocks and grass at 1400–2800 M. It makes dense rosettes of narrowly spatulate, entire, ciliate or glabrous basal leaves 1.5–3 CM long. Erect stems are to 10 CM tall, occasionally twice that height, and carry pale blue to white, narrowly cylindrical flowers to 1.2 CM long in lax, spicate clusters. Propagation is by seed sown in autumn or spring, or by division in spring. Grow it in a sunny crevice in the rock garden or, for the more compact forms, in a trough. It is also suitable for alpine house culture.

Campanula tridentata (synonyms *C. bithynica*, *C. tridens*, *C. tridens* var. *araratica*) comes from Turkey, Armenia, and Georgia, where it grows in alpine meadows, screes, and rocky slopes at 1800–3500 M, usually blooming as the snow

Blue and white *Campanula tridentata*, Trialet, Georgia.

Photo by Vojtěch Holubec

recedes. From a thick rootstock it makes clusters of tight rosettes of oblanceolate-spatulate, slightly hairy, dentate leaves 2–4 cm long that diminish to a short petiole. Ascending to erect stems 5–15 cm tall have a few small, obovate-linear, sessile leaves and light blue to white, erect, solitary, terminal, campanulate to broadly infundibular flowers 2–3 cm long with well-reflexed lobes and a conspicuous white base.

Taxonomists report that there can be some variation between forms in terms of the hairiness of the corolla, especially on the nerves, and this may be part of the reason for confusion within the *C. tridentata* group. For example, although I have described *C. aucheri* as a different species, as do Lewis and Lynch (1998) and the AGS (1993), Ingwersen (1978) suggests that it is just another species within the *C. tridentata* group, which differ from each other only by tiny botanical variations. Crook (1951) found great difficulty in distinguishing between the species in this group and in his own book quoted from a paper read by Ingwersen before the RHS some years earlier, in which he referred to "the confusing group containing *C. ardonensis, C. bellidifolia, C. saxifraga,* and *C. tridentata,* all grading into one another to a bewildering extent."

Campanula tridentata flowers early, commencing in May, and heralds the start of summer. Propagation is by seed sown in autumn or spring. Plant it in a sunny, well-drained spot in the rock garden, or grow it as a pot plant in the alpine house. It may be prone to red spider mite when planted under cover.

Campanula troegerae comes from the Yusufeli area of Turkey, where it grows in partly shaded rock crevices at around 1800 m. It is tufted, with grey-green, pubescent, ovate-cordate, serrate leaves to 4 cm on long petioles. Ascending to erect stems 10–20 cm long have leaves that are similar to the basal tufts but sessile. Pale pink buds on short petioles open to beautiful, crystalline white, almost flat, stellate flowers to 5.5 cm across, with prominent, exserted stigmas. Like *C. choruhensis, C. kirpicznikovii,* and *C. seraglio,* this species is closely related to *C. betulifolia.* Propagation is by seed sown in autumn or spring. Grow it in a sunny spot in the rock garden, but remember that it dies back to a woody rootstock over winter. It makes a lovely pot plant for the alpine house and is often seen on the show bench.

Campanula troegerae.

Photo by Panayoti Kelaidis

Campanula tubulosa comes from central to western Crete, where it grows in a variety of habitats, from shady, moist crevices in limestone rocks and deep limestone gorges at around 100–800 M, to rocks in woodland areas where the trees afford it the shade it needs. It makes rosettes of grey, hairy, lanceolate, crenate basal leaves. Ascending to decumbent, repeatedly branched, faintly hairy stems 15–20 CM long have small, lanceolate leaves, the lower ones on petioles and the upper ones sessile. The erect, violet to pale-lilac, tubular, velvety-hairy flowers are to 2.5 CM long, on short peduncles, and either solitary or in groups of three. Although it takes several years to reach flowering size, this species will die after flowering, and therefore can be treated as a biennial or monocarp. Propagation is by seed, of which it sets plenty, sown in spring or autumn. Like most of the Mediterranean campanulas it resents winter wet and is best grown in the alpine house. However, it will love a summer hot spot in the garden if you can keep the slugs at bay and grow it anew every year.

Campanula turczaninovii (synonym *C. silenifolia*) comes from the Siberian mountains and northern Mongolia, where it grows in the tundra zone and in coniferous forests. From a deep taproot it makes clusters of rosettes of oblong-elliptic to lanceolate, usually entire leaves 5–15 CM long. The many thin, erect stems, 10–70 CM tall, have sessile, lanceolate-linear leaves. The deep blue, narrow, infundibular, pendant flowers are to 4.5 CM long and from one to five on peduncles at the top of the stem. Propagation is by seed sown in autumn or spring, and the plant blooms in its second year. It can be grown in a semi-shaded position in the rock garden or border.

Campanula tymphaea comes from Albania and northern Greece, where it grows among rocks and in meadows from subalpine to alpine levels. It makes rosettes of oblong-spatulate, crenate leaves on petioles. Stems 10–30 CM tall have many bright green, oblong or ovate-lanceolate, sessile leaves. The violet-blue, infundibular flowers to 1 CM long are in terminal clusters of four to seven. Propagation is by seed sown in autumn or spring, or by division in spring. Grow it in the sunny area of a rock garden. The compact forms make good alpine house plants.

Campanula uniflora is a circumpolar and subarctic species that grows in stony limestone formations. It can be found growing in Alaska, Greenland, northern Russia, and the Colorado grassy tundra area at around 3755 M, and in Sweden and

Norway. From a thick, branching rootstock it makes tufts of small, oblong-oval, crenate leaves on short petioles. Thin, erect stems 5–10 CM tall have solitary, mid to deep blue, pendant to almost erect, narrowly infundibular flowers to 1 CM long. I first saw this plant on a field trip to Loveland Pass, Colorado, during the 2003 North American Rock Garden Society conference. It is so small that it is surprising our small group spotted it, and I have to disagree with Crook (1951) when he says that "the interest must be mainly botanical." This is a beautiful but tiny species that I would love to grow, and it deserves more prominence. Hopefully one day it will be seen regularly at the summer shows. Although I have had seed on two occasions, there has been no germination. Propagation is by seed sown in autumn or spring, or possibly by cuttings taken in spring.

Campanula valdensis (synonym *C. carnica* subsp. *puberula*) is simply a hairy form of *C. carnica*. The AGS *Encyclopaedia of Alpines* (1993) also gives the possibility of it being the same plant as *C. carnica* subsp. *puberula*, but I can find no other reference to this and therefore cannot confirm it.

Campanula velebitica is endemic to the Velebit Mountains and Paklenica National Park, Croatia, where it grows in rocky areas. It makes clumps or colonies with erect to ascending stems 15–25 CM tall and many blue or blue-violet flowers to 2 CM long in loose racemes. Propagation is by seed sown in autumn or spring. This is an extreme rarity and highly unlikely to be in cultivation.

Campanula versicolor comes from the Balkan Peninsula and southeastern Italy, where it grows in rocky areas and cliffs in the lower forest region. From a thick taproot it makes rosettes of a few smooth, leathery, ovate to cordate, crenate-dentate leaves on long petioles. Leafy, unbranched stems 20–40 CM tall have one to five erect, pale to mid-lilac flowers to 2.5 CM or more across on peduncles growing from each leaf axil. It is a very floriferous species, with flowers that are almost flat, and stellate, with long spreading lobes and a deep blue-purple centre, making them very attractive. Some references report that the stems grow to 120 CM, but I suspect this applies to the form of this plant that hangs down from rocks, rather than the more usual shorter-stemmed form. The late Jack Elliott once commented that on finding *C. versicolor* for the first time growing out of the rock among the ruins at Mistra in southern Greece, he thought it looked monocarpic but had second thoughts when he saw that it had seed capsules and was in flower

Campanula versicolor

at the same time. Since that occasion he grew and distributed it, considering it to be a good hardy perennial, although it does need a sunny spot and may not come through a harsh winter. It is still rather scarce in cultivation, with most seed coming from various botanical garden distributions. Propagation is by seed sown in autumn or spring, or from basal cuttings taken in spring. Once the plants are a few years old, they produce a number of rosettes that can be carefully removed and used as cuttings if taken with plenty of underground stem. From my research, root cuttings and division are said to work, but I would only try that if I had more than one plant to risk. Try it in the garden, but as previously mentioned, it does need a sunny spot. It makes a good pot plant, but short forms will need to be selected from seed-grown plants. My own plants grown from seed are around 25 CM tall and smothered with flowers.

Campanula waldsteiniana comes from Croatia, growing at around 1600 M in limestone crevices, where it forms superb dwarf cushions. It makes tufts of small, spatulate leaves with many thin, erect, leafy stems 10–15 CM tall. Stem leaves are glaucous, lanceolate-ovate, finely serrate, and acute. The stems terminate in solitary, upturned, blue-violet stars to 2 CM across that have a base of deepest violet and that cover the whole plant. It is a gem of a species and still not in cultivation as much as it should be. For some reason many references suggest it is similar to

*Campanula
waldsteiniana*

C. tommasiniana, but it is a completely different plant in height and flower. Propagation is by seed sown in autumn or spring, or by careful division in spring. Grow it in a tight crevice in the rock garden or as an alpine house plant with a gritty compost. It is quite hardy, but being deciduous it disappears underground over winter.

Campanula witasekiana comes from the eastern Alps and mountains of Slovenia, and the northern Balkan Peninsula, where it inhabits the higher-altitude grassland. It makes tufts of obovate-elliptic, crenate basal leaves. Thin, erect stems, 20–40 CM tall, have lanceolate-linear, entire leaves to 6 CM long. The purple-blue, pendant, campanulate flowers are 1.3–1.6 CM long and in clusters of three or four on short peduncles. Propagation is by seed sown in autumn or spring, or by careful division of the slender rhizomes in spring. Be careful where you plant it in the rock garden, as it increases rapidly, forming large clumps, and can be invasive.

Campanula zoysii is described by Farrer (1918) as "the last and strangest of the race—that minute exquisite rock-jewel which you may see filling the crevices and high chinks of the Karawanken in just such limestone cliffs and crannies as those beloved by *C. raineri* further west." He went on to describe it as "rosettes of tiny-spoon-shaped foliage, glossy and bright green shoots of several inches carrying a number of long pale-blue bells so oddly bulging and puckered at the mouth as to resemble nothing on earth so much as a tiny soda-water bottle with a ham-frill at the end." Such prose is impossible to follow; I can only try to add to the description. The Karawanken mountains are in the southeastern European Alps, where *C. zoysii* grows in crevices among the limestone cliffs. It is tufted, spreading by underground runners that eventually form mats or small mounds. Basal leaves are ovate-obovate and on petioles. Stems to 7.5 CM tall have leaves that are broadly lanceolate-linear. The pale blue to mid-blue flowers are to 2 CM long, narrowly tubular, and crimped at the mouth. These crimped mouths make it very difficult for bees to enter, and in the past I have noticed two different types of bees flying around my plants: a small one that burrowed into the closed end of the flowers to obtain the pollen, and a very large one that just drilled a hole straight through each flower. Half an hour later, all the flowers possessed an extra hole. No seed was set, which made it a pointless exercise as far as I was concerned. Propagation is by seed sown in spring or autumn, by cuttings taken in spring, or by removing rooted side shoots from spring to summer.

Although this is *the* campanula that is always mentioned by rock garden writers and speakers discussing campanulas for growing in tufa and troughs, there are many different clones in the trade, some vigorous and free-flowering and some not. If possible, try to see the plant in flower before you buy it.

It is a fairly easy plant to grow and if grown for exhibition can fill a 15 CM pot in three years. Grown in tufa in a trough outdoors, it remains tight and a delight to see. However, there is one piece of advice I give to everyone who wishes to grow this plant. Although the plant blooms tremendously well, hardly any rosette being without a flowering stem, after flowering the majority of these stems and their rosettes die back, sometimes resulting in the death of the entire plant. You must make it a priority therefore to propagate it before flowering so that you have smaller plants coming on to replace the big one, which inevitably dies.

Its main enemy in the garden is slugs, but perhaps Clarence Elliott (1936) had the right idea when he said, "We get over that difficulty by having *Campanula zoysii* in such quantity that the most gargantuan slugs come over all bilious at the mere sight of our beds."

Campanula zoysii 'Lismore Ice' is a white form raised and christened by Brian Burrow, former nurseryman from England, from wild seed collected in the Julian Alps and distributed through the AGS seed exchange in 1986. It is an exquisite plant but is much more compact than the usual blue form and is slower to increase, with smaller leaves. The tips of the leaves are slightly yellow, but this is a natural characteristic and not, as some writers have said, a sign of chlorosis. Like the usual form of the species, it will grow perfectly well in a trough open to all the ravages of the weather, provided slugs and snails are kept at bay. It takes longer to build up into a large plant, but it seems that continual disturbance (removing rooted pieces, for example) and a deep topdressing of grit will encourage it to survive and produce more side shoots. From a small plant obtained in 1995 I managed to produce at least 20 saleable plants two years later. Cuttings taken in spring will also root fairly easily, as with the more common form of the species. In the late 1990s it appeared that I was the only person in possession of 'Lismore Ice', but I gave one of my plants to the original raiser, who propagated it quickly and in a couple of years had enough to distribute again. He even returned a couple of plants, as my stock had become low. This is what conservation is all about.

Campanula zoysii

Campanula zoysii
'Lismore Ice'

Hybrids

Hybrids between species crop up quite often, but not all are good enough to bring into cultivation, whether for reasons of poor colour, small flower size, difficulty in cultivation, or some other fault. What is required is a vigorous but not particularly invasive plant that is hardy in most parts of the world, easy in cultivation, and that contains the best attributes of both parents. Plants like these are popular with rock gardeners and will stand the test of time. It has been observed that many hybrids have yellow-green leaves, which is probably a symptom of mixing two bloods. Many of the older hybrids have been lost to cultivation, probably as a result of going out of fashion and nurserymen not propagating them at the time. Listed here are some of the old hybrids still in cultivation, as well as many of the new ones. Some are natural garden hybrids, while others resulted from deliberate crossing.

Without doubt, more natural garden hybrids will find their way into the trade over the next decade or two: the willingness for species of *Campanula* to cross will make it happen. More interesting, though, are the deliberate crosses made between species that in the wild may grow on different continents, or between species that are not in flower at the same time. Crosses are also being made between species that individually are already terrific plants, in an attempt to

Campanula raineri var. *alba* × *C. morettiana* var. *alba*.

Photo by Robert Rolfe

produce hybrids that might be even more wonderful. For example, *Campanula raineri* var. *alba* × *C. morettiana* var. *alba* is a cross made by Brian Burrow that produced seed that was sown in January 2003. From this first-generation cross came a lovely blue-flowered form, and Brian hopes to produce second-generation plants that are white-flowered, with flowers just as good as those of the present hybrid.

Campanula **'Abundance'** is, like *C.* 'Spetchley', a cross between *C. rotundifolia* and *C. carpatica* var. *alba*. It is similar to 'Spetchley' but with more and smaller flowers.

Campanula **'Birch Hybrid'** is a cross between *C. portenschlagiana* and *C. poscharskyana* and is intermediate between the parents. It was introduced by Walter Ingwersen and named for his Birch Farm Nursery. The plant has a spread of about 45 CM, and the tough, arching to prostrate stems are 10–15 CM long, with small, evergreen, ovate-cordate, serrate leaves. The upward-facing, purple-blue, campanulate flowers are in large clusters. Although both parents are very invasive, this hybrid can be easily contained by removing some of the rooted side pieces as required. These can also be used for propagation in spring or summer if necessary. This is an excellent plant for the rock garden, flowering profusely all summer, is tough, easy, and can tolerate a wide range of conditions, even dry shade. Although it spreads quickly by underground runners, it is ideal as a groundcover without being too invasive.

Campanula **'Bumblebee'** was introduced by Rick Lupp in the 1990s. It appeared as a seedling in a batch grown from seed collected from *C. piperi* 'Mt. Tahoma' in the nursery of that name. 'Mt. Tahoma' had been growing in close proximity to a tray of *C. lasiocarpa*, and a natural cross was carried out by bees. 'Bumblebee' is a lovely hybrid, with large, upward-facing blooms of a deep blue on 15 CM stems. Its basal growth is much like *C. piperi*, making tufted rosettes of shiny, dark green, leathery, toothed leaves.

Propagation is by division, and it is very quick to reproduce: a small piece potted up when the plant is in active growth will increase in size so quickly that within a couple of months it can be divided yet again into several rooted pieces. If vegetative propagation is done in spring, pieces with no roots can be treated as cutting material in a frame, and rooting in sand will occur within five to six weeks.

Like *Campanula piperi*, attention must be paid to the dead-looking stems over winter, and these should not be removed until the plant is in full growth. This cultivar is very similar in winter appearance and soil requirements to *C. piperi*, although I find it much more agreeable in cultivation than either of its parents. It is a very vigorous plant, quickly filling an 18 CM pot, and can also be grown in a scree or trough. It appears regularly on the show bench.

Campanula 'Bumblebee'

Campanula 'Cantata' was raised by Brian Burrow and is a deliberate cross made between *C. zoysii* 'Lismore Ice' and *C. pulla* var. *alba*. Like its parents it grows from rhizomes, although it is more vigorous than *C. zoysii*. It makes mats of deep green, ovate leaves to 13 MM long and to 9 MM wide on short petioles. Multi-branched stems to 10 CM tall have mid to dark blue, solitary, tubular flowers to 20 MM long and 8 MM wide, with fine hairs on the inside of the mouth of the slightly flared lobes. The blue flowers become darker if the plant is grown in the open garden. From my experience it holds its flowers longer than either of the parents and is a very good pot plant. My plant was awarded an RHS Certificate of Preliminary Commendation in June 2004. Propagation is by division in spring or summer. It grows well in a trough and as a pot plant in the alpine house for exhibition.

Campanula 'Cantata'

Campanula '**Cassini**' is a cross between *C. cenisia* and *C. piperi.* It was raised and introduced by Rick Lupp in about 1995 and like *C.* 'Bumblebee' is a bee hybrid that occurred at Mt. Tahoma Nursery. This cross, made by others in the past, has produced several hybrids, all of which have apparently disappeared from cultivation. Hopefully this one will last longer. It makes tufted mats of small, green-yellow, obovate, serrate leaves that spread from rhizomes. Erect stems to 10 CM tall have blue, stellate flowers. The cultivar name commemorates a NASA space probe that was launched in 1997. Propagation is by division in spring or summer. It is a lovely choice hybrid that is much easier to grow than either parent. Grow it in a trough or as a pot plant in the alpine house.

Campanula '**Covadonga**' (synonym *C. linifolia* 'Covadonga') grows in Covadonga, in the Cantabrian Mountains of northern Spain. It makes short basal tufts of very narrow, lanceolate, serrate leaves to 3 CM long. Thin, multibranched stems grow to 15 CM tall. The solitary, deep blue-purple, campanulate flowers are to 2.5 CM long and 2.5 CM wide at the mouth. Occasionally a plant may have several stems that are like tendrils with tufts of leaves at the ends, and they twist around the plant. Clarence Elliott and Roger Bevan selected this form from plants growing at the foot of a cliff face in the Covadonga area. It is a beautiful plant. Some

Campanula 'Covadonga'

people feel that *C. pulla* has the darkest flowers in the genus, but *C.* 'Covadonga' certainly rivals it. It gained an RHS Award of Merit when shown by Clarence Elliott on 4 July 1939. It was originally exhibited as *C. linifolia*, then *C. scheuchzeri*, and finally settled in the *C. rotundifolia* group, which as we all know is quite variable. However, I feel that 'Covadonga' is quite a distinct plant and should stand on its own.

This is a plant that for some reason in the past became unfashionable. One keen campanula grower commented to me in July 2003, "I remember buying this plant from Joe Elliott way back in the 1970s but, as with a number of Joe's good plants, haven't seen it for some time." I was lucky to obtain my plant in June 2003 as a gift from a customer, and I feel it should be reintroduced if possible.

Propagation is by seed sown in autumn or spring, but there will be a variation of flower size and height with the seedlings, although usually the flowers are the same deep blue as the parent. My own seedlings have produced some beautiful dwarf forms. Rooted underground runners can be found occasionally, and these should be detached and potted up. This is an excellent plant for a sunny trough or the alpine house.

Campanula **'Edward Forrest'** is a cross between *C. betulifolia* and *C. troegerae*. It was raised and introduced by John Forrest and named in memory of his brother, who died in an aircraft tragedy, and for his father, also named Edward Forrest. What is so amazing is that only one seedling survived the cross made in 1990 and yet it turned out to be such a beautiful plant. It makes tufts of leaves intermediate in shape between the parents but also shows some of the pubescence of *C. troegerae*. Lax stems to 15 CM carry deep pink flower buds that open to large, white, tubby cups with an exerted style. It was awarded an RHS Certificate of Preliminary Commendation in June 1995. Propagation is by cuttings taken in summer, although not too much cutting material is produced at that time. One suggestion is to forgo flowers one year and cut back all flowering stems, thus producing plenty of young growth for cuttings. Seed is quite often set, and I have raised a number of plants with a lot of variation. This plant also hybridises well with *C. choruhensis*. Although it will probably grow in the rock garden perfectly alright, it is one of those plants just meant for a pot in the alpine house and for exhibition. Grow it in a very gritty compost.

Campanula 'Edward Forrest'

Campanula **'G. F. Wilson'**, like *C. ×pulloides*, resulted from a cross between *C. carpatica* 'Turbinata' and *C. pulla*, but it leans toward 'Turbinata' in looks and growth. Stems grow to 10 CM tall, with rich purple, pendant, campanulate flowers that have slightly crimped lobes. Plants in cultivation have either green-yellow or green foliage. Propagation is by division in spring or summer. Grow it in a sunny rock garden, but keep splitting and replanting it, as for *C. ×pulloides*. It blooms later than *C. ×pulloides*, being at its best from July to August.

Campanula 'Hallii' is a hybrid between *C. cochlearifolia* and *C. portenschlagiana* but without too much of the invasive qualities of the latter. It makes mats of pale green, glossy leaves intermediate between the two parents. Stems to 10 CM tall have white, solitary, pendant to semi-erect flowers similar to but more open than those of *C. cochlearifolia*. It was raised by Alva Hall in about 1920. Propagation is by division in spring or summer. Grow it in the rock garden.

Campanula 'Haylodgensis' (synonym *C. ×warleyensis*) is a cross between *C. carpatica* and *C. cochlearifolia*. Research suggests that this was originally a single-flowered form, not the double that is accepted nowadays. It has the running habit of *C. cochlearifolia* but with lax stems to 15 CM and light blue, bowl-shaped, double flowers that are larger than those of *C. cochlearifolia* 'Elizabeth Oliver'. It is an old hybrid dating back to 1885 when it was raised by a Mr. Augustine-Henry of Hay Lodge near Edinburgh. Propagation is by division in spring or summer. Grow it in the rock garden or trough.

Campanula 'Hilltop Snow' is a plant I raised in 1997 and named for the cottage "Hilltop" that at the time was owned by Tony and Shirley Barber and situated just outside of Bath, Somerset, United Kingdom. It was from their garden that seed was collected in 1996 from plants mistakenly labelled *C. thessala*. They had blue flowers and were very attractive, somewhat akin to *C. rotundifolia*. The seed was sown in January 1997, and the seedlings were pricked out in small batches, with the more vigorous ones potted up singly. The vigorous plants all flowered in June of that year, and all but one were blue. The exception had white flowers and was grown on for assessment. It was vigorous and propagated easily by division. The divisions were grown on in pots, and one was planted in the garden, where it bloomed in 1998, through summer and well into October. It is a first-rate plant for the rock garden or exhibition and was awarded an RHS Certificate of Preliminary Commendation in June 1998. It makes tight mats of cordate-reniform, crenate basal leaves 1.5 CM long and to 1.2 CM wide. Thin stems to 15 CM tall have linear leaves and pure white, campanulate, nodding flowers to 2.4 CM long and to

2.5 CM wide on short, hair-like pedicels. Propagation is by division in spring or summer. It sets plenty of seed, but any resulting white-flowered plants cannot be named 'Hilltop Snow'. This cultivar is ideal for the rock garden or alpine house, blooming through summer into autumn and standing up well to bad weather.

Campanula 'Hilltop Snow'

***Campanula* 'Joe Elliott'** is a beautiful plant generally accepted to be a hybrid between *C. morettiana* and *C. raineri*. It was raised in the 1970s by the proprietor of Broadwell Nursery in Gloucestershire, the late Joe Elliott. It is a bee hybrid (a natural cross carried out by bees), the seed parent being *C. morettiana*, and Joe admitted having the audacity to name it after himself. A wise choice, as this hybrid ranks among the best. Like many hybrids, it is much more vigorous than the parents and also demonstrates their best characteristics. It forms a mound of soft, greyish green, downy leaves to 15 CM across. Stems are 5–8 CM tall and hold two or three lavender-blue, broadly infundibular flowers to 3.2 CM long and 2.5 CM wide. It blooms for a long period, from June through summer, and in the alpine house continues blooming into autumn. Propagation is by division from spring onward, or cuttings can be taken if required. It grows well in a gritty, limey soil, makes an excellent pot plant for the alpine house, and is often seen on the show bench. If growing it in a pot, make sure it does not dry out over winter or it will not come back to life in spring.

Campanula 'Joe Elliott'

***Campanula* 'John Innes'** (synonym *C.* ×*innesii*) was considered by Crook (1951) to be a hybrid between *C. carpatica* and *C. pyramidalis*, and he agreed with the name *C.* ×*innesii*, but I have to concur with Lewis and Lynch (1998), who call it "an unlikely cross between *C. carpatica* as the seed parent and *C. versicolor* as the pollen parent." Also, the cultivar name seems to be appropriate, as it was raised at the John Innes Institute, England. As *C. pyramidalis* grows so large, to around 2 M tall, I would have thought that any hybrid with this species as one of its parents would grow much taller than 'John Innes'. Furthermore, you only have to look at the flowers of *C. versicolor* to see the similarity between that species and this cultivar. The flower shape is almost exactly the same, but in comparison with *C. versicolor*, whose flowers are pale blue with a deep blue eye, the flowers of 'John Innes' are a lovely, rich purple-blue with a deeper blue eye. 'John Innes' makes tufts of obovate, mildly serrate basal leaves to 2.5 CM wide and 5 CM long on petioles that are almost the same length. Decumbent to ascending stems are to 30 CM or more long, with lanceolate leaves to 4.5 CM long on petioles near the base of the stem, becoming shorter and sessile as they near the top of the stem. The almost flat, upward-facing, deeply cut, star-like flowers are to 4.5 CM across and on pedicels, with up to 15 growing along the length of the stem. Propagation is by cuttings or division in spring. This is an excellent plant for the front of a large rock garden, making a mat some 70 CM or more across. I grow it in a trough, where it hangs down over the side and makes a deep blue waterfall. Watch out for slugs and snails, though, which will crawl up the length of the stem eating all green growth as they go.

Campanula 'John Innes'

***Campanula* 'Lynchmere'** is a cross between *C. elatines* and *C. rotundifolia*. In 1951 Clifford Crook, describing it as "one of the latest introductions," commented: "It is too early to say anything of its behaviour in cultivation but it is certainly showy and appears very promising." As the plant had already been given an RHS Award of Merit in 1948, Crook's observations seem to have been quite an understatement. This cultivar makes a small clump 20–30 CM tall of thin, branching stems with bright green, ovate, crenate, obtuse leaves. The lovely, rich violet-blue, campanulate, pendant, terminal flowers are to 2 CM long and 1 CM across, with slightly reflexed lobes. Unfortunately, it is not seen around too much nowadays. Propagation is by cuttings taken in spring, or by division in spring or summer. It is a beautiful and long-lived plant and is equally at home in a rock garden or pot. If cut back after its first flush it will usually bloom again in late summer.

Campanula **'Maie Blyth'** is a choice little hybrid from New Zealand that appears to have some *C. carpatica* blood in its makeup. It was named for Maie Blyth of Timaru in the South Island, who raised it from a seedling that germinated in a pot of seed from the AGS distribution of wild-collected *C. morettiana* seed. None of that species germinated, but this little plant did. A few plants were released from Maie's nursery in 1979, and the cultivar was listed commercially for the first time in 1981 by Highfield Alpines near Timaru, New Zealand. The owner of that nursery, Lesley Cox, is now the proprietor of Gala Plants in Dunedin, New Zealand, and still lists 'Maie Blyth'. It is a lovely and unusual plant, making a condensed mound of small, crinkled foliage with many flat, blue flowers to 2.5 CM across in dense clusters on stems to 12.5 CM tall.

Several excellent seedlings have been selected and named, including two plants raised by Lesley Cox: 'Blithe Spirit', which is identical to 'Maie Blyth' except that it is white, and 'Silver Chalice', which is very compact but with a larger, silvery lavender flower. Another, selected by Bryan Davies of Christchurch, was originally named 'Moonbeam' but is now in the trade as 'Blue Moon' or 'Blue Moonlight'.

Propagation is by cuttings taken in spring. Seed is quite often set, but of course any seedlings raised from this cannot be named 'Maie Blyth'. It grows well in a sunny trough or rock garden.

Campanula 'Marion Fisher'

Campanula **'Marion Fisher'** was raised by John Fisher of Cheltenham, England, who found it growing on a south-facing scree in his garden. It was growing among a clump of *C.* 'Haylodgensis' as a "root sport" of that plant. Fisher dug it up, propagated it, and passed a number of plants on to a nurseryman. Those plants died out, but luckily some that he propagated appeared on plant sales tables at local shows, and now this plant is widely available and a firm favourite in the trade. It makes congested mats of small, ovate-cordate leaves with stems to 10 CM tall and double white flowers to 2 CM across. Propagation is by division in spring or summer. This is a vigorous plant that grows well in a rock garden or trough.

Campanula **'Mist Maiden'** is thought by many to be a cross between *C. rotundifolia* and *C. tommasiniana*, but that is not certain, and its origin remains a little obscure. It makes mats of linear leaves and slender, wiry stems to 15 CM tall. Pure white, pendulous or horizontal, campanulate flowers are to 2.5 CM in width, about the same in length, and four to five per stem, making the plant appear very floriferous. The whole plant is minutely grey-pubescent, and when seen at a distance its combination of grey foliage and white flowers gives the effect of a mist, making the name 'Mist Maiden' very appropriate. The plant was exhibited by W. E. Th. Ingwersen, received an RHS Award of Merit in July 1981, and was described by Brian Mathew as one of the most graceful of all the white-flowered campanulas. Propagation is by division in spring. Planted at the back of a rock garden, it makes a lovely feature during summer.

Campanula **'Norman Grove'** is reputed to be a hybrid between *C. isophylla* and *C.* 'Stansfieldii', its habit appearing to favour the latter. It makes tufted mats of small, ovate, cordate, dentate leaves. Erect stems to 15 CM tall have few lanceolate leaves. The mid-blue, suberect to erect, campanulate flowers are on relatively long pedicels growing from the leaf axils. It was named for Norman Grove of Sutton Coldfield, England, a campanula enthusiast who exhibited alpines before the First World War. He raised a number of good *Campanula* hybrids that obtained awards, including 'Chastity', a white form, and 'Enchantress'; both are probably no longer in cultivation. Propagation is by division in spring. Grow it in the rock garden, as it may be a bit too robust for a trough. It is fairly long-lived and will eventually grow into a large mat like *C.* 'Stansfieldii'.

***Campanula* 'Polly Henderson'** is a cross between *C. hercegovina* 'Nana' and *C. excisa.* Another bee hybrid, it was found as a seedling in the garden of Keith McMath of Blackpool, England, and raised by him. From a thick mat of underground rhizomes it makes tufts of elliptic-ovate, sharply serrate leaves to 3 CM long. Thin, branching stems to 15 CM tall have leaves similar to the basal tufts near the base of the stem but changing to linear-lanceolate and dentate on the top two-thirds. The solitary, purple-blue, erect, campanulate flowers open to almost stellate and are terminal on the branches. Just before the flowers open, the tips of the petals are still held together, giving the buds a bulbous shape. It is a beautiful and unusual plant. Propagation is by division in spring or summer. Grow it in a rock garden, trough, or alpine house. If growing it as a pot plant, repot it every spring.

Campanula 'Polly Henderson'

***Campanula* 'Pseudoraineri'** (occasionally *C.* ×*pseudoraineri*, *C.* ×*pseudo raineri*) is a name given to a plant widely accepted as a hybrid between *C. carpatica* and *C. raineri*, although it is not as widely recognised as differing from *C. raineri* when seen in the flesh. It makes tufts of grey, cordate leaves and stems with few leaves, 10–15 CM tall. The flowers are blue, 4.5 CM across, and of a more shallow shape than *C. raineri*, more like those of *C. carpatica*. Growth is slow and creeping, similar to *C. raineri*, and it dies back over winter. Unfortunately, seed of this union can crop up in many seed exchange lists, and the plants on many sales tables can be wrongly named as *C. raineri*. It is an attractive plant, however, and much easier to grow than *C. raineri*. Propagation is by division in spring or summer. Grow it in a trough or in the rock garden.

Campanula ×*pulloides* is a garden hybrid that resulted from a cross between *C. carpatica* 'Turbinata' and *C. pulla*. It is very similar to *C. pulla* but with larger foliage and flowers. It makes loose basal rosettes with slender stems to 18 CM tall that have few leaves and carry purple-blue, campanulate, pendant flowers to 2 CM long and often described as looking like slightly crinkled paper. Propagation is by division in spring or summer. Although *C.* ×*pulloides* is of garden origin, it is not a particularly robust plant and should be constantly divided to keep it going. Plant it in full sun and a fertile, well-drained soil, either in the rock garden or as an edger in a bed or border.

Campanula ×*rotarvatica* (synonym *C.* 'Rotarvatica'), as its name implies, is a cross between *C. rotundifolia* and *C. arvatica*, two excellent rock garden plants. The foliage reflects the best of both parents, and it has the longevity of *C. rotundifolia* and the bright blue, starry flowers of *C. arvatica*, on stems 10–15 CM long. Unfortunately, like many of the old but good hybrids, it is not often seen nowadays. Propagation is by division in spring or summer. Grow it in the rock garden or trough.

Campanula 'Ruffles' is another cross between *C. piperi* and *C. lasiocarpa* raised by Rick Lupp, and a sister seedling to 'Bumblebee'. It makes tight mats of small, shiny green, dentate foliage with stems to 10 CM and masses of upward-facing, rich blue, campanulate flowers that become ruffled around the edges as they age. Propagation is by division in spring or summer. Like 'Bumblebee', it makes an excellent plant for a trough or the alpine house.

Campanula 'Sojourner' is a cross between *C. parryi* and *C. piperi*. Another bee hybrid from Mt. Tahoma Nursery, it showed up in a batch of *C. parryi* seedlings at the nursery. It makes tight mats of small, toothed leaves with stems to 10 CM tall and large sprays of rich lavender flowers. It is a superb plant and so easy to grow.

Propagation is by division in spring or summer. It is quite vigorous, following the *C. parryi* type of growth, and needs careful placing, maybe even a trough to itself.

***Campanula* 'Spetchley'** (synonyms *C.* ×*jenkinsae, C.* ×*jenkinsonii*) is generally accepted as being a cross between *C. rotundifolia* and *C. carpatica* var. *alba,* and is roughly halfway between its parents, although leaning slightly toward *C. rotundifolia.* Stiff, erect stems grow to 30 CM tall, with four to six white, broadly campanulate, pendant flowers on short pedicels.

***Campanula* 'Stansfieldii'** (occasionally *C.* ×*stansfieldii*) is thought by some to be a cross between *C. tommasiniana* and *C. carpatica,* although Farrer (1918) suggests it could be a natural hybrid from Monte Maggiore, Italy, and proposes *C. tommasiniana* or *C. waldsteiniana* and *C. pulla* as possible parents. Personally I cannot see any *C. waldsteiniana* blood in it, but it is highly unlikely this puzzle will ever be solved. Suffice it to say that it is an excellent garden or exhibition plant. It makes mats of pale green, lanceolate, dentate, hairy leaves to 1.3 CM wide and to 2.5 CM long on short petioles. Erect, hairy stems 7.5–15 CM tall carry racemes of up to 12 or more deep violet-blue, campanulate flowers to 1.9 CM long and 2.5 CM wide. Although all plants of this hybrid in theory should be the same, quite surprisingly there appear to be several different clones. Two examples grow

Campanula 'Stansfieldii'

in my alpine house: both have stems less than 7.5 CM tall, but the flowers, although the same colour, are different sizes. However, there could be a simple answer to this. In July 2004 at an AGS show, I saw two forms exhibited with flowers apparently different in colour. On examination I found they were both exhibited by the same person, and one was a division from the other. Although the exhibitor could not explain why the flowers were different shades of blue, it was probably due to the variation in compost used, watering regime, and amount of light received by each plant in the alpine house. Propagation of 'Stansfieldii' is by division in spring or summer, and as it quickly spreads by rhizomes, division can be carried out several times in a season. It is easily grown in the rock garden and in any reasonable soil. It also makes a good pot plant for exhibition but requires deadheading if it is to be kept looking nice.

Campanula **'Timsbury Perfection'** is a lovely introduction from *C. rotundifolia* subsp. *arctica* 'Mt. Jotunheimen' seed that was raised by myself in 1999. I have had a number of good forms from this seed and grown them in my garden. This one was selected for its wealth of bloom and ease of propagation, and feeling it was near perfection for the grower or nurseryman, I named it to honour the village where I live. It makes a congested mat of small, reniform-cordate, crenate leaves on long petioles in early growth, becoming linear to 17 MM long and 1.5 MM wide

Campanula 'Timsbury Perfection'

later in the season. Many-branched stems to 15 CM tall are covered with short, white, spreading hairs and have linear leaves. The pale blue, narrowly campanulate flowers are to 1.2 CM long and on slender pedicels. If continually deadheaded, the plant will be in flower for many weeks. In July 2001 it was awarded a Certificate of Preliminary Commendation by the RHS Joint Rock Garden Plant Committee. Propagation is by division in spring or summer. It does set seed, and it is quite likely that some seedlings will be as good if not better than the parent. However, none can be given the same name as the parent plant. It is an excellent plant for a rock garden, trough, or alpine house, and makes a good exhibition plant. If grown in pots, however, it must be repotted or divided every year to keep its vigour.

Campanula topaliana × ***C. calaminthifolia*** is a nice plant combining the best of both parents, although like them it is a short-lived perennial or biennial.

Campanula topaliana ×
C. calaminthifolia

Basal stem leaves are orbicular-cordate, and stem leaves are ovate-lanceolate, coarsely serrate, and to 7.5 CM long. This is a vigorous, spreading plant that prefers partial shade or partial to full sun and moist soil.

Adenophora maximowicziana comes from Japan. Its thin, arching stems are 40–60 CM long, with terminal, broad panicles of blue, campanulate flowers to 1 CM long. Radical leaves are ovate to cordate and on long petioles. Stem leaves are narrowly lanceolate, 8–20 CM long, and have appressed teeth. This species blooms well into autumn.

Adenophora megalantha comes from China. It has erect stems to 45 CM tall, with racemes of campanulate, purple-blue to deep blue flowers that grow to 4 CM or more. Stem leaves are ovate to elliptic, coarsely serrate, 6–10 CM long, and hairy on both sides. This species is suitable for pot culture and with its large flowers can be very showy and good for exhibition.

Adenophora nikoensis (synonyms *A. coronopifolia*, *A. polymorpha*) comes from Japan. Its erect stems are 20–40 CM tall and carry many pendant, campanulate, pale blue flowers, 2–2.5 CM long, in loose racemes. The flowers have toothed and

Adenophora nikoensis.

Photo by Aalt Musch

linear calyx lobes. The leaves are linear to lanceolate, serrate, slender-pointed, and 4–10 CM long. It is a very good plant for pot culture. *Adenophora nikoensis* var. *alba* is a beautiful white form. There are two varieties that are slightly different from the usual form of the species: variety *petrophila*, which is slightly taller and has falcate-lanceolate leaves, and variety *stenophylla* (synonym *A. nipponica*), which has lanceolate, untoothed calyx lobes.

Adenophora pereskiifolia (synonym *A. latifolia*) comes from northeastern Mongolia and southeastern Siberia. Its erect stems grow to 45 CM, occasionally with short side branches, and carry racemes of campanulate blue flowers that are to 2 CM long. Basal leaves are ovate and on long petioles. The stem leaves are in whorls and are 3–8 CM long, ovate-oblong, pointed, and coarsely serrate.

Adenophora sinensis (synonym *A. chinensis*) comes from China. It has erect stems 30–75 CM tall, with campanulate violet-blue flowers to 2 CM long carried in simple racemes. Stem leaves are narrowly ovate, heavily serrate, and to 7.5 CM long.

Adenophora takedae comes from Japan. It has thin, arching stems to around 60 CM long that have campanulate, violet-blue flowers 1.5–2.5 CM long in few-flowered, leafy racemes. Stem leaves are 7.5–15 CM long, narrowly ovate to linear, and serrate. *Adenophora takedae* var. *howozana* grows in the high mountains and is much smaller than the more common form of the species. Its stems grow to 15 CM tall and have much smaller flowers.

Adenophora tashiroi (synonym *A. polymorpha* var. *tashiroi*) comes from Japan and Korea. Its decumbent or spreading stems are 10–30 CM long and hold campanulate, violet-blue flowers 1.5–2 CM long, either solitary or a few to a raceme. The lower stem leaves are ovate, coarsely serrate, and 1.5–3 CM long. The upper leaves are shorter and narrower.

Asyneuma

There are about 50 species of perennials and biennials within the genus *Asyneuma*, and all are closely related to *Phyteuma*, often being included within that genus. Their habitat ranges from Europe and the Mediterranean to the Caucasus, except for one species that grows in eastern Asia. They are tufted to mound- or mat-forming, with stems that vary from very short to erect, tall, and leafy. Flowers are small, campanulate, and divided almost to the base to form five narrow lobes, and are mainly held in spikes, racemes, or panicles but can be solitary. They bloom from late spring to summer. Will Ingwersen (1978) considered this genus to be of little interest to rock gardeners, but several fine species have been introduced since that statement was made, and these plants should challenge the skills of the most experienced alpine grower.

Propagation is by seed sown in spring, by basal cuttings taken in spring, or by division in autumn or spring. Although most of the species described here are tall and only suitable for the perennial border, several can be grown in the rock garden, raised bed, trough, or alpine house. Two in particular are high-alpine species that resent any moisture left on their foliage. All require well-drained soil and a sunny site.

Asyneuma anthericoides (synonyms *A. grandiflorum*, *Phyteuma anthericoides*, *Podanthum anthericoides*) comes from the rocky calcareous slopes of Bulgaria, southeastern Romania, and Serbia and Montenegro. It forms clumps of linear to narrowly oblanceolate basal leaves 4–6 CM long. Erect stems 25–40 CM tall have a few smaller leaves. Purple to blue flowers to 1 CM long are in loose panicles.

Asyneuma campanuloides (synonym *Phyteuma campanuloides*) grows on steep, stony hillsides in the gorges of the central and eastern Caucasus. It makes clumps of ovate, dentate basal leaves that are hairy on the underside. Stems are 30–50 CM tall, and the stem leaves are lanceolate and smaller than the basal leaves. The 5–8 CM long, deep violet-blue flowers are terminal, in long compounded racemes, generally growing three together on very short pedicles from the leaf axils. This gives the plant a tall spike of bloom. When it was in the genus *Phyteuma*, this species had the common name of three-flowered phyteuma.

Asyneuma canescens (synonyms *Phyteuma canescens, Podanthum canescens*) comes from southeastern Europe, Croatia, Hungary, Romania, and Macedonia, where it grows in steppe and mountain grassland. Stems 40–60 cm tall have many lanceolate-oblong, dentate leaves that are 4–6 cm long and become abruptly smaller near the uppermost part of the stem. The lilac to violet-blue flowers are to 1 cm long in spicate panicles. *Asyneuma canescens* subsp. *cordifolium* (synonym *A. cordifolium*) comes from southern Macedonia and differs from the usual form of the species only in that the stem leaves are broadly ovate and become progressively smaller as they go up the stem.

Asyneuma compactum (synonym *Campanula compacta*) comes from Turkey, where it grows in crevices on exposed limestone ridges at 400–2400 м. It is sometimes described as the gem of the genus. Greyish green, glossy, oblanceolate to spatulate leaves are 1–3 cm long and make mats and low cushions to 5 cm high and 30 cm wide. The solitary (occasionally two), erect, amethyst blue flowers have narrow petals, a dark style, and are on very short stems. The calyx is narrowly dentate. This is a very choice species for the alpine house.

Asyneuma filipes (synonym *A. lobelioides* var. *filipes*) comes from Turkey, where it grows on grassland and rocky slopes at 1800–3200 м. Erect stems 20–40 cm tall have serrate, linear-lanceolate, abaxially verrucose leaves 2–8 cm long on short petioles. The blue flowers, 8–15 мм long, are rarely crowded and are in lax panicles.

Asyneuma fulgens comes from the Himalaya in Nepal to Myanmar, southwestern China, and Sri Lanka, where it grows in grassland at 1500–3000 м. It makes tufts of lanceolate to elliptic basal leaves to 5 cm long. The blue flowers are 6–10 мм long and in interrupted racemes or spikes 30–50 cm tall.

Asyneuma limonifolium comes from the Balkan Peninsula and southeastern Italy, where it grows among calcareous rocks. It makes low rosettes of dark green, undulate, oblong to lanceolate leaves. Wiry, almost leafless stems are to 25 cm tall, with spikes of star-like, violet-blue flowers that are 1 cm long. It is a lovely species and grows well in a sunny scree.

Asyneuma linifolium comes from Turkey, where it grows in limestone crevices at 1500–2600 M. It makes clumps of greyish green, obovate to linear, dentate leaves in rosettes to 5 CM across. Ascending stems 5–15 CM tall have spikes of purple-blue, starry flowers to 1 CM long with dark brown anthers. *Asyneuma linifolium* subsp. *eximium* has stem leaves with entire margins, and the flowers are in spikes more compact than those of the more common form of the species. These are excellent plants for a trough or the alpine house.

Asyneuma lycium (synonym *Phyteuma lyceum*) comes from the Lycian Taurus area of Turkey, growing at 1400–2300 M. From a central, fleshy rootstock it makes tight, compact tufts of minute, green, spatulate, entire leaves that taper to long petioles. The solitary, terminal, slate blue flowers have five open, linear lobes with an exserting red stigma, and are on wiry stems growing to 5 CM long. This is one of two excellent species introduced by Peter Davies and makes a superb alpine house plant.

Asyneuma pulvinatum comes from western Turkey, where it grows in crevices in the sheer faces of hard limestone cliffs and rocks at 1500–2000 M. It makes a tight, rounded cushion to 10 CM high of minute, silvery green, narrowly elliptic to lanceolate leaves. The open, lilac to blue flowers with five narrow petals are to 6 MM long and in terminal, compact racemes. Propagation is by cuttings, as wild seed is rarely, if ever, available. This is the second species introduced by Peter Davies. It is ideal for alpine house culture in a gritty compost or piece of tufa, or in a trough that is covered in winter. The cushion is very prone to fungal infections during autumn and winter, and a free flow of air must be given to combat this.

Asyneuma trichostegium comes from central Turkey, where it grows on rocky volcanic slopes at around 2400–3200 M. It makes small tufts of linear-lanceolate, dark green leaves to 4 CM long. Ascending stems 5–15 CM long carry spikes of stellate, deep blue-violet flowers. Grow it in a trough or alpine house.

CODONOPSIS

The genus *Codonopsis* is a very attractive member of the Campanulaceae, and the herbaceous, non-twining species fit neatly into the context of this book. The first and most important matter to address before growing anything from this genus is the naming of the species. *Codonopsis* species suffer greatly from misidentification, and many plants and seeds of the herbaceous species in circulation are *C. clematidea*, regardless of what is stated on the label. It is definitely worth seeking out accurately named material, however. The flowers of these plants are beautifully marked and add a subtle elegance to the summer garden.

Some *Codonopsis* species, such as *C. clematidea*, *C. ovata*, and *C. obtusa*, are very easy to cultivate and can be grown in the garden for a number of years, while others are more challenging. The more easily cultivated species are readily raised from seed, which is regularly and generously set. Germination is good and the seed has quite a long viability. Do not sow the seed too thickly, however, as the young seedlings are very delicate and not easy to separate. If you do sow too generously, it is possible to leave the young plants in the seed pan until the top growth has died down in the winter, and then it is a matter of separating the small tuberous roots, which at this stage are like small single carrots.

Members of this genus are not particular as to the pH of the soil, but waterlogged soils would not be suitable, nor would very hot, dry sites. A good garden loam is ideal.

Codonopsis bhutanica was introduced from Bhutan by Frank Ludlow, George Sherriff, and J. H. Hicks in 1949 but not named until 1972. It does not rank among the showiest of plants, either in size or colour of flower, but it is of interest to the specialist grower in spite of its difficulty in cultivation. It has a sprawling habit, with stems to 30 CM and small, ovate leaves to 2.5 CM long and 1.5–2 CM wide. The delicate, purple flowers are to 2 CM long and 1–1.2 CM wide. The flower colour is similar to that of a typical *Fritillaria meleagris*. This species is available from a few nurseries and via seed exchanges.

Codonopsis cardiophylla is a bit of a mystery. There have been various descriptions over the years, all referring to "a thickened white margin to the leaves." This description was first quoted in *A Revision of the Genus Codonopsis* by T. F. Chipp, printed in the *Journal of the Linnean Society* in 1908, and has been continually repeated over the years. Assuming that the description is accurate, Jane Leeds, a considerable authority on herbaceous *Codonopsis*, queries whether *C. cardiophylla* is still in cultivation, as all the plants she has seen offered under this name have been poor-colour forms of *C. clematidea*. However, *C. cardiophylla* is listed in the *RHS Plant Finder* as being available from a number of nurseries.

Codonopsis clematidea is the most commonly encountered species in cultivation and comes from the mountains of central Asia. It is very easy to grow and has a fairly lax habit. Branched stems to 45 CM are sparsely hairy, green in the lower part, and with a purple tinge higher up. The leaves are glabrous, 2.8–3 CM long and 1.6–1.8 CM wide on petioles 8–10 MM long. The delicate, pale blue, campanulate flowers to 3 CM long and to 2 CM wide are usually solitary and terminal on the branches. The interior is exquisitely marked with a purple band about halfway up the tube and with a pattern of orange and purple near the base. It flowers from the end of June into July. The whole plant has a somewhat unpleasant, foxy smell when bruised, and a white milky sap weeps from any wounds on the stems. These negative features are small, however, and should not deter plant lovers from growing this species.

Codonopsis dicentrifolia comes from the central Himalaya, from central Nepal to Sikkim, and is a gem. It has a lax habit, with stems to 45 CM tall. The leaves are small, about 1–1.5 CM long, green above, and deep purple beneath. The long, straight-sided, campanulate flowers are to 3 CM long and mottled mauve and white. This is a challenging species and in cultivation seems to need cool, shady conditions. It doesn't appear to be a long-lived plant, and seed is not set as generously as with the other species.

Codonopsis meleagris is native to southwestern China, where it grows in clearings in pine woodland. It is a very desirable plant, making a basal rosette (which is unusual for the genus) of dark green leaves that are indented with veins and glabrous beneath. Stems to 45 CM tall are smooth and green, with some purple at the neck. The flower is to 4 CM long, to 2 CM wide, suffused with greenish yellow, and marked with a network of very obvious purple veining. It can be propagated from root cuttings and does best when grown in a shady spot. Hybrids of this species are often seen in cultivation, something that is not normally seen with other *Codonopsis* species.

Codonopsis obtusa comes from the Panjshir Valley in Afghanistan, where it grows in scrub at about 2500 M. The usual form seen in cultivation originated from seed collected by Paul Furse in the middle of the 20th century. Branching stems grow to 35 CM tall and are green with a slight purple hue where they branch, near the flowers and at ground level. The ovate, finely glabrous leaves are 3.6–3.9 CM long and 2.4–2.8 CM wide, on petioles 7–8 MM long. The campanulate, soft ice blue flowers are to 2.5 CM long and taper from 2.5 CM to 1.6 CM wide. They have a silver-grey sheen and are subtly marked on the inside, the blue gradually fading toward the base, where the green of the calyx shows through and contrasts well with the cream stamens, which have purple lines on them. One of the charming characteristics of this species is the way the flowers change shape. In bud they are very obviously round and balloon-like, but as they mature and the petals separate and recurve strongly, they evolve to become substantial bells. This species can develop into bushy plants with an overall width of some 30 CM.

Codonopsis obtusa.
Photo by Jane Leeds

Codonopsis ovata has a restricted distribution in the wild, growing in the western Himalaya, Pakistan, and Kashmir. Although first introduced in 1856, it is still a comparatively rare plant in gardens, due mainly to misidentification. It is more refined than *C. clematidea*, displaying much grace and delicacy, and is also far less

Codonopsis ovata.

Photo by Jane Leeds

fetid. Stems are branching and erect, with a few occasionally lax, grow to 20 CM tall, and are green and slightly hairy. The ovate leaves are to 2.5 CM long, to 1.7 CM wide, green above, glabrous beneath, and similarly slightly hairy. The soft blue, campanulate flowers have flared lobes, are to 3.2 CM long and to 3.5 CM wide, and taper gracefully to the base. They have delicate, darker longitudinal veining. A mature plant will have a spread of about 30 CM. It is definitely worthwhile seeking out a correctly named plant of this species, and then keeping it going with seed. In the middle of July you will have a plant displaying flowers of much beauty and refinement.

CRATEROCAPSA

Craterocapsa is a genus of perennial plants from the Cape and KwaZulu-Natal in South Africa. They are prostrate and have short stems and blue flowers.

Craterocapsa congesta makes a tight, compact mound to 15 CM high covered with blue, sessile flowers that have well-reflexed, pointed lobes. It makes an excellent specimen for pot culture.

Craterocapsa congesta.

Photo by David McDonald

Craterocapsa tarsodes, the carpet bellflower, grows in shallow soil in rocky montane grassland at 1200–2500 M. From a thick taproot it makes mats or carpets of apical rosettes of lanceolate, ciliate leaves 7–30 MM long. The short stems carry solitary, axillary, infundibular, sessile, blue flowers, with five lax, rounded lobes, to 2 CM wide. It is used in a herbal remedy for the treatment of epilepsy by the

Craterocapsa tarsodes.

Photo by David McDonald

Northern Sotho people of South Africa. Propagation is by seed sown in autumn or spring, or by division after flowering. Grow it in a warm spot in the rock garden or as an alpine house plant.

CYANANTHUS

There are approximately 23 species in the genus *Cyananthus*, all native to western China, Kashmir, Punjab, and Nepal, where they grow in alpine pastures at medium to high altitudes. They flower in late summer to autumn and are suitable for a rock garden, raised bed, deep scree, or wall. These plants do well in semi-shade or shade, with a well-drained but humus-rich and moisture-retentive soil, and are tolerant of high summer rainfall. However, it might be best if plants that are grown in the garden have their dormant roots covered during wet winters. Although *Cyananthus* species are often thought to be plants for peat beds only, in the wild many grow on limestone. They also make excellent alpine house plants, grown in a gritty, humus-rich compost. All have prostrate stems that grow from a clump of woody roots, and flowers with five flat, star-like, spreading lobes that vary in width and a tube that varies in length. Flowers are variable in colour, from deep blue to violet, with white forms also found. Although there are annuals in this genus, all those described here are perennial. Propagation is by seed sown in spring, by stem cuttings taken before the flowers develop, or by division in spring. In addition to the plants described here, the hybrid *Cyananthus lobatus* × *C. microphyllus* has violet to deep blue flowers and makes a mat 5 CM high and to 70 CM across. It requires peaty soil and partial shade.

Cyananthus delavayi (synonyms *C. barbatus*, *C. microrhombeus*) comes from China, where it grows in grassland, disturbed forests, and thickets along north-facing ravines and on sandstone slopes at 2300–4000 M. Procumbent, thin, branched, hirsute stems have tiny, reniform, greyish green leaves that are whitish on the underside. The deep blue to violet-blue, solitary, terminal, stellate flowers are 1.5–2 CM across. The lobes have a tuft of hairs at the base. This species was introduced into cultivation by George Forrest and Francis (Frank) Kingdon-Ward.

Cyananthus formosus comes from southwestern China and was described by Austrian botanist Heinrich Handel-Mazzetti (1927), who saw it while travelling in the area during the First World War, as a wonderful plant of the limestone screes, growing alongside *Cremanthodium smithianum*, *Eriophyton wallichianum*, *Aconitum tatsienense*, and *Corydalis calcicola*. It can also be found growing on shale slopes in the alpine meadows, vegetated slopes, and scree at 4250–4600 M. It is in effect a larger version of *C. delavayi*, with deep blue to violet-blue flowers 2.5–4 CM across.

Cyananthus incanus comes from India, Nepal, and Sikkim, where it grows at 2700–5300 M. Thin, procumbent stems grow 12–15 CM long with greyish green, ovate, sinuate leaves. The solitary, terminal, blue flowers are stellate and long-tubed, to 2.5 CM wide, with a white tuft of silky hairs in the throat. This species flowers more freely than *C. lobatus*.

Cyananthus lobatus is an easy and vigorous perennial that ranges from northwestern India eastward along the length of the Himalaya, where it grows at around 4200 M. Many prostrate, branched stems grow to 30 CM long from the woody rootstock. Leaves 6–10 MM long are slightly hairy and pinnately lobed. The

Cyananthus lobatus.

Photo by Panayoti Kelaidis

pale to deep blue, purple, or white, stellate flowers have open, flat lobes to 3–4 CM across and short tubes. They are hairy in the throat, and the calyx is covered with short black hairs. This is the most popular species grown in gardens. *Cyananthus lobatus* var. *insignis* has flowers to 5 CM wide, and *C. lobatus* 'Sherriff's Variety' has large blue-violet flowers.

Cyananthus longiflorus (synonyms *C. argenteus*, *C. obtusilobus*) comes from Yunnan (China), where it grows in grassland at 2800–3600 M. Thin, reddish, procumbent to ascending stems to 15 CM or more have many tiny, elliptic, sessile, greyish green leaves. The solitary, terminal, erect, light to dark blue or violet, stellate flowers have narrow lobes and a very long tube with a whitish throat. This is a beautiful species rarely seen in cultivation.

Cyananthus microphyllus (synonyms *C. integer*, *C. linifolius*) comes from the western Himalaya, Nepal, and Tibet, where it grows in pastures at 3300–5000 M. It is one of the smallest species of *Cyananthus*. Thin, reddish, procumbent stems to around 15 CM long have tiny, heath-like, elliptic, sessile, dark green leaves. The violet-blue, solitary, terminal, star-like flowers are 2–2.5 CM wide and have wide lobes and a short tube with a throat that is pale blue and hirsute inside. Although

Cyananthus microphyllus.

Photo by Mike Ireland

it grows in full open exposure in its native Nepal, it does better in a lightly shaded site when planted in the garden.

Cyananthus sherriffii (synonym *C. napalensis*) comes from the eastern Himalaya, Tibet, where it grows in grassland at 4400–5000 M. It makes mats of lax, procumbent stems with silvery grey, sessile, ovate, obtuse, crenate leaves 5–8 MM long. The solitary, terminal, light blue, stellate flowers are 2–3 CM across, with flat, wide lobes rounded at the tips, a bearded throat, and a short tube. This is the gem of the genus but unfortunately is also the most difficult to grow, as I have found to my cost. It does not like drought or winter wet and therefore must be cultivated in the alpine house, but beware of hot, dry summers, and keep it moist.

Flowers of *Cyananthus sherriffii*

EDRAIANTHUS

There are between 10 and 24 species in the genus *Edraianthus*, depending on what taxonomists have agreed on at any one time. They come from southeastern Europe, ranging from the Balkan Peninsula to the Caucasus, and make small mats or hummocks, with crowded, narrow leaves and relatively large, tightly clustered flowers nestled close to the ground. The campanulate flowers are lilac to violet-blue or white.

You may occasionally see some of the species described here appearing in plant catalogues as *Wahlenbergia*, a genus to which *Edraianthus* is closely related. Taxonomists continually change species from one genus to the other, as Clarence Elliott (1936) observed: "When I first knew *E. serpyllifolius* and *E. pumilio* they were called *Edraianthus*. Later they were lumped into *Wahlenbergia* and yet within my lifetime they were once again back into *Edraianthus*." Just give a thought to the poor nurserymen who have to write and rewrite their catalogues.

There are a number of botanical differences between *Edraianthus* and *Wahlenbergia*, the easiest being that *Edraianthus* has bracts immediately below the flowers, which can be solitary but are more frequently in terminal clusters, whereas in *Wahlenbergia* the flowers are usually solitary on long peduncles with no bracts immediately below them.

Edraianthus species are ideal perennials, being very attractive and easily grown in the rock garden, raised bed, trough, or alpine house. They thrive in a sunny spot with well-drained soil. Propagation is by seed sown fresh in spring, or by cuttings taken in spring. Wild-collected seed will produce a variety of forms.

Edraianthus dalmaticus (synonym *E. caudatus*) comes from screes in western Serbia and Montenegro. It makes dense mats or tufts of linear-lanceolate leaves 3–5 CM long. The white-ciliate, erect stems are 3–7 CM tall, with up to ten violet-blue flowers to 2 CM long in a terminal tight cluster surrounded by bracts. The outer bracts are up to twice the length of the corolla. It is glabrous throughout.

Edraianthus dinaricus (synonym *E. serpyllifolius* subsp. *dinaricus*) comes from rocky slopes in western and central Serbia and Montenegro. The ascending to erect stems are 2–6 CM tall and sparsely leafy. The leaves are linear, almost subulate, white-ciliate above, white-hirsute below, and 2.5–4 CM long. The violet-blue flowers are 1.2–1.5 CM long, campanulate-tubular, terminal, solitary, and erect. This species is often confused with *E. pumilio*, the only difference being that the leaves of *E. dinaricus* are wider, the stems longer, and it has fewer leaves.

Edraianthus graminifolius (synonym *E. kitaibelii*) ranges from the Mediterranean to eastern Europe, where it grows on limestone slopes. Commonly known as grassy bells, it makes tufts of lustrous, grassy foliage to 15 CM tall that eventually

*Edraianthus
graminifolius.*

Photo by Panayoti Kelaidis

*Edraianthus
graminifolius* subsp.
niveus

form cushions. Ascending to erect, hairy stems are 5–10 CM tall, with linear-lanceolate leaves 5–15 MM long and ciliate at the base. The violet-blue flowers, 1.3–3 CM long, are in terminal clusters of three to six. The bracts are no longer than the corollas. *Edraianthus graminifolius* subsp. *niveus* (synonym *E. niveus*) is a white form.

Edraianthus owerinianus comes from the Caucasus and resembles a tight form of *E. pumilio*. It makes silver buns with solitary, almost stemless, deep blue, campanulate flowers. It flowers very early in its life when grown from seed. A very beautiful species.

Edraianthus parnassicus comes from the mountains of southern, central, and northwestern Greece, where it grows in limestone crevices. It makes tufts of oblong-lanceolate to obovate or spatulate basal leaves, 1–4 CM long and 5–10 MM wide. Ascending to erect stems 10–15 CM tall have violet flowers 1–1.5 CM long in spherical terminal clusters of three to four.

Edraianthus pumilio (synonym *Wahlenbergia pumilio*) comes from western Serbia and Montenegro, and Croatia, where it grows at around 1750 M in limestone crevices. It makes very compact cushions 3–15 CM wide, with tufts of very narrow,

Edraianthus pumilio

linear-lanceolate leaves 8–20 MM long that are green underneath and have a whitish silvery sheen above. Densely leafy stems are 1–3 CM long and hold large, solitary, sessile, violet-blue, campanulate-tubular flowers, 1–3 CM long, that sit tight on the cushion May–June. The calyx teeth are one and a half to two times the length of the ovary. Forms vary from compact to more lax, and leaves can be just green. This is one of the gems among the Balkan species. It makes a wonderful plant for pot culture in the alpine house, where its interesting, compact, silvery foliage makes a show before the flowers appear and cover the foliage completely. In the rock garden it needs sunny scree conditions, a dry rock crevice, or planting in a trough.

Edraianthus serbicus (synonym *E. dalmaticus* subsp. *serbicus*) is endemic to western Bulgaria and eastern Serbia. As it occupies a rather limited area, it is classed as being ecologically vulnerable by European standards. In Bulgaria its distribution is limited to the calcareous frontier mountains on open, rocky terrains and rock crevices, or on terrains with large outcrops of the base rock having a southern, western, or eastern exposure. It closely resembles *E. graminifolius* but is more compact, often being described as halfway between *E. pumilio* and *E. graminifolius*. The linear leaves are 5–8 CM long, with fine hairs, and the violet-blue, campanulate flowers are to 3 CM long and in clusters of 6–12 on short, prostrate stems.

Edraianthus serpyllifolius (synonym *Wahlenbergia serpyllifolia*) comes from Croatia, western Serbia and Montenegro, and northern Albania, where it grows in limestone crevices on rocky slopes at around 1750 M. It is tufted and makes compact cushions 2–12.5 CM across, with rosettes of shiny, dark green leaves that are linear-lanceolate to spatulate, obtuse, and glabrous but with stiff, white hairs at the margins. The deep violet flowers are 1.5–2.5 CM long, solitary, and terminal, with a dark red calyx, on prostrate to ascending reddish stems 2–5 CM long. This is one of the best species in the genus.

    Edraianthus serpyllifolius var. *major* (synonym *Wahlenbergia serpyllifolia* 'Major') has larger flowers than the more common form of the species and makes a stunning pot plant, but I find it more difficult to grow. There is a white form, too, that is just as compact as the usual form. All are suitable for trough culture.

Edraianthus tenuifolius (synonym *E. bosniacus*) comes from Albania, Serbia and Montenegro, and Greece, where it grows on rocky slopes. It makes tufts of lance-olate-linear, entire leaves with stems to 8 CM tall and dense clusters of 3–15 deep violet flowers, 2 CM long, that often have a whitish base and very fine hairs inside. It closely resembles *E. graminifolius* but has narrower leaves, to 1.5 MM wide, that are ciliate up to the apex, and also has bracts at least as long as the corolla. *Edraianthus tenuifolius* var. *alba* is a nice white form, but plants raised from its seed cannot be guaranteed to come true to colour.

Edraianthus wettsteinii comes from the montane to subalpine rocky slopes of Serbia and Montenegro, and northern Albania. It closely resembles *E. pumilio*, but the leaves are narrower and the calyx teeth are longer. The densely hairy, blue-violet flowers are 1–1.2 CM long and one to three to a stem. There are reports of plants with five flowers to a stem, but this is extremely rare and probably does not occur in cultivation.

JASIONE

There are approximately 15 species of annuals and perennials within this genus, often referred to as shepherd's scabious or sheepsbit. Their habitats range from Europe to southwestern Asia, the Mediterranean, and the northeastern United States, where they grow in poor, sandy soil in full sun. They are tufted, with stems of varying heights and with many tiny, five-petalled flowers in dense, globular heads, similar to the flowers of *Scabiosa*. Flowering season is from May to September. Propagation is by seed sown in autumn or spring, or by division in spring. These plants are suitable for a warm, dry part of the rock garden, where they are likely to be long-lived, but they cannot tolerate rich, moist soil. Several make good alpine house plants.

Jasione bulgarica is a perennial from Bulgaria, where it grows in subalpine grass-land and among thickets. It is similar to J. laevis, but the leaves and involucral bracts are glabrous. Stems 15–23 CM tall have oblanceolate leaves and pale blue or blue-lilac flowers to 2 CM across.

Jasione bulgarica,
Bulgaria.

Photo by Ann Borrill

Jasione crispa (synonym *J. humilis*) comes from southwestern Europe, particularly the Pyrenees and Sierra Nevada, where it grows on acid soil in meadows and screes to 2500 M. It makes tufts of hairy, oblong-lanceolate, occasionally dentate leaves. Stems 15–30 CM tall have leaves to only halfway up the stem and hold heads of blue flowers. This species is perennial.

Jasione crispa subsp. *amethystina* (synonym *J. amethystina*) is endemic to the Sierra Nevada, growing at around 2000–2900 M. It makes low, dense tufts of leaves similar to the more common form of the species, with stems to 10 CM tall holding heads of blue flowers. It is also perennial and makes a good alpine house plant.

Jasione heldreichii (synonyms *J. dentata*, *J. jankae*) is a biennial that is similar to *J. montana* and ranges from the Balkan Peninsula to Romania and Turkey, where it grows in dry, stony grassland. It has lanceolate, shortly setose leaves on long petioles. Stiff stems 10–20 CM tall have heads of blue flowers to 1 CM across.

Jasione laevis (synonyms *J. perennis*, *J. pyrenaica*) ranges across western and west-central Europe, growing in dry areas. It is a tufted perennial with stems 20–45 CM tall, narrowly oblong, ciliate leaves to 4 MM wide, and soft violet-blue

Jasione montana.

Photo by Panayoti Kelaidis

flower heads to 4 cm wide. Although easy to grow from seed, it is variable, but it will bloom all summer and is suitable for the dry rock garden or border.

Jasione laevis 'Blue Light' (or 'Blaulicht') has stems to 20 cm tall. *Jasione laevis* subsp. *carpetana* comes from the mountains of central Spain and is 10–15 cm tall. Subspecies *orbiculata* comes from the Balkan Peninsula, Romania, and southern Italy and has stems 5–10 cm tall. Subspecies *rosularis* comes from the mountains of southwestern Spain and has stems 30–50 cm tall, with oblanceolate leaves to 8 mm wide.

Jasione montana, known as sheepsbit or mountain sheepsbit, ranges over most of Europe, including the United Kingdom, and also western Turkey, North Africa, and the northeastern United States, where it grows in open grassland on acid, sandy, stony places, banks, and hedgerows to 1700 m. It is a variable species with stems 15–45 cm tall that have oblong-linear, occasionally dentate, often undulate, sessile leaves and blue, white, or pink flower heads 1.5–3.5 cm across.

Jasione supina comes from Turkey, where it grows on screes and rocky slopes at 1900–4000 m. It is a densely tufted perennial with oblong to spatulate basal leaves to 1.5 cm long. Prostrate to ascending stems 5–10 cm long have ovate to lanceolate leaves to 1 cm long and blue flower heads to 1.5 cm across. This species makes a good alpine house plant. There are three subspecies, all with slight botanical or geographical variations: *J. supina* subsp. *akmannii*, *J. supina* subsp. *pontica*, and *J. supina* subsp. *tmolea*.

LIGHTFOOTIA

Lightfootia is a genus of about 46 species of woody shrubs with small, stellate, pale lavender or yellow flowers that grow in South Africa, although it was suggested in 2004 (Cupido) that the genus may be moved into *Wahlenbergia*. Panayoti Kelaidis, curator of Denver Botanic Gardens, Colorado, United States, described it to me as follows:

> *Lightfootia* is a genus of very strange plants. I found them here and there in the Karoo, forming the most bizarre shrubs, very dense and sculptural and only a foot or two high, like something out of a fairy tale: one with

witches and dark woods. They had very woody parts with tiny, adpressed, almost black leaves and miniature yellow or lavender flowers that do look campanulaish. The shrubs had a woody base and were substantial, almost like a tree trunk, only wildly asymmetrical and molded. It is one of the oddest plants I have ever seen.

Two of the more common species are *Lightfootia tenella* and *L. longifolia.*

PETROMARULA

This genus, whose scientific name translates from the Greek *petra* ("rock") and *marouli* ("lettuce"), has the obvious common name of rock lettuce. It contains just one species and is endemic to Crete.

Petromarula pinnata grows on calcareous rocks, cliffs, and abandoned terraces, occasionally near the sea. It makes basal rosettes of light green, pinnate or pinnatisect leaves 10–30 CM long with large, glabrous, dentate segments. The erect stems 20–50 CM tall have much smaller leaves and carry spikes of pale blue, starlike flowers to 1 CM across, with a darker blue centre and five very narrow lobes, on short pedicels growing from the leaf axils. Propagation is by seed sown in autumn or spring, but if collecting your own seed, be aware that much of the seed may be taken and eaten by insects before you can get to it. Although best grown in the alpine house as a pot plant, this species may be cultivated outdoors if planted in a warm, well-drained position.

PHYSOPLEXIS

Physoplexis comosa (synonym *Phyteuma comosum*) existed in the flora of the Tertiary period, before the start of the Ice Age, and must be the weirdest yet most beautiful flower of all the Campanulaceae. To describe it stretches anyone's imagination and eloquence to the limits, and yet it still cannot be described accurately. All you can do is look at it in wonder and agree that the common name, devil's claw, suits it admirably.

From a fat, fleshy rootstock grow tufted rosettes of shallow to deeply toothed, reniform leaves 1.9–2.5 CM long. The erect to decumbent stems have smaller, short-stalked, lanceolate leaves and are 5–10 CM long. Tight, globular heads of up to 20 flowers or more, each to 2.5 CM long, are held at the ends of each stem, and each flower is a delicate object in itself. It can only be described as a pale lilac inflated flask or club-like base that, as it tapers to a very thin neck, changes colour to a deep or almost blackish purple. From the end of the thin neck protrudes the deep purple, forked and twisted stigma. The shorter the stems the more the plant appears like a giant pincushion as it is completely covered with flowers in June and July.

It grows in narrow, lofty crevices of limestone cliffs in the southern Alps and the Dolomites to around 2000 M, where the roots creep through any narrow cracks and anchor the plant firmly to the rocks. There is no humus in the crevices, but a very sandy substratum. Franz Hadacek observes (personal communication):

> I have never seen the plant growing in any other place. It prefers to grow on shady, damp, limey rocks, and you will look for it in vain on sunbathed prominent rocky peaks. You may find it in damp ravines. Sometimes you can see it from the car on the cliffs next to the road. It does not like low winter temperatures nor dry, hot summers, but a humid and cool climate. Very rarely white forms or red coloured may occur.

Clarence Elliott, in the days when collectors were rife in the mountains, commented (1936) that when attempting to remove a plant of *Physoplexis* from its rock crevice, a collector would often come away with a plant having only a small piece of root attached, but that it would willingly grow when brought home. Of course, in these days of conservation we cannot do this, but it may be worth trying with garden-grown plants, slicing a piece of root away with foliage attached and potting it up. However, I believe *P. comosa* has to be grown exclusively from seed if you can get it, and it is occasionally offered in commercial seed lists. There is great difficulty in collecting your own seed, as the dried seed capsule is very small and usually combines with the base of the dead flower, making seed collecting almost impossible. In cases like this, I advise crushing both the capsule and dead flower base between thumb and forefinger and sowing the resultant "dust," or examining it with a magnifying glass for viable seed.

For the seed compost, use a gritty soil with a generous proportion of tufa or lime mortar (if available) if the soil is lime-free. A pretreatment of the seed with

Physoplexis comosa

gibberellins is recommended. In the first year, only a few seeds may germinate, but in the second year most of the rest will appear. Prick out the seedlings, place them in clay pots in a mixture similar to the seed compost, and keep the pots in an open frame.

In the rock garden this plant needs partial shade and placement in a tight crevice. As it grows well in tufa, this medium can be used to grow it in the rock garden or in a pot in the alpine house. This plant is like caviar to slugs and must be well protected wherever it's grown.

According to Hadacek, he is successful with *Physoplexis* when he grows it in troughs in which he has placed bigger tufa blocks drilled with holes 2.5 CM in diameter. The holes reach to the bottom of the block. The seedlings are then planted in these holes, using the same mixture used to make the seed compost. Since this mixture is very poor, he adds fertiliser a few times during the growing season. He also drills holes into the sides of the troughs for other plants. The troughs are in partial shade and exposed to rain and snow, and the plants live sometimes up to 10 years. The same cultivation method is successful using a pot rather than a trough to hold the tufa, and exhibits like this can be seen at AGS shows in summer.

There is one habit of *Physoplexis* that can be rather alarming. Fairly soon after it blooms, the top growth goes suddenly dormant, remaining so until the following spring. This habit also causes alarm in spring as gardeners anxiously wait for new shoots to appear, since this doesn't usually occur before the end of March.

PHYTEUMA

There are about 40 species of *Phyteuma*, all perennials from the Mediterranean, Europe, and Asia and collectively known as rampion. They are tufted to clump-forming, with a thick fleshy rootstock and simple leafy stems. A solitary terminal inflorescence of dense globular heads or spikes have small sessile or subsessile flowers that are tubular, wide at the base but becoming very narrow, with five slender, deep corolla lobes that only open after the pollen has been shed. The flower colour ranges from pale to deep blue, violet-blue, blackish purple, and greenish white, and all are summer-flowering. Propagation is by seed sown in autumn or spring, or by division in spring. All *Phyteuma* are best grown in a rock garden with well-drained soil and a sunny aspect. The small forms make good trough or alpine house plants.

Phyteuma betonicifolium, the betony-leaved rampion, comes from the European and Italian Alps, where it grows in meadows and woods to 2650 M. It forms clumps of ovate-lanceolate, serrate basal leaves to 20 CM long, cordate at the base and on long petioles. Stems 30–50 CM tall have linear, serrate, sessile leaves that are 50 MM long and 5 MM wide. The reddish blue to deep blue flowers are in terminal, cylindrical spikes to 4 CM long.

Phyteuma charmelii ranges from the Pyrenees to the Apennines, where it grows in rocky limestone areas to around 1500 M. It makes basal tufts of thin-textured, lanceolate-ovate, deeply serrate leaves on long petioles, and the margins curl inward toward the midrib. The basal leaves tend to wither at flowering time. Stem leaves are linear-lanceolate, deeply serrate, and to 15 CM or more. Stems to 40 CM tall have blue heads of flowers to 2.5 CM wide.

Phyteuma confusum (synonyms *P. hemisphaericum* subsp. *confusum*, *P. nanum*) comes from the eastern European Alps, Bulgaria, where it grows on acid rocks and screes. It makes basal tufts of oblong-spatulate, blunt-toothed leaves. Stems 5–15 CM tall have dense, terminal, rounded heads of deep blue flowers.

Phyteuma cordatum (synonym *P. balbisii*), the maritime rampion, is a rare species that comes from the Maritime and Ligurian alps, where it grows on lime-stone rocks to 2000 M. It makes tufts of orbicular-reniform, serrate basal leaves, cordate at the base and on long petioles. Thin, flexible stems 15–25 CM tall have cordate-ovate, serrate leaves on short petioles and terminal globular or roundish heads of pale blue flowers.

Phyteuma globularifolium (synonym *P. pauciflorum*), the rosette-leaved rampi-on, comes from the eastern European Alps, where it grows among acid rocks and screes at 2000–3000 M. It makes basal rosettes of short, spatulate, crenate leaves on short petioles. The erect, almost leafless stems are 5–10 CM tall and have dense, deep violet-blue, globular heads. This makes a lovely alpine house plant. *Phyteuma globularifolium* subsp. *pedemontanum* (synonym *P. pedemontanum*) is taller, has pointed leaves, and grows at 1300–2600 M.

Phyteuma hedraianthifolium, the rhaetian rampion, comes from the central and eastern European Alps, where it grows in rocky and stony places and in woodland at 1400–3100 M. It makes tufts of linear, finely serrate basal leaves. Erect to ascend-ing stems to 15 CM or more have linear, serrate leaves and globular heads of dark blue to violet flowers.

Phyteuma hemisphaericum, the globe-headed rampion, comes from the Euro-pean Alps, where it grows in meadows and on stony slopes, screes, and acid rocks to around 2900 M. From a fleshy rootstock it makes tufts of erect, lanceolate-linear, acute, almost grass-like leaves. Erect to ascending stems 3–30 CM tall have dark violet-blue, globular heads of flowers to 2 CM wide.

Phyteuma humile (synonym *P. carestiae*), the dwarf rampion, comes from the central and southwestern European Alps, where it grows in stony meadows and on acid rocks, screes, and moraines at 1800–3250 M. It makes large basal tufts of linear-oblanceolate, barely serrate leaves to 10 CM or more. Stiff, erect stems 2–12 CM tall have linear leaves and globular heads of dark violet-blue flowers.

Phyteuma hemisphaericum, Matterhorn, Switzerland.

Photo by Ann Borrill

Phyteuma michellii comes from the southern Alps, where it grows in subalpine meadows and occasional screes to 2300 M. It makes tufts of linear-lanceolate, serrate leaves that have hairy margins at the base and are on long petioles. The leaves are often withered at flowering time. Erect stems 25–40 CM tall have linear, serrate leaves and cylindrical spikes of bright blue to blue-lilac flowers. It is similar to but not as tall as *P. scorzonerifolium.*

Phyteuma nigrum (occasionally *P. nigra*), the black rampion, comes from the northeastern Alps, where it grows in acid woodland and subalpine meadows to 1200 M. Populations have also been recorded in the Czech Republic, Holland, and Belgium. It makes clumps of ovate-cordate, crenate basal leaves that are to 5 CM long and on petioles almost as long. Stiff, erect stems 30–60 CM tall have lanceolate, crenate, sessile leaves and oval or cylindrical heads of blackish violet, occasionally blue or white, flowers.

One interesting thing about this species is that in 1999 a single stand was found at Vierrageahči, northeastern Norway, on disturbed ground by an old road. In addition, *Phyteuma spicatum* has been reported from two sites in Sør-Varanger, Finnmark, northeastern Norway, at Fredheim (first recorded 1998) and Pikevann (first recorded 1980), growing in meadows and forest glades. All three of these stations are close to German World War II camp sites. When this

Phyteuma nigrum.

Photo by Panayoti Kelaidis

information is assessed together with recordings of a number of other nonnative taxa found in the same areas, it strongly suggests that both *Phyteuma* species were introduced accidentally between 1941 and 1944 with hay imported from central Europe for horse fodder. With these populations still in existence after nearly 60 years, the Sør-Varanger sites must be the world's northernmost occurrences of both *P. nigrum* and *P. spicatum*.

Phyteuma orbiculare, the round-headed rampion, ranges over much of Europe, including England, where it grows in dry meadows and on rocky ground, often on limestone, to 2600 M. It makes tufts of lanceolate to cordate, serrate basal leaves on long petioles. The erect, slender stems are to 30 CM tall and have lance-olate leaves, becoming sessile as they progress up the stem. Dark blue to violet-blue or occasionally white flowers are in dense, globular heads to 2.5 CM across. It is a variable species, and it is possible to find many varieties described that have only small botanical differences. In England, where this species is known as *P. tenerum*, it is restricted to sites on chalk downs in the southern part of the country and grows to 50 CM tall. There are reports that in the Chalk Pit, part of a nature reserve in Lancing Village, West Sussex, it occurs in small numbers where the chalk is near the surface and the grass is short.

Phyteuma ovatum (synonym *P. halleri*), the dark rampion, comes from the Pyre-nees, European Alps, and Apennines, where it grows in subalpine meadows to 2400 M. This species is similar to *P. spicatum* but has blackish violet flowers.

Phyteuma scheuchzeri, the horned rampion, comes from the southern Alps and Apennines, where it grows on rocky slopes to 2600 M. It makes tufts of thick, bluish green, lanceolate-cordate, serrate leaves on long petioles. Stems to 40 CM have lanceolate, sessile leaves and globular heads to 2.5 CM wide of deep blue flowers.

Phyteuma scorzonerifolium, the scorzonera-leaved rampion, comes from the southwestern and south-central European Alps and the northern and central Apennines, where it grows in meadows and open woodland to 2200 M. It makes tufts of lanceolate, serrate basal leaves to 20 CM or more long. Strong, erect stems to 60 CM or more have shorter, linear, serrate leaves. The pale blue to bluish lilac flowers are in cylindrical spikes to 5 CM long, small in relation to the height of the stems.

Phyteuma sieberi (synonym *P. orbiculare* var. *sieberi*) comes from the southeastern European Alps, where it grows on limestone rocks at 1600–2600 M. It is very much like *P. orbiculare* but has broader, lanceolate-ovate, sessile stem leaves and stems 25–30 CM tall. It is reported to be a horrible self-seeder.

Phyteuma spicatum, the spiked rampion, is widespread from Britain to Scandinavia and the Pyrenees, through the European Alps, growing in meadows and woods, usually on limestone, to 2100 M. It makes tufts of ovate-cordate, crenate-serrate leaves on long petioles to 15 CM or more. Strong, erect stems 40–80 CM tall have linear, sessile leaves and cylindrical spikes, to 15 CM or more, of yellowish to greenish white flowers. Blue to violet forms have also been found.

Phyteuma vagneri is endemic to the Carpathians. It makes basal tufts of ovate-cordate leaves on long petioles. Stiff, erect stems to 30 CM or more carry ovoid-spherical heads of blackish violet flowers. This species is similar to *P. spicatum*, but the flower heads are shorter. Although it is a very striking plant, self-sown seedlings can become a menace.

PLATYCODON

This monotypic genus is native to northern China, eastern Siberia, Korea, and Japan, where it grows on grassy hillsides or mountain slopes among an occasional pine tree. Although the usual form of *Platycodon grandiflorus* is probably too large for most rock gardens, there are many good forms, both in colour and size, that are suitable, not just for the rock garden but also for pot culture. Another attractive side to platycodons is that they have inflated buds, caused by the petal lobes being held together until the flower finally opens. This gives the genus the common name balloon flower. Although there are "double-flowered" forms in the trade, all seem to be what is commonly known as semi-double, having just two rows of petals.

Propagation of platycodons is by seed or very careful division in spring. Variations in colour and size may occur if seed has been collected from garden-grown plants. These plants have deep taproots, and great care must be taken if digging them up for division. They do resent disturbance.

Platycodons are herbaceous, dying back below ground level over winter and coming into growth in late spring. Grow them in a sunny or partially shaded spot, and mark the spot so that the plants will not be damaged when you are digging around in the winter and early spring. Learn to be patient with this genus, as it is late to come into growth. Although platycodons will grow perfectly well in limey soil, they will do better if the soil is slightly acid. Slugs and snails will treat themselves to a meal on the newly emerging shoots.

Platycodon grandiflorus forms small clumps with stems growing 60–70 CM tall. Leaves are 4–7.5 CM long and to 4 CM wide, grow only on the stems, and are elliptic to narrowly ovate, serrate, dark green above, and slightly glaucous below. The balloon-like buds open to purple-blue, five-petalled, saucer-shaped stars, to 5 CM across, with darker blue veins. They can be solitary or grouped together at the top of the stem, and bloom in July–August. A wide range of cultivars are available, with single, semi-double, or double flowers of white, pink, and blue, and growing to varying heights. All are suitable for the border or rock garden.

Platycodon grandiflorus var. *apoyama* (synonym *P. grandiflorus* 'Apoyama') was discovered growing on the slopes of Mt. Apoi in Hokkaidō, Japan, by Brian Halliwell. It is a natural dwarf form, growing 10–30 CM tall, and has deep violet flowers, although a form with pure white flowers is also available.

Platycodon grandiflorus Astra series is a specially developed range of F1 hybrid cultivars. For example, 'Astra Blue' is rich violet-blue, 'Astra Pink' is pink with

Buds of *Platycodon grandiflorus*

Double form of
Platycodon grandiflorus

darker pink veins on each petal, and 'Astra White' is pure white. All grow 10–15 CM tall and often flower well in their first year from seed.

Among the other cultivars available are 'Double Blue', to 60 CM tall, with double violet-blue flowers; 'Double White', to 60 CM tall, with double white flowers; 'Fairy Snow', 20–37.5 CM tall, with white flowers that have violet-purple veins on the inside and a violet-blue flush on the outside; 'Mariesii', 30–45 CM tall, with deep blue flowers; 'Mariesii Albus', with white flowers; 'Pumilus', a cultivar of long standing, 15–20 CM tall, with good, open, blue-violet flowers; 'Roseus', with lilac-pink flowers; 'Semiplenus', with semi-double flowers in white, pink, or blue; and 'Sentimental Blue', a very low-growing dwarf form, just 15 CM tall, with profusely blooming blue flowers.

ROELLA

Roella is a genus of small shrubs named for G. Roelle, an 18th-century professor of anatomy in Amsterdam. There are 24 species within the genus. Most species come from the southwestern Cape in South Africa, with only one extending into the Eastern Cape and KwaZulu-Natal. Their habitat is mainly on stony mountain slopes, and the large, mainly blue flowers are borne on the tips of branches in groups or singly. For another enthusiastic description of South African flora, I turn once again to Panayoti Kelaidis:

> *Roella* is simply fantastic, with huge upturned deep blue bells (often fantastically painted) on short stems with very thick blue-green leaves attractive in their own right. I was astonished when I ran across it the first time growing *wild* at Kirstenbosch, and then other places in South Africa. I have grown them and they are not hard to grow. They all hail from the Fynbos (as a consequence not very hardy in Denver, say), but they would thrive in an alpine house and are truly spectacular.

Roella amplexicaulis is a shrublet that grows 30–50 CM tall, with whitish blue flowers.

Roella ciliata grows to 50 CM tall and has low, tightly branched stems with bright green, needle-like, evergreen leaves and masses of stemless, star-like, upward-facing, mauve-blue flowers to 4 CM across, with dark purple blotches. If the plant is continually deadheaded, it will bloom for a long time right into autumn.

Symphyandra

There are 14 species within this genus, their habitats ranging from eastern Europe to central Asia and Korea. It is a small group of plants, many of which are biennial or even annual. They are related to and resemble the campanulas but are separated botanically by the anthers, which instead of being free are joined into a tube that surrounds and is closely pressed against the lower part of the style. These plants have attractive basal rosettes, leafy stems, and clusters of nodding, white to purple, campanulate flowers, which bloom in late spring, summer, and, in suitable weather, autumn. They are excellent and very floriferous plants for the large rock garden and perennial border. Propagation is by seed, which is usually set abundantly, and the plants often self-sow, although if you do not want this it is best to deadhead the plant as the flowers go over. Any self-sown seedlings can be potted up if required and planted out later. These plants thrive when given sun or light shade, a light, well-drained soil, and moderate watering.

Symphyandra antiqua comes from the Caucasus and is endemic to the gorges and limestone rock fissures of Georgia (Abkhazia).

Symphyandra armena grows in rock crevices in the Caucasus, Turkey, and Iran but is equally at home in the garden where it has room to spread out. It is a herbaceous perennial, occasionally biennial, sending up branching, erect to decumbent, pubescent stems to 40 CM tall. The many branches start almost at ground level, growing from each leaf axil. Each branch terminates in racemes of three to six faintly hairy, campanulate, powder blue, occasionally white, flowers to 2 CM long and 2 CM wide, with the lobes curled back. It blooms June–August. Stem leaves are on long, thin petioles and are ovate, cordate, heavily serrate, densely pubescent, and to 25 CM long, becoming shorter and sessile near the top of the stem. Although it does seed itself about, it never gets out of hand.

Symphyandra armena

Symphyandra asiatica (synonym *Hanabusaya asiatica*) comes from Korea, where it grows in grassland. It has few basal leaves, and they are ovate to broadly lanceolate, coarsely dentate, slightly pubescent above, and practically smooth below. They grow to 8 CM long on equally long petioles. Stems are 20–70 CM tall and have few branches, with leaves restricted to the lower half. The light purple, campanulate, pendant flowers are solitary, terminal, to 5 CM long and to 2.5 CM across, and have very short and slightly spreading lobes.

Symphyandra cretica is a perennial species from Crete and the Aegean Islands, where it grows on shady, rocky outcrops, steep banks, and walls at 50–1700 M. It has a cylindrical, fleshy rootstock from which grow loose rosettes of pale green, ovate-cordate, coarsely serrate leaves to 15 CM long and 4 CM wide on long petioles. Unbranched stems, 30–50 CM tall, are sparsely leaved, the leaves gradually becoming narrower and more sessile toward the top of the stem. Blue to white, smooth, pendant, campanulate flowers to 3 CM long have relaxed lobes and are in racemes of one to four.

    Symphyandra cretica subsp. *samothracica* is a slightly shorter form with leaves to 4 CM long and usually blue flowers. *Symphyandra cretica* subsp. *sporadum* (synonym *S. sporadum*) comes from the Sporades Islands. It makes basal rosettes of obtuse, crenate leaves 1–3 CM long that have long petioles. Stem leaves are ovate-cordate or reniform, and sessile. A few simple, erect stems grow to 25 CM, and the pale blue, pendant, campanulate flowers, inflated in the middle and with short, smooth lobes, are in loose racemes of one to five. Crook (1977) suggests that although both of these subspecies vary in height from the more common form of the species, it is not certain that these differences would persist if the plants were grown in cultivation under identical conditions.

Symphyandra hofmannii comes from Serbia and Montenegro, and Bosnia and Herzegovina, where it grows in rocky places. From a thick, branched, fleshy rootstock it makes rosettes of leaves that are 5–15 CM long, ovate-lanceolate, coarsely serrate, pubescent, and on long petioles. Strong, many-branched, erect to decumbent stems 30–60 CM tall rise from the centre of the rosettes. Stem leaves are similar to the basal ones, becoming smaller and sessile nearing the top of the stem. The pendant flowers are hairy externally, to 3 CM long, creamy white, and broadly campanulate, with short, rounded, revolute lobes. Although a very desirable garden plant, this species is likely to be short-lived and is best regarded as a biennial only.

Symphyandra hofmannii.

Photo by Panayoti Kelaidis

Symphyandra lazica comes from Turkey, where it grows among rocks at around 1200–1800 M. Tufts of cordate-ovate, sharply and doubly serrate leaves 4–8 CM long have petioles at least as long, grow from a thick, branched rootstock. Thin, flexible, ascending to decumbent stems grow to 40 CM with leaves that are smaller than the basal leaves and on shorter petioles. Pale red, tubular, campanulate flowers 3–7 CM long are solitary or in small terminal clusters. It is a perennial species.

Symphyandra lezgina is a perennial species from the eastern Caucasus, where it grows in vertical rock fissures at 900–2000 M. The many ascending or subpendant stems, simple and few-branched, are to 45 CM tall and have solitary flowers. Stem leaves are small, oblong-lanceolate, crenate-dentate, faintly ciliate, and gradually narrow to short petioles. The whole foliage is greyish glabrescent. The blue-violet, broadly campanulate flowers have lobes to about half their length, with bearded edges.

Symphyandra ossetica is a perennial that comes from the Caucasus, where it grows in rock fissures at 2000–2400 M. It makes basal rosettes of ovate, coarsely serrate leaves to 7 CM long that have white, silky hairs at the margins and are on long petioles. The stiff, erect, leafy stems grow to 45 CM tall, are branched at the upper half, and carry solitary flowers at the stem tips. The pale blue flowers are narrowly campanulate, with slightly hairy lobes that are half their length. In some ways this species resembles *S. pendula*, but it is more erect and has fewer and narrower flowers.

Symphyandra pendula comes from the Caucasus, where it grows in rock fissures on calcareous and clay shale, and in the middle forest belt. It makes a basal tuft of light green leaves that are to 15 CM long, broadly ovate-cordate, doubly serrate and acuminate, and glabrous-rugose on both surfaces, with long petioles. The ascending to decumbent stems are to 45 CM tall and branched. The creamy white, campanulate flowers to 5 CM long are lobed to about a third of their length and are in short panicles almost hidden in the leaves. This plant is best seen at eye level in the rock garden—tumbling over a rock, for example—as the decumbent stems tend to hide the flowers. It is also a good plant for the perennial border, where it can grow to over 30 CM wide.

Symphyandra wanneri.

Photo by Panayoti Kelaidis

Symphyandra transcaucasica (synonym *S. pendula* var. *transcaucasica*) is more or less restricted to the western Caucasus. It is very similar to *S. pendula*, but its stems are shorter and more branched, and it is much more floriferous. The leaves also differ in that they are ash grey, softly hairy, and much more cordate.

Symphyandra wanneri comes from the mountains of Romania, Bulgaria, and Serbia and Montenegro, where it grows on shady cliffs or rocky outcrops. It is quite a popular plant in cultivation and although short-lived, either monocarpic or biennial, is well worth having, as it makes large mounds and brings a lovely splash of colour to the rock garden throughout the summer. It forms rosettes of ovate-lanceolate, sharply dentate leaves 5–10 CM long that gradually reduce to winged petioles. The erect, many-branched, solitary stem to 30 CM tall has smaller and sessile leaves. Both the main stem and the branches carry small leafy panicles of pendant, violet-blue flowers, 2–3.5 CM long, narrowly campanulate, with short lobes that are shortly reflexed. The whole foliage is slightly hairy. I have read one report of a free-flowering dwarf form of this species that grows in Austria and is just 15 CM tall. If this is correct it would make an excellent addition to the rock garden or alpine house.

Symphyandra zangezura is a perennial that comes from the rocky, mountainous regions of Armenia. It makes neat hummocks of small, grey-green basal leaves to 30 CM or so across, from a thick, herbaceous rootstock. The leaves are orbicular, palmately lobed, deeply incised, and often described as geranium-like. Wiry, erect to decumbent stems grow to 30 CM tall and have broad, triangular, dentate leaves on petioles that become smaller as the leaves near the top of the stem. The lavender-violet flowers are 5 CM long, pendant, broadly campanulate, lobed to half their length, and on long peduncles growing from the leaf axils. This is a delightful plant for the rockery or front of the border, where the stems often bend with the weight of the flowers. It is described by Crook (1977) as "the most graceful member of the genus." *Symphyandra zangezura* 'Pale Lilac' is a cultivar available from some commercial seed lists.

TRACHELIUM

The genus *Trachelium* has been very confusing in the past, with some species being moved to *Diosphaera* and then back again, while others have been moved into *Campanula*. They all come from the Mediterranean region and are woody-based perennials, most of them growing to 100 CM tall or more. The name of the genus is derived from the Greek and means "rough throat," a reference to the medicinal use of these plants to treat neck and throat disorders. The genus is commonly known as blue throatwort for the same reason. The two most interesting species are described here.

Trachelium asperuloides is a beautiful cushion species from southern Greece, where it grows in rock crevices. Its makes tight, crowded rosettes of small, shiny green, entire, obovate-orbiculate, sessile leaves to 5 MM long. The lilac flowers are terminal in clusters of one to five, with five spreading lobes to 3 MM long, and a tube that is 6 MM long. Propagation is by seed sown in spring, or by cuttings taken in spring or summer. It is best grown in an alpine house, as it is unlikely to survive winter wet in the rock garden unless well protected. As an exhibition plant it is well known at the summer shows, and for this purpose it is usually grown in a well-drained compost in light shade, kept reasonably dry over winter, and given

Trachelium asperuloides.

Photo by Paul Ranson

Trachelium jacquinii
subsp. *rumelianum.*

Photo by Panayoti Kelaidis

an annual clipping after flowering to keep it compact (a job I assume the local goats do in the wild).

Trachelium jacquinii (synonym *Diosphaera jacquinii*) comes from Crete and northeastern Greece, where it grows in rock crevices. It has a woody rootstock and makes tufts of green, leathery, narrowly ovate or oblong, dentate, sessile leaves. Stems grow to 15 cm and carry bluish lilac, five-lobed flowers, with the lobes and the tubes both about 5 mm long. The flowers are in compact, terminal heads. Denver Botanic Gardens in Colorado, United States, is well known for its ability to cope with Mediterranean plants. Panayoti Kelaidis, the curator, had this to say during a discussion of this species:

> *Trachelium jacquinii* is a minor weed for me, but a lovely one. We probably have several hundred sowing around the Alpine Garden. Most years I must get at least a quarter cup if not a half cup of seed off them: that probably translates to several million seed. If the flowers lasted a bit longer it would be a first-rate plant for us. It blooms in the middle of our summer, often when the weather is especially sultry, and the flowers rarely last more than a week. During that week they are stunning, however. We have had plants with fifty or more flower heads. They are actually growing out of solid rock here in some areas, although my greatest concentration is in the crevice garden facing north at the back of the Alpine House. I would rate this as an easy alpine here.

Trachelium jacquinii subsp. *rumelianum* (synonym *T. rumelianum*) comes from Greece and Bulgaria, where it grows at around 1200–1300 m in meadows and near coniferous forests, including Pirin National Park. It makes a sprawling clump to 60 cm across. Stems to 30 cm long have terminal heads of tubular lilac flowers. Stem leaves are glossy green, ovate, serrate, and thin-textured. Propagation is by seed sown in spring, or by cuttings taken in spring or summer. If you have conditions like those found at Denver Botanic Gardens (low humidity year-round, precipitation coming primarily as snow in March and April, very sporadic though sometimes heavy rain from May to September, and often very dry, cold, and sunny autumns and winters), grow it in the open rock garden. Otherwise give it some winter protection.

WAHLENBERGIA

The genus *Wahlenbergia* was named by German botanist H. A. Schrader in 1814 in honour of Georg Göran Wahlenberg (1780–1851), professor of botany at Uppsala University, Sweden, who was noted for his studies of European plant geography. The number of species within this genus is variable, as species included in other genera are often moved into *Wahlenbergia* and then out again. They are mainly from the southern hemisphere, and nearly all are confined to South Africa, Australia, New Zealand, and South America. This genus is closely related and similar to *Campanula*, but in *Wahlenbergia* the seed capsule opens at the apex, while in *Campanula* the capsule opens by side pores or valves. The collective common name for *Wahlenbergia* is bluebell. Propagation is by seed sown in spring, by cuttings taken in late spring, or by division in spring or autumn. In addition the stems of some species root as they spread, which makes it easy to propagate by removing the rooted side shoots.

Most *Wahlenbergia* species are short-lived or verging on tender in cold regions of the northern hemisphere. If grown in the open garden, the majority will need sunny, dry rock crevices, poor soil, and protection from winter wet. For any species listed here that require conditions different from this, the conditions are described. A number of these species make good pot plants for the alpine house. All are summer-flowering.

Wahlenbergia albomarginata comes from the South and Stewart islands of New Zealand, where it grows on rocky slopes, open tussock grassland, and stream banks at 700–1700 M. It makes tufts of spatulate leaves to 5 CM long (smaller in drier habitats) with distinct, thick, white margins. The erect stem is 5–20 CM tall, with white to pale blue, campanulate flowers that are to 3 CM long and have darker-coloured veining and deeply incised petals. It can grow to form large patches, spreading by vigorous rhizomes. This species is generally recognised as the easiest and most perennial of the genus. Several good cultivars are available that were selected for hardiness and colour, one of which is *W. albomarginata* 'Blue Mist'.

Wahlenbergia brockiei is endemic to the limestone soils near Castle Hill in the Kura Tawhiti Conservation Reserve, Canterbury, New Zealand. It is tufted and makes rosettes of linear, dark green leaves to 3 CM long. The flowering stems are thin and leafless, 5–10 CM tall, with pale blue, solitary flowers that have flared lobes and are to 2 CM across. The inside is lighter and marked with fine, dark lines.

Wahlenbergia cartilaginea grows in the South Island of New Zealand, in the drier mountains of Marlborough and Nelson, low- to high-alpine areas, usually on screes. It is rhizomatous and makes lax rosettes of fleshy, grey to purple, spatulate leaves, 5–20 CM long and as much as 1.5 CM wide, with white margins. Flowering stems are thin, erect, 2–5 CM tall, and hold solitary, white to light blue or lavender flowers 1 CM across with widely flared lobes. This plant requires gritty, humus-rich, moist soil.

Wahlenbergia ceracea comes from the Australian states of New South Wales, Tasmania, and Victoria, where it grows in moist areas and grassland at high montane to alpine levels, spreading by slender rhizomes. It is tufted, with alternate leaves 2–3 CM long, obovate or oblanceolate, becoming spatulate to lanceolate further up the stem, and sinuate or flat. Flower stems are decumbent to ascending or erect and 10–60 CM long, with flowers that are pale blue to violet outside, lighter inside, and 2.5–4.5 CM across. The flowers are pendant in bud but later become erect. It requires a humus-rich, moist soil that becomes drier in winter and also needs some shading in summer.

Wahlenbergia congesta (synonyms *W. saxicola* var. *congesta*, *W. tasmanica*) comes from the South Island of New Zealand, where it grows on rocks and in sand dunes on the west coast up to 100 M. It is a mat-forming species with creeping rhizomes. Leaves are to 2.5 CM long, orbicular to oblong, and on long petioles. The flowering stems are very thin and have solitary, white to pale blue flowers to 1.2 CM wide and with flared lobes.

Wahlenbergia cuspidata comes from the Cape, KwaZulu-Natal, and Lesotho in South Africa, where it grows among rocks at 1500–3000 M on eastern slopes. It is tufted, with hirsute, semi-amplexicaule leaves. Stems to 30 CM tall have blue flowers to 1.5 CM across.

Wahlenbergia fasciculata comes from KwaZulu-Natal and Lesotho in South Africa, where it grows among rocks and in grassland at 1500–2400 M. It is tufted, with simple, solitary stems 10–30 CM tall, with blue flowers to 1.5 CM across that are sessile, axillary, and crowded. Leaves are short, narrow, and fasciculate.

Wahlenbergia gloriosa.

Photo by Richard Wilford

Wahlenbergia gloriosa comes from Australia, where it is restricted to the high mountain forests and woodlands of the Australian Capital Territory (ACT), southeastern New South Wales, and eastern Victoria, above about 1300 M. It makes lax rosettes of obovate-spatulate, sinuate, dentate, dark green leaves 2–3 CM long and usually opposite. Erect, slender stems 7.5–20 CM tall have solitary, flat flowers to about 3 CM in diameter. They are deep blue to violet-purple with a white centre, hence the common name of royal bluebell. The colour of the flowers makes this plant easy to identify in the natural areas around Canberra, and it is protected in the wild. In 1981 a committee was formed to advise the Minister for the Capital Territory, Michael Hodgman, on a suitable floral emblem for the ACT. On 26 May 1982 it was announced that *W. gloriosa* had been chosen. Propagation is by seed or by division of its branching rhizomes. This plant needs a cool, shady site with humus-rich, moist soil in the rock garden, but its deep flower colour and ease of growing make it a very attractive species for the alpine house.

Wahlenbergia gracilis, the sprawling bluebell, is a variable species that comes from New Zealand, where it grows from coastal lowland to montane rocky slopes, open forests, and woodlands. The procumbent to ascending stems are square, hairy, many-branched, and grow to 40 CM. Lower leaves are opposite, spatulate-obovate, 1–4 CM long, with a thickened or cartilaginous margin, and shallowly dentate. The white to pale lavender flowers, 1–2 CM wide, are solitary, flat, stellate, and erect, but nodding while in bud.

Wahlenbergia gymnoclada was discovered in Tasmania in 1985 and introduced into cultivation the same year. It grows in open forest and coastal scrub, and in the central mountains to 760 M. It is tufted, with linear, green leaves that are 2–3 CM long and pubescent underneath. The slender flower stems, to 25 CM tall, are occasionally branched near the base and carry terminal, outward-facing to erect, rich violet-blue flowers. These flowers are less campanula-like than others in the genus, the tube being very short and the corolla lobes wide-spreading. It is commonly known as the naked bluebell. Although probably not hardy enough for a northern hemisphere rock garden, this is a showy species for the alpine house, its flowering period lasting throughout the summer.

Wahlenbergia hederacea.

Photo by Trevor Cole

Wahlenbergia hederacea (synonym *Campanula hederacea*) grows throughout western Europe, including the British Isles, in damp to boggy grassland. The leaves are orbicular, 5–15 MM long, and shallowly lobed, giving it the common name of the ivy-leaved bellflower. Flowering stems are filiform and to 5 CM tall. The pale blue flowers are solitary, campanulate, and 5–15 MM long, with flared lobes. It is a creeping species that forms small mats but is short-lived, requiring a humus-rich, moist site in sun or semi-shade.

Wahlenbergia huttonii comes from the Cape and KwaZulu-Natal steppes of South Africa, where it grows at around 500–2000 M. It is tufted, with a woody rootstock. Leaves are linear, sessile, crowded, and spreading. Erect stems are 10–30 CM tall and carry blue, sessile flowers 6–10 MM across in small terminal clusters. The petals are deeply emarginate.

Wahlenbergia krebsii comes from South Africa, where it grows in subalpine to alpine grassland. It is tufted, with linear, sinuate leaves that are crowded at the base of the stem. Thin, erect, branched stems are 20–30 CM tall. The stem leaves are dentate and sessile, and the whole foliage is bluish green. The lavender-blue, cup-shaped flowers are deeply lobed, 1–2.5 CM across, with pointed petals, and are in lax panicles. It can make dense mats 60–90 CM across. It is easy and fast-growing in suitable parts of the world and best planted in a humus-rich soil with full sun exposure. After it blooms, cut it back to 5 CM tall and top-dress with garden compost just before midspring.

Wahlenbergia matthewsii comes from the South Island of New Zealand, where it ranges from the hottest and driest spots in the lowlands right up to around 1000 M, growing on limestone bluffs and debris (hence its common name, the limestone harebell). It is a tufted and taprooted species with crowded, linear, coriaceous leaves, 2–5 CM long, usually with white margins. The stem is ascending, 20–30 CM tall, and often branched. The white to pale blue flowers are solitary, 2–3 CM across, and broadly campanulate. It is one of the easiest and most satisfactory of the genus for garden cultivation, usually surviving mild winters in the northern hemisphere. However, it seeds around prolifically and also spreads by masses of thread-like stolons, over a very wide area if allowed to. Although it is a very pretty plant, it is suggested that it be grown in a pot or trough, at least till you are satisfied with its habit.

Wahlenbergia pygmaea comes from both North and South islands of New Zealand, where it grows in subalpine to low-alpine scrub, grassland, tussock herbfields, and rocky slopes. It is tufted, with small, shallowly dentate leaves to 1.5 CM long. Stems 1.5–2.5 CM tall have pale blue flowers with a white throat. This species is similar to but smaller than *W. albomarginata* in all its parts, apart from the corolla tube, which is wider.

Wahlenbergia pygmaea subsp. *tararua* is found only in the Tararua Range and is one of New Zealand's most threatened native species. It has flat leaves with four to seven marginal teeth. Its flowers are white, with one fine blue vein beneath each petal. It occurs in herbfields above the tree line.

Wahlenbergia rivularis is a perennial species from South Africa that blooms throughout the summer. It makes spreading mats of soft green leaves with stems to 30 CM and beautiful white to cream campanulate flowers. Over winter it goes semi-dormant but retains its green foliage.

Wahlenbergia rivularis.

Photo by Ellen Hornig

Wahlenbergia saxicola (synonym *W. tasmanica*), the mountain bluebell, is endemic to the Cradle Mountain area of Tasmania, where it grows in screes and on ridges. It forms glossy green mats of leaves that are 1–3 CM long, spatulate to

Wahlenbergia saxicola.
Photo by Richard Wilford

obovate or lanceolate, shallowly dentate to crenate, and shiny on the upper surface. Stems 5–10 CM tall hold pale blue, erect, campanulate flowers 1 CM across. In cultivation it needs a gravelly, humus-rich, moist soil and a sunny position. It resents drying out.

Wahlenbergia stricta (synonyms *Campanula erecta*, *W. consimilis*) is found in all the states of Australia except the Northern Territory, and is probably the most common *Wahlenbergia* species in the country, where it is often seen in masses on the roadside. Its habitat is generally plains, grassland, red gum woodland, wet and damp valleys, dry sclerophyll forest, and grassy, low, open forest. It is a taprooted, tufted perennial with erect, slender stems 20–90 CM tall. The lower leaves are softly hairy, ovate-linear, opposite, with undulate margins, and 1–7 CM long. The upper leaves are smaller and lanceolate to linear. The pale to deep lilac-blue or occasionally white flowers have a white throat, are erect, campanulate, and 1.5–3.5 CM wide, with a conspicuous tube.

Wahlenbergia trichogyna grows on rocky slopes in Australia and in one small location in New Zealand. From a deep taproot it forms tufts, making lax rosettes of leaves that are spatulate or obovate to lanceolate, shallowly dentate, sinuate to crisped, and to 3 CM long. The erect to decumbent stems are 30–60 CM tall. The solitary blue flowers are 2–3 CM across, have purplish shading, and are pendant in bud but later erect.

Wahlenbergia undulata (synonyms *Campanula undulata*, *W. dinteri*) comes from the southwestern Cape and KwaZulu-Natal in South Africa, where it grows on stony grassland or in seasonally moist places. It is like *W. ceracea* but usually larger and more robust, giving it the common name the giant bellflower. In full bloom it makes cushions to 60 CM high. From the base of the plant the woody older stems continually fork, gradually becoming softer and greener toward the flower-bearing tips. The linear-lanceolate, sinuate, sessile leaves are to 3 CM long and 1 CM wide, and grow on the bottom half of the stems. The margins are always undulate, and tiny white hairs are scattered along the stems and leaves. The pale lavender to soft mauve flowers are 3.5–5 CM across and often pendant when in bud. In the garden this plant is best treated as a tender perennial or annual, and it sets plenty of seed. Seed of an annual named *W. undulata* 'Melton Bluebird' is available from seed lists.

Glossary

Abaxial. On the side away from the axis

Acuminate. Gradually tapering to a point, the sides somewhat concave

Acute. Sharply pointed

Amplexicaule. Clasping the stem, as a leaf base or stipule

Appendage. A growth in the gaps between the calyx lobes

Appressed. Lying close and flat against another part

Arcuate. Arching or curved like a bow

Ascending. Growing obliquely upward, often curving

Axillary. Located in or arising in an axil

Barbate. Bearded with long stiff hairs

Biennial. Living for two years, usually flowering and setting seed the second year

Caespitose. Growing in tufts

Calyx. The outer whorl of the flower, which in the genus *Campanula* is made up of five sepals or calyx lobes (with or without appendages, according to species)

Campanulate. Bell-shaped, as opposed to infundibular or tubular

Capsule. A dry fruit or seed case that splits to shed seed

Ciliate. Having marginal hairs (cilia) that form a fringe, as on leaves, stipules, or sepals

Cordate. Heart-shaped

Coriaceous. Leathery

Corolla. The whole whorl of petals

Corymb. A flat-topped or convex racemose flower cluster, the lower or outer pedicels longer, their flowers opening first

Crenate. Having margins with rounded teeth

Crenulate. Having irregularly wavy margins

Crisped. Curled, wavy

Cuneate. Wedge-shaped

Decumbent. Resting on the ground but with the tip of the stem ascending

Deltoid. Triangular

Dentate. Having margins with teeth that are not directed forward

Denticulate. Minutely dentate or toothed

Dichotomous. Repeatedly forking in pairs

Emarginate. Having a small notch at the apex

Erect. Upright in relation to the ground, as opposed to pendant

Exserted. Protruding, as with stamens or stigma projecting from the corolla

Falcate. Sickle-shaped

Fasciculate. Connected or drawn into a bundle

Filiform. Thread-like

Geniculate. Abruptly bent

Glabrate. Becoming glabrous with age

Glabrous. Smooth, without hairs

Glaucous. Covered or whitened with a bloom, as with a cabbage leaf

Hirsute. Rough, with coarse, stiff hairs

Hispid. Rough, with stiff or bristly hairs

Hispidulous. Minutely hispid

Infundibular. Funnel-shaped, not campanulate nor with the petals reflexed

Lanate. Wooly; densely covered with long, tangled hairs

Lanceolate. Lance-shaped

Linear. Long, narrow, with parallel margins, as with blades of grass

Lobes. Divisions or segments, as of a leaf or petal

Lyrate. Lyre-shaped; pinnatifid, with the terminal lobe large and rounded, the lower lobes small

Margin. The edge of a leaf

Monocarpic. Flowering or bearing fruit only once and then dying

Monotypic. Having one representative, as a family with one genus or a genus with one species

Oblanceolate. Inversely lance-shaped

Obovate. Shaped like the longitudinal section of an egg, with the broadest part toward the tip

Obtuse. Blunt to almost rounded at the end

Orbicular. Circular

Orbiculate. Nearly circular

Ovate. Shaped like the longitudinal section of an egg, with the broadest part toward the stem

Panicle. A repeatedly branched inflorescence

Papillose. Having small nipple-like projections

Pedicel. The stalk of a single flower in a flower cluster

Peduncle. The stalk of a flower or of a flower cluster

Pendant. Hanging downward

Petiole. A leaf stalk

Pinnatifid. Pinnately cleft into narrow lobes that do not reach the midrib

Pinnatisect. Pinnately cut to the midrib

Pistil. The central reproductive organ of a flower consisting of ovary, style, and stigma

Polymorphic. Occurring in more than two distinct forms

Pore. A small opening in a capsule through which seed is shed

Procumbent. Trailing on the ground but not rooting

Pubescent. Covered with short, stiff hairs

Radical. Belonging to or proceeding from the roots

Reflexed. Abruptly bent or curved downward

Reniform. Kidney-shaped

Reticulate. Having a network of veins

Rosette. A cluster of leaves at ground level

Rugose. Wrinkled

Sclerophyll forest. An Australian ecosystem, classified into two types, wet or dry, both types comprised of plants with short, tough, often spiky leaves

Sepal. The lobe or segment of the calyx

Serrate. Having margins that are saw-like, with sharp, forward-pointing teeth

Sessile. Attached directly to the base, not stalked, as a leaf without a petiole

Setose. Beset with bristles

Simple. Undivided, used to describe unlobed leaves or unbranched inflorescences

Sinuate. Having strongly wavy margins

Spatulate. Spoon-shaped

Spicate. Having the form of or arranged in a spike

Stamen. The male or pollen-producing organ of a flower

Stellate. Star-shaped

Stigma. The terminal portion of a pistil, which receives the pollen

Stolons. Slender modified stems that run along the ground, often rooting at the nodes, as with strawberries

Subulate. Awl-shaped

Tomentose. Covered with dense, matted, wooly hairs

Tubular. Long and tube-like, as a campanula flower, with or without flared lobes

Undulate. Wavy; having wavy margins

Verrucose. Warty

Winged. Not round but having wings, or flanged along its length, as used to describe a petiole

Campanulas for Different Situations

As a nurseryman I am continually asked, "What campanula should I plant here?" or "Is this campanula better in a trough than a rock garden?" I hope this list of suggestions goes some way toward answering those questions. You have to bear in mind, though, that what is suitable in one part of the world is quite likely unsuitable in another. Climate will control most of the planting. Is a particular campanula hardy where you live? Only you can answer that. What about winter rain? That answer, again, will depend on where you live. This list is mainly meant to give some idea of what to plant where. If I suggest a species should be grown in the alpine house, it doesn't mean you have to exhibit the plant. So many people say to me, "I don't have an alpine house because I don't want to show." An alpine house is not just for exhibitors. Its main purpose is to protect the plant from winter wet—and remember, it keeps the rain from the grower as well!

I have made a list of species, hybrids, and cultivars that I consider suitable for growing in the border, rock garden, trough, and alpine house. The rock garden can include a scree if you wish, and a cold frame can be substituted for an alpine house. These suggestions are by no means set in stone: if you already grow a campanula successfully in a place different from where I suggest, by all means carry on.

It is possible that many of these campanulas will not be available where you live, in which case you will need to seek out an appropriate seed list, specialist nurseryman, or search the Internet. Visit shows, if possible, to see the plants exhibited, and then trawl the trade stands. Seek and you will (probably) find.

FOR THE BORDER

Campanula albovii
Campanula alliariifolia
Campanula alliariifolia 'Ivory Bells'
Campanula collina
Campanula dichotoma
Campanula divaricata
Campanula dolomitica
Campanula glomerata
Campanula glomerata var. *alba*
Campanula glomerata 'Joan Elliott'
Campanula komarovii

Campanula lanata
Campanula lingulata
Campanula loefflingii
Campanula makaschvilii
Campanula medium
Campanula patula
Campanula pelviformis
Campanula persicifolia
Campanula portenschlagiana
Campanula poscharskyana
Campanula propinqua

Campanula punctata
Campanula punctata 'Alba'
Campanula punctata 'Bowl of Cherries'
Campanula punctata 'Cherry Bells'
Campanula punctata 'Flashing Lights'
Campanula punctata var. *hondoensis*
Campanula punctata 'Pink Chimes'
Campanula punctata 'Plum Wine'
Campanula punctata 'Rubiflora'
Campanula ramosissima 'Meteora'
Campanula recta

Campanula rhomboidalis
Campanula rigidipila
Campanula rotundifolia
Campanula sarmatica
Campanula serrata
Campanula sibirica
Campanula spatulata
Campanula speciosa
Campanula spicata
Campanula thyrsoides
Campanula turczaninovii

FOR THE ROCK GARDEN

Campanula acutiloba
Campanula aghrica
Campanula albanica
Campanula albovii
Campanula alliariifolia
Campanula alpestris
Campanula alpina
Campanula andrewsii
Campanula argaea
Campanula argyrotricha
Campanula arvatica
Campanula arvatica var. *alba*
Campanula atlantis
Campanula aucheri
Campanula barbata
Campanula betulifolia
Campanula 'Birch Hybrid'
Campanula carpatica
Campanula carpatica 'Blue Clips'
Campanula carpatica 'Bressingham White'.
Campanula carpatica 'Hannah'
Campanula carpatica 'Isabel'
Campanula carpatica 'Riverslea'
Campanula carpatica 'Turbinata'
Campanula carpatica 'White Clips'
Campanula chamissonis
Campanula choruhensis

Campanula cochlearifolia
Campanula cochlearifolia 'Blue Tit'
Campanula cochlearifolia 'Cambridge Blue'
Campanula cochlearifolia 'Elizabeth Oliver'
Campanula cochlearifolia 'Lilacina'
Campanula cochlearifolia 'Miranda'
Campanula cochlearifolia 'Miss Willmott'
Campanula cochlearifolia 'R. B. Loder'
Campanula cochlearifolia 'Silver Bells'
Campanula collina
Campanula conferta
Campanula cymbalaria
Campanula dichotoma
Campanula drabifolia
Campanula elatines
Campanula elatinoides
Campanula elegantissima
Campanula excisa
Campanula fenestrellata
Campanula formanekiana
Campanula fragilis
Campanula garganica
Campanula garganica 'Blue Diamond'
Campanula garganica 'Dickson's Gold'
Campanula garganica 'W. H. Paine'

Campanula 'G. F. Wilson'
Campanula hagielia
Campanula 'Hallii'
Campanula hawkinsiana
Campanula 'Haylodgensis'
Campanula hedgei
Campanula hercegovina
Campanula hercegovina 'Nana'
Campanula heterophylla
Campanula hieracioides
Campanula 'Hilltop Snow'
Campanula incurva
Campanula involucrata
Campanula isophylla
Campanula jaubertiana
Campanula 'Joe Elliott'
Campanula 'John Innes'
Campanula kirpicznikovii
Campanula kolenatiana
Campanula komarovii
Campanula ledebouriana
Campanula leucosiphon
Campanula lingulata
Campanula loefflingii
Campanula 'Lynchmere'
Campanula lyrata
Campanula macrostyla
Campanula 'Maie Blyth'
Campanula malicitiana
Campanula 'Marion Fisher'
Campanula massalskyi
Campanula 'Mist Maiden'
Campanula moesiaca
Campanula 'Norman Grove'
Campanula oligosperma
Campanula olympica
Campanula oreadum
Campanula orphanidea
Campanula pallida
Campanula parryi
Campanula persica
Campanula persicifolia var. planiflora

Campanula persicifolia var. planiflora
   f. alba
Campanula petrophila
Campanula piperi
Campanula 'Polly Henderson'
Campanula portenschlagiana
Campanula portenschlagiana
   'Resholdt's Variety'
Campanula postii
Campanula prenanthoides
Campanula 'Pseudoraineri'
Campanula ptarmicifolia
Campanula pulla
Campanula pulla var. alba
Campanula ×pulloides
Campanula quercetorum
Campanula raddeana
Campanula radicosa
Campanula radula
Campanula raineri
Campanula ramosissima
Campanula ×rotarvatica
Campanula rotundifolia
Campanula rotundifolia 'Ned's White'
Campanula rupestris
Campanula ruprechtii
Campanula sarmatica
Campanula scabrella
Campanula scheuchzeri
Campanula scouleri
Campanula serrata
Campanula shetleri
Campanula 'Sojourner'
Campanula spatulata
Campanula 'Spetchley'
Campanula 'Stansfieldii'
Campanula stefanoffii
Campanula stevenii var. beauverdiana
Campanula strigillosa
Campanula suanetica
Campanula telephioides
Campanula thessala

Campanula 'Timsbury Perfection'
Campanula tommasiniana
Campanula trachyphylla
Campanula tridentata
Campanula troegerae
Campanula turczaninovii
Campanula ×*tymonsii*
Campanula tymphaea

Campanula versicolor
Campanula waldsteiniana
Campanula 'Warley White'
Campanula witasekiana
Campanula ×*wockei*
Campanula ×*wockei* 'Puck'
Campanula zoysii

For Troughs

Campanula acutiloba
Campanula aghrica
Campanula alpestris
Campanula alpina
Campanula andrewsii
Campanula anomala
Campanula argentea
Campanula argyrotricha
Campanula arvatica
Campanula arvatica var. *alba*
Campanula atlantis
Campanula autraniana
Campanula bayerniana
Campanula bessenginica
Campanula betulifolia
Campanula bornmuelleri
Campanula 'Bumblebee'
Campanula calaminthifolia
Campanula candida
Campanula 'Cantata'
Campanula carpatha
Campanula cashmeriana
Campanula 'Cassini'
Campanula celsii
Campanula cespitosa
Campanula chamissonis
Campanula chamissonis 'Oyobeni'
Campanula choruhensis
Campanula choziatowskyi
Campanula cochlearifolia

Campanula cochlearifolia var. *alba*
Campanula cochlearifolia 'Baby Bell'
Campanula cochlearifolia 'Blue Tit'
Campanula cochlearifolia 'Cambridge Blue'
Campanula cochlearifolia 'Elizabeth Oliver'
Campanula cochlearifolia 'Lilacina'
Campanula cochlearifolia 'Miranda'
Campanula cochlearifolia 'Miss Willmott'
Campanula cochlearifolia 'R. B. Loder'
Campanula cochlearifolia 'Silver Bells'
Campanula collina
Campanula coriacea
Campanula 'Covadonga'
Campanula cymbalaria
Campanula davisii
Campanula dzaaku
Campanula elegantissima
Campanula garganica
Campanula grossheimii
Campanula hakkiarica
Campanula hercegovina 'Nana'
Campanula herminii
Campanula incanescens
Campanula jaubertiana
Campanula 'Joe Elliott'
Campanula 'John Innes'
Campanula kirpicznikovii

Campanula lasiocarpa
Campanula ledebouriana
Campanula ledebouriana subsp.
  pulvinata
Campanula lourica
Campanula 'Lynchmere'
Campanula macrorhiza
Campanula 'Maie Blyth'
Campanula 'Marion Fisher'
Campanula morettiana
Campanula myrtifolia
Campanula oreadum
Campanula petrophila
Campanula piperi
Campanula 'Polly Henderson'
Campanula pulla
Campanula pulla var. *alba*
Campanula raineri
Campanula ×*rotarvatica*

Campanula rotundifolia subsp. *arctica*
  'Mt. Jotunheimen'
Campanula rotundifolia 'Mingan'
Campanula 'Ruffles'
Campanula samarkandensis
Campanula sartorii
Campanula saxatilis
Campanula scabrella
Campanula scheuchzeri
Campanula seraglio
Campanula shetleri
Campanula stefanoffii
Campanula stevenii var. *beauverdiana*
Campanula telephioides
Campanula teucrioides
Campanula uniflora
Campanula waldsteiniana
Campanula ×*wockei* 'Puck'
Campanula zoysii

For the Alpine House

Campanula aghrica
Campanula albertii
Campanula alpestris
Campanula alpina
Campanula andrewsii
Campanula anomala
Campanula argentea
Campanula argyrotricha
Campanula aristata
Campanula atlantis
Campanula aucheri
Campanula autraniana
Campanula barbata
Campanula bayerniana
Campanula bessenginica
Campanula betulifolia
Campanula bornmuelleri
Campanula 'Bumblebee'

Campanula buseri
Campanula calaminthifolia
Campanula cana
Campanula candida
Campanula 'Cantata'
Campanula carpatha
Campanula carpatha var. *alba*
Campanula cashmeriana
Campanula 'Cassini'
Campanula celsii
Campanula cenisia
Campanula cespitosa
Campanula chamissonis 'Oyobeni'
Campanula choruhensis
Campanula choziatowskyi
Campanula conferta
Campanula coriacea
Campanula 'Covadonga'

Campanula crispa
Campanula cymbalaria
Campanula davisii
Campanula dzaaku
Campanula 'Edward Forrest'
Campanula elegantissima
Campanula excisa
Campanula filicaulis
Campanula formanekiana
Campanula fragilis
Campanula fragilis subsp. *cavolinii*
Campanula fruticulosa
Campanula garganica 'Dickson's Gold'
Campanula garganica 'W. H. Paine'
Campanula hakkiarica
Campanula hawkinsiana
Campanula hedgei
Campanula hercegovina 'Nana'
Campanula heterophylla
Campanula hieracioides
Campanula hierapetrae
Campanula 'Hilltop Snow'
Campanula humillima
Campanula hypopolia
Campanula incanescens
Campanula involucrata
Campanula isaurica
Campanula jaubertiana
Campanula 'Joe Elliott'
Campanula kirpicznikovii
Campanula kolakovskyi
Campanula kryophila
Campanula lasiocarpa
Campanula ledebouriana
Campanula ledebouriana subsp.
  pulvinata
Campanula leucosiphon
Campanula lourica
Campanula lyrata
Campanula 'Maie Blyth'
Campanula mairei
Campanula 'Marion Fisher'

Campanula massalskyi
Campanula modesta
Campanula mollis
Campanula morettiana
Campanula morettiana var. *alba*
Campanula myrtifolia
Campanula myrtifolia 'Helmi'
Campanula oligosperma
Campanula oreadum
Campanula orphanidea
Campanula paradoxa
Campanula persicifolia var. *planiflora*
Campanula persicifolia var. *planiflora*
  f. *alba*
Campanula petrophila
Campanula piperi
Campanula piperi 'Snowdrift'
Campanula piperi 'Townsend Ridge'
Campanula piperi 'Townsend Violet'
Campanula 'Polly Henderson'
Campanula postii
Campanula 'Pseudoraineri'
Campanula pulla
Campanula pulla var. *alba*
Campanula quercetorum
Campanula radchensis
Campanula raddeana
Campanula raineri
Campanula raineri var. *alba*
Campanula rotundifolia subsp. *arctica*
  'Mt. Jotunheimen'
Campanula rotundifolia 'Mingan'
Campanula 'Ruffles'
Campanula rupestris
Campanula rupicola
Campanula ruprechtii
Campanula samarkandensis
Campanula saxatilis
Campanula scabrella
Campanula seraglio
Campanula shetleri
Campanula 'Sojourner'

Campanula 'Stansfieldii'

Campanula stefanoffii

Campanula stevenii var. *beauverdiana*

Campanula strigillosa

Campanula suanetica

Campanula teucrioides

Campanula thessala

Campanula 'Timsbury Perfection'

Campanula tommasiniana

Campanula topaliana

Campanula trachyphylla

Campanula tridentata

Campanula troegerae

Campanula tubulosa

Campanula tymphaea

Campanula versicolor

Campanula waldsteiniana

Campanula ×*wockei* 'Puck'

Campanula zoysii

Campanula zoysii 'Lismore Ice'

Societies and Sources

SOCIETIES

A number of specialist societies deal specifically with the cultivation of alpine plants, including members of the Campanulaceae, and I encourage readers to join at least one. Many offer regular bulletins with photos and articles relating to campanulas and their relatives, annual seed lists that include a wide range of Campanulaceae that can be obtained, and regular shows at which a wonderful range of plants are exhibited and grown to a high standard. Anyone interested should contact the societies directly.

Alpine Garden Society
AGS Centre
Avon Bank
Pershore
Worcestershire
WWR10 3JP
England

Scottish Rock Garden Club
A. D. McKelvie
43 Rubislaw Park Crescent
Aberdeen
AB15 8BT
Scotland

North America Rock Garden Society
Jacques Mommens, Executive Secretary
P.O. Box 67
Millwood, New York 10546
United States

Rock Garden Club—Prague
Klub skalnickaru Praha
Maríkova 5
162 00 Praha 6
Czech Republic

MAIL-ORDER NURSERIES

The following nurseries sell a wide range of Campanulaceae.

Lesley Cox
Gala Plants
21 Sproull Drive
RD 1
Dunedin
Otago
New Zealand

Graham's Hardy Plants
"Southcroft"
North Road
Timsbury
Bath
BA2 0JN
England

Mt. Tahoma Nursery
28111 112th Avenue East
Graham, Washington 98338
United States

Parham Bungalow Plants
Parham Lane
Market Lavington
Devizes
Wiltshire
SN10 4QA
England

Seed Lists

Alplains
32315 Pine Crest Court
Kiowa, Colorado 80117
United States

Euroseeds
Marcela Ryparova
Hromuvka 1511
753 01 Hranice N. M.
Czech Republic

Josef Halda
Box 110
501 01 Hradec Kralove 2
Czech Republic

Rocky Mountain Rare Plants
1706 Deerpath Road
Franktown, Colorado 80116
United States

Wild Seeds
Vojtěch Holubec
Sidlistni 210
CZ-165 00
Praha 6
Czech Republic

World Seeds
Vladislav Piatek
Záhumenní 2129
708 00 Ostrava-Poruba
Czech Republic

Wild Seeds of Exquisite Alpines
Josef Jurášek
P.O. Box 251
Praha 5 152 00
Czech Republic

Bibliography

Aichele, D. 1978. *A Field Guide in Colour to Wild Flowers*. Octopus Books: London.

Alm, T., M. Piirainen, and A. Often. 2000. Krigsspredte arter i Sør-Varanger, Finnmark: vadderot *Phyteuma spicatum* og svartvadderot *P. nigrum*. Abstract from *Blyttia* 58: 46–54. http://www.toyen.uio.no/botanisk/nbf/blyttia/20000a3.htm. Accessed 2005.

Alpine Garden Society. 1993. *Encyclopaedia of Alpines*. 2 vols. Ed. K. Beckett. AGS: Pershore, United Kingdom.

Annie's Annuals. 2005. *Campanula incurva*. http://www.anniesannuals.com/signs/B%20-%20C/Campanula_incurva.htm. Accessed 2005.

Apostolova, I., and A. Ganeva. 2000. New Data on *Edraianthus serbicus* (Kern.) Petrovic in Bulgaria. *Phytologia Balcanica* 6 (1): 65–71. http://www.bio.bas.bg/~phytolbalcan/2000-6-1/2000-6-1-06.pdf. Accessed 2005.

Archibald, J., and J. Archibald. 1993–1994. Seed list. Jim and Jenny Archibald: Llandysul, Wales.

Behçet, L., and O. Karabacak. 2003. The Presence of *Campanula radula* Fischer in Turkey. Yüzüncü Yil University, Faculty of Science and Art, Department of Biology: Van, Turkey.

Botanic Gardens Trust. 2005. PlantNET, the Plant Information Network System of Botanic Gardens Trust, Sydney, Australia. Version 2.0. http://plantnet.rbgsyd.nsw.gov.au. Accessed 2005.

Brickell, C., ed. 1996. *The Royal Horticultural Society A–Z Encyclopedia of Garden Plants*. Dorling Kindersley: London.

Brightman, C. 1992. Some Interesting Plants at the Shows, 1990–91. *Quarterly Bulletin of the Alpine Garden Society* 60 (1): 54.

Candolle, A. 1830. *Monographie des campanulées*. Veuve Desray: Paris.

Crook, H. C. 1951. *Campanulas*. Country Life: London.

Crook, H. C. 1977. The Genus *Symphyandra*. *Quarterly Bulletin of the Alpine Garden Society* 45 (3): 246–254.

Cupido, C. 2004. Family: Campanulaceae. South African National Biodiversity Institute, South Africa. http://www.plantzafrica.com/plantcd/campanulac.htm. Accessed 2005.

Dewey, H. 2000. Alpine-L. The Electronic Rock Garden Society: For Rock Gardening and for Dwarf and Alpine Plants, Including Their Botany. http://www.thealpinegarden.com/alpine-L.htm. Accessed 2005.

Douglas, G. W., G. B. Straley, and D. Meidinger. 1989. The Vascular Plants of British Columbia, Part 1: Gymnosperms and Dicotyledons (Aceraceae through Cucurbitaceae). British Columbia Ministry of Forests. http://www.for.gov.bc.ca/hfd/pubs/Docs/Srs/Srs01/Srs01-4.pdf. Accessed 2005.

Elliott, C. 1936. *Rock Garden Plants*. Reprint. Edward Arnold: London.

Euphrasia. 1989. A Spanish Dignitary. *Quarterly Bulletin of the Alpine Garden Society* 57 (3): 203.

Euphrasia. 1990. Parental Pride. *Quarterly Bulletin of the Alpine Garden Society* 58 (1): 11.

Farrer, R. 1918. *The English Rock Garden*. T. C. & E. C. Jack: London. 199–200, 205–206.

Grey-Wilson, C., and M. Blamey. 1979. *The Alpine Flowers of Britain and Europe*. Collins: London.

Halliwell, B. 1985. *Campanula bayerniana*. *Quarterly Bulletin of the Alpine Garden Society* 53 (4): 384.

Hamblett, R. 2000, 2003. The Chalk Pit. Lancing Village Nature and History. http://lancingvillage.co.uk/nature/FOLR/chalkpit.htm. Accessed 2005.

Handel-Mazzetti, H. 1927. *Naturbilder aus Südwest-China*. Österreichischer Bundesverlag: Vienna.

Heath, R. E. 1981. *Collectors' Alpines*. Collingridge: Surrey, United Kingdom.

Hebe Society. 2005. Hebe Society. http://www.hebesoc.vispa.com/. Accessed 2005.

Hilton, E. 1978. A Rock Wall. *Quarterly Bulletin of the Alpine Garden Society* 46 (2): 105.

Hulme, J. 1989. Some Interesting Plants at the Shows, 1987–88. *Quarterly Bulletin of the Alpine Garden Society* 57 (1): 78.

Hyde, M., and B. Wursten. 2002–2005. Flora of Zimbabwe. http://www.zimbabweflora.co.zw/index.php. Accessed 2005.

Ingwersen, W. 1978. *Ingwersen's Manual of Alpine Plants*. Will Ingwersen and Dunnsprint: Eastbourne, United Kingdom.

Jaume Saint-Hilaire, J. H. J. 1828–1833. *La flore et la pomone françaises*. 6 vols. Chez l'auteur: Paris. http://www.mbgpress.org/rarebooks.htm. Accessed 2005.

Kelaidis, G. 1993. Rocky Mountain Rare Plants seed catalogue. Denver, Colorado, United States.

Lewis, P., and M. Lynch. 1998. *Campanulas.* Timber Press: Portland, Oregon, United States.

Mansfield, T. C. 1942. *Alpines in Colour and Cultivation.* William Collins: London. 61.

Mathew, B. 1976. Some Interesting Plants at the Shows, 1975–76. *Quarterly Bulletin of the Alpine Garden Society* 44 (4): 298.

Mathew, B. 1981. Plant Awards, 1980–81. *Quarterly Bulletin of the Alpine Garden Society* 49 (4): 357.

Mathew, B., and B. Starling. 1978. Plant Awards, 1977–78. *Quarterly Bulletin of the Alpine Garden Society* 46 (4): 299.

Missouri Botanical Garden. 1995–2005. Ornamental Plants of Horticultural Value: *Campanula.*
http://www.mobot.org/MOBOT/Research/russia/campanula.shtml. Accessed 2005.

Missouri Botanical Garden. 1995–2005. Ornamental Plants in Their Natural Habitats: The Caucasus.
http://www.mobot.org/MOBOT/research/russia/caucasus.shtml. Accessed 2005.

Missouri Botanical Garden. 1995–2005. Ornamental Plants in Their Natural Habitats: Georgia.
http://www.mobot.org/MOBOT/Research/russia/georgia.shtml. Accessed 2005.

Missouri Botanical Garden. 1995–2005. Rare, Endangered and Vulnerable Plants of the Republic of Georgia.
http://www.mobot.org/MOBOT/research/georgia/cfamily.shtml,
http://www.mobot.org/MOBOT/research/georgia/checklist.pdf. Accessed 2005.

Mowle, D. 1985. Some Plants at the Shows, 1983–84. *Quarterly Bulletin of the Alpine Garden Society* 53 (1): 26–60.

New Ornamentals Society. 2003. NOS Campanula Page.
http://newplants.tripod.com/camp311.html. Accessed 2005.

New Zealand Plant Conservation Network. 2005. New Zealand Plant Conservation Network. http://www.nzpcn.org.nz. Accessed 2005.

Oganesian, M. E. 1995. Synopsis of Caucasian Campanulaceae. *Candollea* 50: 275–308.

Rolfe, R. 1997. Plant Awards, 1996–97. *Quarterly Bulletin of the Alpine Garden Society* 65 (4): 429–430, 434–435.

Scoggan, H. J. 1978–1979. *The Flora of Canada*. 4 vols. National Museum of Natural Sciences, National Museums of Canada: Ottawa, Ontario, Canada.

Shetler, S. G. 1963. A Checklist and Key to the Species of *Campanula* Native or Commonly Naturalized in North America. *Rhodora* 65: 319–337.

Shulkina, T. 2004. *Ornamental Plants from Russia and Adjacent States of the Former Soviet Union: A Botanical Guide for Travelers and Gardeners*. Missouri Botanical Garden Press: St. Louis, Missouri, United States.

Slabý, P. 1990–2005. Rock Garden Plants Database. Version 3.0. http://web.kadel.cz/flora. Accessed 2005.

Society for Growing Australian Plants. 1997. Australian Plants Online. Number 8, December 1997. http://farrer.riv.csu.edu.au/ASGAP/APOL8/ac97-4.html. Accessed 2005.

Suncrest Nurseries. 2000–2005. Descriptive catalogue. http://www.suncrestnurseries.com. Accessed 2005.

Tools of the Adventure. 2005. Castle Hill Ethics. http://www.tota.co.nz/castlehill/ethics.html. Accessed 2005.

Turland, N. 1990. Cretan Bellflowers and St. John's Worts. *Quarterly Bulletin of the Alpine Garden Society* 58 (4): 319–320.

Turland, N. 1993. Cretan Cliff-Dwellers. *Quarterly Bulletin of the Alpine Garden Society* 61 (4): 382–384.

University of Alberta Devonian Botanic Garden. 1997–2005. University of Alberta Devonian Botanic Garden. http://www.discoveredmonton.com/devonian/getgro25.html. Accessed 2005.

USDA, NRCS. 2005. PLANTS Database. Version 3.5. Data compiled by Mark W. Skinner. National Plant Data Center: Baton Rouge, Louisiana, United States. http://plants.usda.gov. Accessed 2005.

Van der Werff, D., ed. 1999. PLANTS. http://www.plants-magazine.co.uk/plants/index.html. Aquilegia: Hartlepool, United Kingdom. Accessed 2005.

Welsh, S. L. 1974. *Anderson's Flora of Alaska and Adjacent Parts of Canada*. Brigham Young University Press: Provo, Utah, United States. 724.

Woodward, B. 1973. Plants of North America. *Quarterly Bulletin of the Alpine Garden Society* 41 (3): 246–255.

Conversion Tables

Inches	Centimetres	Feet	Metres
¼	0.6	1	0.3
½	1.25	6	1.8
1	2.5	8	2.4
2	5.0	10	3.0
3	7.5	20	6.0
4	10	25	7.5
5	12.5	30	9.0
6	15	50	15
7	18	100	30
8	20	1000	300
9	23	2500	750
10	25	5000	1500
15	37	7500	2250
20	51	10,000	3000

Temperatures

$$°C = 5/9 \times (°F - 32)$$
$$°F = (9/5 \times °C) + 32$$

Index of Plant Names